ISBN 1-58023-086-5

TORAH
OF THE EARTH

EXPLORING 4,000 Years
of ECOLOGY in Jewish Thought
Vol. 1
Biblical Israel & Rabbinic Judaism

Perhaps the most profound Jewish statement about the relationship between human beings and the earth is bound up in two words of Hebrew—two words that do not even need a sentence to connect them:

Adam. Adamah.

The first means "human being"; the second, "earth." The two words intertwine to teach us that the human and the earth are intertwined. In Hebrew no one is able to say the name of the earth or of humanity without hearing an echo of the other.

—from the Introduction

Four millennia of human responses to the natural world come to life in this groundbreaking resource that provides a diverse group of ecological and religious voices. It offers us a thought-provoking key to understanding the intersection of ecology and Judaism.

More than 30 leading scholars and experts—including Abraham Joshua Heschel, Judith Plaskow, Arthur Green, Tikva Frymer-Kensky and Erich Fromm—enlighten, provoke, and provide a guided tour of ecological thought from four major Jewish viewpoints: Biblical Judaism, Rabbinic Judaism, the Zionist movement, and the Eco-Judaism movement.

"Waskow gathers thinkers, ideas and inspiration from Jewish tradition that provide us with wisdom and critical thinking.... A needed and timely and prophetic work!"

—Matthew Fox, President, University of Creation Spirituality, and author of *The Reinvention of Work* and *Original Blessing*

"Finally, a comprehensive anthology of Judaism and the Earth that explores these concerns and challenges us to action! . . . [An] invaluable resource."

—Rabbi Warren G. Stone, Chair, Environmental Committee, Central Conference of American Rabbis

ARTHUR WASKOW is recognized as one of the leading thinkers of the Jewish renewal movement. He has been at the forefront of creating Jewish renewal theory, practice and institutions. Rabbi Waskow founded and directs the Shalom Center, and is a Pathfinder of ALEPH: Alliance for Jewish Renewal, an international network. He is founder and editor of the journal *New Menorah*, and helped found the Fabrangen Cheder and the National Havurah Committee. His previous books include *The Freedom Seder; Seasons of Our Joy;* and *Down-to-Earth Judaism.* He is the co-editor of *Trees, Earth, Torah: A Tu B'Shvat Anthology* (Jewish Publication Society), and author of *Godwrestling—Round 2: Ancient Wisdom, Future Paths* (Jewish Lights), which was named "Best Religion Book of the Year."

He and his wife, Phyllis Berman, who is also a leader of Jewish renewal, often join to lead retreats and workshops in many Jewish and interreligious settings. Together they wrote *Tales of Tikkun: New Jewish Stories to Heal the Wounded World.*

Waskow lives in the Philadelphia area. He has two grown children of his own, is "associate parent" for two others, and has one son-in-law and one daughter-in-law.

"Compelling reading both for those new to thinking about the Jewish response to environmental questions and for those already acquainted with this rapidly growing field."
—**Mark X. Jacobs,** Director, Coalition on the Environment and Jewish Life

For People of All Faiths, All Backgrounds

JEWISH LIGHTS Publishing
www.jewishlights.com

COVER DESIGN: CASEY NUTTALL

TORAH

OF THE EARTH

EXPLORING

4,000 Years of

ECOLOGY in

Jewish Thought

VOL. 1

BIBLICAL ISRAEL:
One Land, One People

RABBINIC JUDAISM:
One People, Many Lands

EDITED BY
ARTHUR WASKOW

For People of All Faiths, All Backgrounds
JEWISH LIGHTS Publishing

Torah of the Earth: Exploring 4,000 Years of Ecology in Jewish Thought
Vol. 1: Biblical Israel & Rabbinic Judaism

Library of Congress Cataloging-in-Publication Data

Torah of the earth : exploring 4,000 years of ecology in Jewish thought / edited by Arthur Waskow.
p.   cm.
Includes bibliographical references.
ISBN 1-58023-086-5 (v. 1) — ISBN 1-58023-087-3 (v. 2)
1. Human ecology—Religious aspects—Judaism. 2. Nature—Religious aspects—Judaism.
3. Human ecology—Israel. I. Waskow, Arthur Ocean, 1933–
BM538.H85T67 2000
296.3'8—dc21

                                                                                    00-008696

First Edition

ISBN 978-1-68336-466-5 (hc)

Manufactured in the United States of America
Printed on recycled paper

Cover design: Casey Nuttall
Text design: Sans Serif Inc.

Published by Jewish Lights Publishing
www.jewishlights.com

For our children
Shoshana and Michael, David and Ketura, Morissa, Joshua;
For their children
and the children of their children;
For all children:

May you live to see your world fulfilled, your planet healed.
May you be our link to future worlds, and may your hope
    encompass all the generations of all life yet to be.
May your heart conceive with understanding, may your mouth speak
    wisdom, and your tongue be stirred with songs of joy.
May your gaze be straight and sure, your eyes be lit with
    Torah's lamp, your face aglow with heaven's radiance,
    your lips speak words of knowledge.
May your innards rejoice in foods whose seeds are righteousness.
And may you always rush with eagerness to hear the truths
    of the Unity who is more ancient than all time
    and ever present in all beings.

Talmud Bavli: B'rachot 17a
(adapted from translation by Joel Rosenberg in the
Reconstructionist prayerbook, *Kol Haneshamah*)

CONTENTS

EARTH AND EARTHLING, *ADAM* AND *ADAMAH*

Perhaps the most profound Jewish statement about the relationship between human beings and the earth is bound up in two words of Hebrew—two words that do not even need a sentence to connect them: *Adam. Adamah.*

The first means "human being"; the second, "earth." The two words are connected to teach us that human beings and the earth are intertwined. In English, this connection would be obvious only if the everyday word for "human being" were "earthling," or perhaps if the ordinary word for "earth" were "humus." With either of these configurations, no one could say the name of earth or of human without hearing an echo of the other. Intertwined. Not identical, but intertwined.

What differences make us not identical? Genesis 2:5–7 explains:

There was no *adam* to serve/work the *adamah,* but a flow would well up upon the ground and water all the face of the *adamah.* And YHWH [by some understood as "Breath of the World," from the sound of the letters "pronounced" with no vowels, producing only an outbreath] shaped the *adam* out of dust from the *adamah,* and blew into its nostrils the breath of life, and the *adam* became a living being, a breathing being.

The human being lost the breathing "-ah" sound at the end of *adamah.*

At the level of individual life-history, the human being loses the unconscious placental breathing that connects the enwombed human with the all-enfolding earth—and gains a new, more conscious, more deliberate breath.

At the level of the evolutionary history of humankind, *adam* lost the unconscious breathing that connected the earliest human beings with the earth from which they had just emerged—little different, to begin with, from the other primates round about them. And that "-ah" was replaced with a new kind of breath—a conscious breath from the Breath of the World. In separating from the earth, in being born, the *adam* becomes more conscious.

The earth-human relationship takes on a complex, ironic tone. Small wonder that humans eat what the earth grows in a way that bespeaks their alienation and brings upon them and the earth a still deeper alienation: "Damned be *adamah* on your account; with painful labor shall you eat from it."

If this is a myth of births and beginnings, it is also a myth of every new beginning. Not once only has the human race separated itself from the earth, but over and over.

On each occasion, as our sacred stories and our secular histories teach us, we have had to learn a new depth of connection and community with the earth from which we have separated. When we did not, we shattered the localities and regions of our earth and birth—and were shattered in return. For none can eat unscathed from the food into which they have poured out poison.

Today we are living in a crisis of this spiral. Epoch after epoch, the more and more knowledgeable human race has alienated itself more deeply, then realized more deeply its need for connection and built some new sense of community with the earth. Once this meant learning to raise fewer goats in fragile local ecosystems. Now it means learning not to destroy the global ozone layer. The upward turning of the spiral of human power to Make and to Do has faced every community and tradition on the planet with the task of learning better how to Be and how to Love.

In some ways it is in our own generation that we have most vehemently gobbled up that fruit of plenty that grew from the Tree of Knowing, and in our own generation that we face most sharply the danger that the earth will war against us.

So during this past generation Jews have been looking back, with much more urgency, into our own teachings about *adam* and *adamah*. We who were once a down-to-earth people, an indigenous people—what can we learn and teach to heal ourselves and our neighbors and the neighborhood itself—*adam* and *adamah?*

This Jewish conversation has only begun. Much of it has been carried out in a muttered undertone, mostly among a few people who were especially knowledgeable and concerned. This book brings together some of the most important explorations, to make the conversation more public and to make it more possible for the Jewish people as a whole to assess its own part in addressing a planetary crisis.

There have been four basic life-stances from which the Jewish people has addressed these questions: Biblical Israel, Rabbinic Judaism, Zionism, and most recently, Eco-Judaism. These four stances are not merely chronological periods (indeed, the last two of them overlap in time); they embody four different ways of connecting with the earth. For that reason, they have seemed to offer an organic pattern for organizing this book.

Connections of Land and People

Four millennia ago, among Western Semitic nomads in the land of Canaan, there were stirrings of response and resistance to the new imperial agriculture of Babylonia. At some point in the next five hundred years, one of the communities that emerged from this simmering stew began to tell stories of a clan that became the seedbed of the people that came to call itself the Children of Israel—the Godwrestlers—and *Ivrim,* "Hebrews" in rough transliteration but, more important, in translation "boundary-crossers."

For they wrestled with the deepest questions of the universe, and they crossed the boundaries not only of territorial fiefdoms but of cultures and proprieties and social structures.

As they crossed over and wrestled, wrestled and crossed over, they drew from their hearing of the universe words they told and retold and wove into new patterns and turned into stories, poetry, drama, law, daily life-practice, philosophical musings.

These words became what we call the Bible, and one of its great themes was how to make a sacred relationship with the earth. In the Biblical Era that ensued, these Israelites/Hebrews/Jews not only lived intimately with a particular piece of earth but lived in a way that made them—collectively, as a people—responsible for how human beings acted toward the earth and how the earth responded.

This Biblical Era finally was shattered. There followed almost two thousand years in which one of the defining characteristics of Jewish life was that the people Israel no longer had a direct physical connection with the land of Israel. During these centuries of what we call Rabbinic Judaism, Jews shaped the *adam/adamah* relationship much more as scattered households or communities than as a united people.

The Rabbinic community developed some loose guidelines

for a sacred relationship to the earth. Since the lands of the Diaspora were so distant and so different from each other as ecosystems, and since interhuman relationships seemed of higher priority during this period, Rabbinic thought sketched a broad concern for protecting the earth, but with few definitive specifics. The Rabbis were often less concerned with protecting the earth than with explaining how to use its resources to meet the urgent needs of their scattered, often impoverished, people.

In the nineteenth century, the Zionist movement focused on renewing the Jewish connection with the land in a way that would allow and require the making of a Jewish policy toward the piece of earth called Eretz Yisrael. As the State of Israel emerged, so did a set of policies. Over the years, the numbers, the technology, the religious and philosophical perspectives, and the political arrangements of Israelis—in short, the Land, the People, and the State—have all changed in relationship to one another. So, therefore, have policies toward the land.

Meanwhile, the Jewish community in the United States in the second half of the twentieth century found itself politically empowered in unprecedented ways at just the same moment that Jews, Americans, and human beings in general were realizing that the troubled relationship between *adam* and *adamah* had reached the point of planetary crisis. This confluence seemed to a growing number of American Jews to invite—even demand—a collective Jewish response to this planetary crisis.

From many seeds and roots—the Bible reexamined, the Rabbis renewed, secular Jewish poetry and other nature-focused literature, feminist theologies of relationship, Kabbalah and Hasidism—came a gathering of thought that might be called Eco-Judaism, a Judaism that had close to its very center a concern for the healing of the earth.

Although this book treats Eco-Judaism as one of four different expressions of the Jewish relationship with the earth, the book itself, of course, is also an outgrowth of that collective energy. Indeed, it is very likely that almost none of the essays gathered in this book—not even those that examine Biblical, Rabbinic, and Zionist thought, Jewish worldviews that emerged long before a sense of planetary crisis—would have been written had that sense of crisis not emerged in the last generation.

For Jews of this past generation, facing a growing sense of worldwide ecological transformation, have returned to older Jewish writings to understand what Jewish wisdom might have to say. What guidance could it give, what mistakes could it warn against? Guidance and warning not only for our own behavior but for the approaches of other spiritual communities, of the broader societies of which we are a part, of the human race as a whole.

What makes us think that looking back at ancient teachings might be of any help, as we try to dance in the midst of a planetary earthquake?

The Jewish people has faced such earthquakes before, when both political and technological/ecological transformations shook the seemingly solid ground on which we were walking. Indeed, the emergence of the people Israel and the Hebrew Bible in the form in which we know about them may have been themselves the result of such an upheaval, as imperial agriculture made its way from Babylonia into the region of the Western Semites. And the emergence of Rabbinic Judaism, with the Talmud and all its codes and commentaries, was clearly the result of such an upheaval—the triumph of Roman-Hellenistic civilization in the Mediterranean basin.

ANCIENT TEXTS, FUTURE LIFE-PATHS

In all these situations, Jews have valued the wisdom of the past, without letting it straitjacket them. The practice of midrash, in which an old text was turned in a new direction to afford new meaning, was not just a verbal trick but a deep assertion that the wisdom of previous generations was still important, even when changes needed to be made.

Why did Jewish culture and spirituality feel so strongly this need to affirm, and transcend, the past? The past represented an achieved sense of community and identity, which was being jarred by new technologies, new economics, new politics. Riding the wave of the new might be necessary, but to lose the past entirely was to lose communal—and ecological—health. The *adam* who is born again and again and again from the *adamah* dares not lose touch with it.

That need continues in our present crisis, as it has before. So we encounter in this book materials from, and about, the most ancient of Jewish sources as well as the most recent.

Indeed, not only from ancient Israel to now, but also within each era and worldview, we affirm this pattern of reconnecting with a text while taking it in new directions. So each section of this book begins with texts that spring from the worldview of that era and then continues with writings that analyze, study, respond to, and elaborate upon those texts.

What about the sources that we do not find? Yemenite Jewish women cooks, Ethiopian Jewish farmers, Polish dairymen, all dealt with the earth. As the need and desire grows for a revitalized and earth-conscious Judaism to draw on these myriad experiences of Jews around the earth, let us hope that scholars will begin to unearth these materials as many have struggled to unearth the silenced voices of Jewish women.

Meanwhile, for what we already have we sing *Dayenu!*—It is enough for us!—even as we know that after this chorus, this pause to celebrate what we have learned so far, we will sing another verse of further learning.

We can all hope that now the scattered comments of the many who in this past generation have tuned their minds to eco-Jewish teaching can become a fuller conversation, within and beyond the Jewish people.

May the One Who sends the Rainbow to renew the covenant with all of life remind us of our share in giving life to all the many-colored cultures and species of this planet.

Arthur Ocean Waskow
On the 27th Yahrzeit of
Rabbenu Abraham Joshua Heschel
18 Tevet 5760
December 27, 1999

PART I

Biblical Israel:
One Land, One People

For thousands of years, biblical and Rabbinic Jews mostly dealt with biblical texts from within the texts themselves. Recombining one text with another, inside the system, was the way in which they did midrash, that is, they reworked the texts so that without abandoning them they could draw new meaning from them as the world changed and new meaning became necessary.

Then, in the nineteenth century, came a burst of modern scholarly historical analysis of biblical texts. That kind of scholarship stepped back from the texts themselves and from the classic Jewish way of dealing with them. Historians focused on the *contexts* of the texts, began to understand them from the outside, to see them as a reflection of the historical periods in which they emerged. For decades this approach drained the texts of their *torah,* their teaching force, their claim to aim toward wisdom. They became mere cold facts, dead objects on the page. But this dead-ening—like the falling of dead fruit from a tree—turned out to be filled with seed potential.

For now it is possible to move back to the texts at a new level: to unite the historians' and the midrash-makers' modes of study. To treat the ancient text as filled with wisdom because it encodes the ongoing struggles of spiritual seekers to reshape their lives in history. To understand the text as neither dictum nor dead, but as a record of living struggle that we can learn from and transcend.

In other words, the "Sabbath" in which we paused from the kind of textual analysis done in Rabbinic Judaism allowed us to make a spiral turn and to reenter the process of learning from the text not just with new midrash but a new kind of midrash.

Not to hear the ancient content as only a summed-up understanding of the dead past or only a demand for how to live in the present, but to hear beneath the content the process as a guide to the living future.

This is what the three writers we are about to read have done with the sacred texts and the history of Biblical Israel. They have taken the sacred texts and symbols of Israel (two of them took also the symbols and texts of Babylonia) as crystallizations of the sacred efforts of these peoples to understand the earth and the role of human beings in relation to it.

In the historical period that first formed the identity of the Jewish people, the ancient Israelite community lived close to the earth, in the land of Canaan/Israel. Its efforts to understand its own relationship with the land both drew on and differed from the teachings of the nearby Babylonian culture that overlapped with the Israelites in the lands they shaped and were shaped by.

Our authors draw on a variety of texts and histories. Yet this first section, like those that follow, begins with a few specific texts from within the period. Why begin this way?

Because these primary texts give us as direct a window as possible into the ancient Hebrew (translated by the editor), so that it can speak to us for itself, before we turn to hear the voice of midrash and the voice of history.

We find two different styles of biblical teaching:

- Two psalms that celebrate the awesome grandeur and the overflowing joy of the web of life, as woven by YHWH. These are from the aspect of Torah known as *aggadah* ("telling"), which comprises philosophical, spiritual, and emotional wisdom intended to inform the whole person, not necessarily to define a specific action or give lawful boundaries to a life-path. *Aggadot* are sometimes contradictory, as different sages speak different wisdoms.
- Passages from the five books of Torah (and briefly from Chronicles) on the seven-year and fifty-year cycles of rest that human beings must provide for the land and for society, and on what happens if that spiral of work and rest is violated. These are from that aspect of Torah called *halakhah* ("walking a path"), which details the steps of a lawful course of action.

In these texts the Name of God that often appears is the four-letter, unvoweled Hebrew *Yod-Hei-Waw-Hei*. The convention for translating this Name into English is to use "Lord." Here we find instead the more mysterious YHWH, a transliteration rather than a translation. This points toward an aspect of the Name that seems especially apt for Eco-Judaism: Sounded out with no vowels at all (thus not "Jehovah" or "Yahweh"), this Name is simply a breathing.

And so one way to translate it is "Breath of Life" or "Breath of the World." Using YHWH in this way points toward a certain understanding of the Divine: that It is not only transcendent, beyond the world, but also immanent in the world, including the world of earth, rain, wind, sun. The Breath is both beyond us and within us. It connects all life forms with each other.

As a metaphor for the Divine, "Breath of Life" has the virtue of speaking in all languages and in all species, reminding us that what we breathe in is what the trees breathe out; what the trees breathe out, we breathe in: We breathe each other into life.

After these initial texts from the world of the Bible come three examinations from our own era of what we might call "Biblical Eco-Judaism." This is, of course, an anachronistic label. In the biblical culture it was simply a truth of life that any celebration of the sacred would include the sacred intertwining of the Breath of Life. Just as there could be no Judaism divorced from food or sex or money, so there could be no relationship to the earth that was devoid of the Divine. It is only today, after a long alienation of Judaism from connection with the earth, that we might need to call Eco-Judaism into renewed life and give it a special name.

Two of the three commentaries make a point of the interplay between Babylonian and Israelite ways of living with and thinking about the earth. They do this for somewhat different reasons.

Evan Eisenberg explores in considerable depth how the economics/ecologics of the Babylonian and Canaanite/Israelite societies draw them toward different worldviews. He shows how many of their dominant metaphors and symbols grew out of their relationship with the earth. In this way he gives us a new prism through which to view much of the Hebrew Bible and Jewish wisdom, which has usually been understood as drawn from political, not ecological, history—from a history of slavery, wandering, self-government, subjugation, exile.

Eisenberg draws on some of the specific texts created by the two cultures, but focuses less on these than on their different ecological life-paths, and on how these became encoded in two archetypal poles: the Mountain and the Tower, wilderness and city. He sees Israelite tradition as emerging from the experience of shepherds and hill farmers, therefore upholding the primacy of wilderness; Babylonian culture, from the experience of an elaborately irrigated agricultural empire, hence focused on the Tower, the city.

Eisenberg reminds us that no city can live without the nourishment it takes from an untamed wilderness. Yet human beings have tamed themselves, are now tame animals; and wherever they go, they tame the Mountain and make it a Tower. And then what wilderness will nourish us?

Even today we face the question, How can we resolve these dilemmas? For even in this writing on the cultures of three thousand years ago, tomorrow keeps intruding.

Tikva Frymer-Kensky compares Babylonian and Hebrew texts from a different perspective. She is especially interested in whether (as is often charged) the Hebrew Bible denigrates the earth, especially when compared with the ancient "pagan" traditions of Babylonia.

To examine this question, she chooses fewer Babylonian and Hebrew texts than Eisenberg and goes into them more deeply. She points out that the Babylonian *Atrahasis Epic* expresses great concern about overpopulation, which incites the gods to send famines and droughts that violate the earth and limit human powers. The purpose of the earth is to nourish humans, who nourish the gods. The gods need human beings; they care much less about the earth except to use it as a weapon to control their human servants.

By contrast, she suggests, the biblical creation story asserts that just as the dry land cannot exist separate from the trees and grasses (they are all created on the third day), so human beings cannot exist separate from animals (they are both created on the sixth day). This universe is intertwined from the beginning. It is humans who weaken the fruitfulness of earth, and even when God intervenes directly with the Flood, it is in response to lawless human behavior.

We may see more similarity between these stories than does Frymer-Kensky. We might see the gods in Babylonia and the God of the Flood as the delivery system for "what you sow, that's what you reap"—that is, the processes by which human behavior and the rest of the "natural world" are linked. Overpopulate the earth, and these processes (= "the gods") will bring on famine. Flood the earth with ruinous corruption, and through those processes (= "God") the corruption overflows to sweep us all away.

One difference that is especially important from an ecological perspective stands out: Where Babylonia feared overpopulation, Israelite culture celebrated human procreation and fertility. Perhaps this represents the difference between an urban culture, built on imperial agriculture and a population explosion, and a pastoral people, worried perhaps about an overflowing Babylonian empire staring down upon it and therefore far less concerned to limit its own numbers.

And Frymer-Kensky points toward a more basic difference: The overpopulation that leads to the Babylonian Flood is a biological process. For the Israelites, the causes of disaster are vaguer but more in the realm of ethics. And as Frymer-Kensky then shows in more detail, Israelite prophets and priests both cry out about human ethical failures that will pollute the land—physically, politically, and spiritually. Her point is that, today, the "pagan" biologically focused

Babylonian outlook may do less to heal the earth from human damage than the ethical focus of the Israelites.

Finally, in an essay on the rhythm of Doing and Being, and especially the provisions for Rest and Release as they appeared in Israelite land policy, the editor shows how the social and ecological—meeting the needs of the earth and of the poor—were fused into one practice by the sabbatical/Jubilee cycle.

Perhaps this was the answer of nostalgic former nomads to the encroachments of an imperial system of fenced-in property. To surrender entirely: unthinkable. To preserve the old way of life unaltered: impossible.

From reading these writings, the questions we may ask ourselves are:

- What should we do when the ethical/political and the bioecological intertwine, as they seem to do in the present era?
- Can we learn from the teachings of both a small, edgy, pioneering people and a great imperial power?
- Can our generation renew the life-giving spiritual rhythms of the past, and the sense of community they encouraged, while drawing on some of the benefits of the newer technological global civilization?

A. *AGGADAH:* JOY IN CREATION—TWO PSALMS

Translated by Arthur Waskow

Bless YHWH/Breath of Life, O my breathing;
O YHWH, my God, You are very great;
You are cloaked in glory and majesty,
wrapped in a robe of light;
You spread the heavens like a tent,
In the world-wide waters You set the beams of Your planet-wide pavilions,
You make the clouds Your chariot,
move on the wings of the wind.
You make the winds Your messengers,
fiery flames Your servants.
You set the earth on its foundations,
so that it shall never totter.
You robed the earth with ocean waves,
the waters stood above the mountains.

They fled at Your blast,
rushed away at the sound of Your thunder,
Mountains rising, valleys sinking—
to the place You established for them.
You set bounds they must not pass
so that they never again cover the earth.
You make springs gush forth in torrents;
they make their way between the hills,
giving drink to all the wild beasts;
the wild donkeys quench their thirst.
The birds of the sky dwell beside them
and sing among the foliage.
You water the mountains from Your loftiest sources;
the earth is fulfilled with the fruit of Your work.
You make grass grow for the cattle,
and grain for human labor
that we may get food out of the earth—
wine that cheers the human heart,
oil that makes the face shine,
and bread that sustains a human life.
The trees of YHWH drink their fill—
the cedars of Lebanon, Your own planting,
where birds make their nests;
the stork has her home in the junipers.
The high mountains are for wild goats;
the crags are a refuge for rock-badgers.
You made the moon to mark the seasons;
the sun knows when to set.
You bring on darkness and it is night,
when all the beasts of the forests stir.

The lions roar for prey,
seeking their food from God.
When the sun rises, they come home
and couch in their dens.
Then we go out to do our work,
to labor till the evening.
How many are the things You have made, O YHWH;
You have made them all with wisdom;
the earth is full of Your creations.
There is the sea, vast and wide,
with its creatures beyond number,
living things, small and great.
There go the ships,
and Leviathan that You formed to play with.
All of them look to You
to give them their food when it is due.

Give it to them, they gather it up;
open Your hand, they are well satisfied;
hide Your face, they are terrified;
take away their breath, they perish
and turn again into dust;
send back Your breath, they are created,
and You renew the face of the earth.
May the glory of YHWH endure forever;
may YHWH rejoice in Your works!
You look at the earth and it trembles;
You touch the mountains and they smoke.
I will sing to YHWH as long as I live;
all my life I will chant hymns to my God.

May my prayer please You;
I will rejoice in YHWH.
May sinners disappear from the earth,
and the wicked be no more.
Bless YHWH, O my breathing.
Hallelu Yah!

(Psalm 104)

Hallelu-YAH!
Praise YHWH/the Breath of Life from the heavens,
Praise It in the heights,
Praise It, you messengers; Praise It, you multitudes!
Praise It, sun and moon
And all you light-filled stars!
Praise It, Heavens beyond the heavens.
Praise It, waters beneath the heavens.
Praise the Name of YHWH/Breath of Life,
For through Its intertwining all comes to Be,
Each finds its place in the dance of All:
YHWH carves them a role that no one can erase.
So sing praise, all that is earthy and grounded,
All that flows in the deeps like the great sea-monsters,
Fire and hail, snow and fog,
Storm-winds blowing from the Mouth of God.
Lofty mountains, gentle hills,
Fruit trees and evergreens,
Roaring beasts and lowing herds,
Crawly bugs and soaring birds,
Powerful rulers and empowered peoples,
Prosecutors and public defenders,
Men and women sprouting promise,

Bearded elders bent by life and beardless youth not yet on path,
All sing praise to the Breath of Life—
For It stands alone in radiance,
Filling with splendor earth and sky,
Making Its people a horn of plenty.
For the sake of all who love It
Or who come near through Wrestling God,
Let us praise the Breath of Life—Hallelu-YAH!

(Psalm 149)

B. *HALAKHAH*: REST FOR THE EARTH—THE SABBATICAL/ JUBILEE TRADITION

YHWH/Breath of Life spoke to Moses on Mount Sinai, saying: Speak to the Children of Israel and say to them: When you enter the land that I give you, the land is to restfully-cease a Sabbath-ceasing of YHWH. For six years you are to sow your field, for six years you are to prune your vineyard, and to gather in its increase. But in the seventh year there shall be a Sabbath of Sabbath-ceasing for the land, a Sabbath of YHWH. Your field you are not to sow, your vineyard you are not to prune, the aftergrowth of your harvest you are not to harvest. . . .

It shall be a Sabbath of Sabbath-ceasing for the land. You may eat whatever the land during its Sabbath will freely produce—you, your male and female servants, your hired hand, resident-settlers who sojourn with you, and your domestic-cattle and the wild-life in your land may eat all its yield. (Lev. 25:1–7)

Every seventh year you shall practice Nonattachment. This shall be the nature of the Nonattachment: Every holder of a loan shall release what he has lent to his neighbor. He shall not oppress his neighbor or kinsman, for the Nonattachment proclaimed is from YHWH. (Deut. 15:1–2)

You shall count off seven Sabbath-cycles of years—seven times seven years—so that the period of seven Sabbath-cycles of years gives you a total of forty-nine years. Then you shall sound the ram's horn loud; in the seventh New Moon, on the tenth day after the New Moon—on the Day of Atonement—you shall sound the ram's horn throughout all your land. And you shall hallow the year, the fiftieth year.

You shall proclaim Nonattachment throughout the land for all its inhabitants. It shall be a Home-bringing/Jubilee for you: Each of you shall return to his holding and each of you shall return to his family. That fiftieth year shall be a Home-bringing/Jubilee for you: You shall not sow, neither shall you reap the aftergrowth or harvest the untrimmed vines, for it is a Home-bringing/Jubilee. It shall be holy to you: You may only eat the growth direct from the field. (Lev. 25:8–12)

In this year of Home-bringing/Jubilee each of you shall return to your holding. When you sell property to your neighbor, or buy any from your neighbor, you shall not wrong one another. In buying from your neighbor, you shall deduct only for the number of years since the Home-bringing/Jubilee; and in selling to you, he shall charge you only for the remaining crop years: The more such years, the higher the price you pay; the fewer such years, the lower the price; for what he is selling you is a number of harvests. Do not wrong one another, but fear your God; for I YHWH am your God. (Lev. 25:8–17)

You shall act upon My carved-out patterns-of-reality; My judgings you shall keep and act upon, that you may live upon the land in security; the land shall yield its fruit and you shall eat your fill, and you shall live upon it in security. And should you ask, "What are we to eat in the seventh year, if we may neither sow nor gather in our crops?" I will connect My blessing to you in the sixth year, so that it shall yield a crop sufficient for three years. . . . But the land must not be sold beyond reclaim, for the land is Mine; you are but strangers and visitors with Me. (Lev. 25:18–21, 23)

If you follow My laws and faithfully observe My commandments, I will grant your rains in their season, so that the earth shall yield its produce and the trees of the field their fruit. Your threshing shall overtake the vintage, and your vintage shall overtake the sowing; you shall eat your fill of bread and dwell securely in your land. . . . I will grant peace in the land, and you shall lie down untroubled by anyone; I will give the land respite from vicious beasts, and no sword shall cross your land.

I will establish My Dwelling-place in your midst, and I will not spurn you. I will be ever present in your midst: I will be your God, and you shall be My people. I YHWH am your God who brought you out from the land of Narrow Straits/the Egyptians to be their slaves no more, who broke the bars of your yoke and made you walk erect.

But if you do not obey Me and do not observe all these commandments, if you reject My laws and spurn My rules, so that you do not observe all My commandments and you break My covenant. . . . (Lev. 26:3–15)

. . .Your land shall become a desolation and your cities a ruin. Then shall the land make up for its Sabbath-ceasing years throughout the time that it is desolate and you are in the land of your enemies; then shall the land restfully-cease and make up for its Sabbath-ceasing years.

Throughout the time that it is desolate, it shall restfully-cease as it did not restfully-cease in your Sabbath-ceasing years while you were dwelling upon it. (Lev. 26:33–35)

For the land shall be forsaken of them, making up for its Sabbath years by being desolate of them, while they atone for their iniquity; for the abundant reason that they rejected My rules and spurned My laws. (Lev. 26:43)

Those who survived the sword he exiled to Babylon, and they became his and his sons' servants till the rise of the Persian kingdom, in fulfillment of the word of YHWH spoken by Jeremiah, until the land paid back its Sabbaths; as long as it lay desolate it kept Sabbath, till seventy years were completed. (II Chron. 36:20–21)

THE MOUNTAIN AND THE TOWER: WILDERNESS AND CITY IN THE SYMBOLS OF BABYLON AND ISRAEL

Evan Eisenberg

Two ways of looking at the world arose in the ancient Near East and are with us yet. For one, the heart of the world is wilderness. For the other, the world revolves around the city, the work of human hands.

A cartographer's quibble? Hardly. It is a fundamental dispute about the way the world works and what our role in it should be. From the point of view of ecology, there is no more important question one can ask about a civilization than which of these views

Evan Eisenberg is the author of *The Ecology of Eden* and *The Recording Angel.* His writing on nature and culture has appeared in *The Atlantic, The New Republic, The Nation, Natural History,* and other publications. A sometime cantor and former gardener for the New York City parks department, he lives in Manhattan with his wife, an urban planner, and their daughter.

it adopts and acts on. Indeed, the prospects of our own civilization may hinge on whether we can, at this late date, change our minds.

The two great world-views I am speaking of belonged to two kinds of civilization: those of the hilly uplands and those of the great river valleys.[1]

The first kind is typified by the Canaanites, the second by the Mesopotamians. The peoples of the hills, narrow valleys, and narrow coastal plains made their living from small-scale mixed husbandry. This was a much refined but still modest descendant of the earliest farming known, which had arisen in those same hills. The peoples of the great river valleys were more ambitious. They practiced large-scale, irrigated agriculture that was not so different, at heart, from what large corporations do in California today.

Tied to these different ways of living on the land were different economies, different social structures, different political forms, and different ways of looking at the world. Above all, the hill peoples and the valley peoples had different world-poles.[2]

The world-pole is the axis on which the world turns. It is the heart of the world, the source of all life. Nearly every people has a world-pole, but they do not all agree on its shape. For the Canaanites, the world-pole was the Mountain: the wild place sacred to the gods, the font of life-giving water. For the Mesopotamians, it was the Tower: the ziggurat that rose in the midst of the city.

If there is one thing all cosmogonies agree on, it is the need for division. Pine as they may for a time of perfect oneness, all peoples know that a world undivided cannot stand. For life to feed and reproduce itself, there must be division: between heaven and earth, male and female, man and beast and god. But for life to flourish—and on this point, too, all cosmogonies agree—there must be some place where all these things are reconnected. That is the world-pole.

As a rule, the world-pole is the source of life. Like the trunk of a tree, the world-pole is something through which life flows. It is at once phallus and vulva, ram's horn and cornucopia. It is the uterus from which all creatures crawled and the teat from which they continue to suck. If a man or woman—a shaman, a hero, a prophet—would ascend to the heavens or descend to the underworld, here is the stairwell. Here the adept can pow-wow with gods and animals, even merge with them, as all of us used to do at the beginning of time.

THE CANAANITES

The fact that Canaan—the region now occupied by Israel, Lebanon, and Syria—contains the lowest dry land on the planet (the shore of the Dead Sea) as well as deserts, coastal plains, and steppe only makes its great mountains the more imposing.[3] The ranges of Persia and Anatolia sprawl for so many hundreds of miles that it is hard for any one peak to seem a World Mountain; but the Lebanon, Anti-Lebanon, and Ammanus ranges are so compact that they were spoken of in ancient times almost as if they were monadnocks. The Lebanon and Anti-Lebanon ranges reach heights of 10,131 and 9,232 feet, respectively; the Ammanus of 7,418 feet. Their splendor was a byword throughout the Near East, as was the price their timber could bring: in particular, the huge ancient cedars that grew on the upper western slope of the Lebanon.

It is no surprise, then, that in Canaanite poetry both the elder god El and the younger god Baal have their houses or tents on mountaintops. For that matter, so does Baal's sister and bride, the goddess Anat. The Mountain of El is preeminent, being the place where the gods meet in council, to dine and haggle, and the fate of the universe is decreed. El lives at "the source of the Two Rivers, in the midst of the Pools of the Double-Deep." (The last phrase can also be rendered "headwaters of the Two Oceans" and may refer to the male ocean of the heavens and the female ocean that undergirds the earth.) From El's mountain flow the waters that bring life to the world. It is proof of his power that he has broken and yoked the primal waters, and that instead of breaking out and swamping the world they run dutifully in two rivers that give the world life. El does not merely sit by the waters like a poet; he sits on them, keeps a lid on them, and ladles them out.

Nevertheless, by the time of the great Ugaritic epics the waterworks are being handed over in part to a younger and abler god, El's son Baal. Baal's mountain is called Mount Zaphon (or Sapanu), from a root meaning "to look out" or "spy out." That it is a place where heaven and earth fruitfully meet is hinted at in a message he sends to Anat:

> *Pour out peace in the depths of the earth,*
> *Make love increase in the depths of the fields . . .*
> *The speech of wood and the whisper of stone,*
> *The converse of heaven with the earth,*
> *Of the deeps with the stars . . .*
> *Come, and I will seek it,*
> *In the midst of my mountain, divine Zaphon . . .* [4]

Whether the "speech of wood and the whisper of stone" refers, as some think, to the palace or temple which Baal plans to build on his mountain, or rather to the wooded mass of the mountain itself, the role of Zaphon as world-pole is clear. In his message, Baal calls Anat to his side. The flow of love and fertility will be clinched, it seems, by a sacred marriage between Baal and Anat: icing on the cake of his victory and enthronement on Zaphon.

THE WORLD-POLE
AS ECOLOGICAL FACT

To say that the world-pole is a mountain is to state, in mythic shorthand, an ecological fact. There are certain places on earth that play a central role in the flow of energy and the cycling of water and nutrients, as well as the maintenance of genetic diversity and its spread by means of gene flow. Such places provide many of the services that keep the ecosystems around them (and the biosphere as a whole) more or less healthy for humans and other life forms. They help control flooding and soil erosion. They regulate the mix of oxygen, carbon dioxide, water vapor, and other ingredients in the air and keep its temperature within bounds. They are spigots for the circulation of wildness through places made hard and almost impermeable by long human use. All such places are more or less wild; many are forested; many are mountainous, and from them great rivers flow.

The mountains of Lebanon, Syria, and Armenia are the source of water for much of the Near East. From their slopes flow the headwaters of the Jordan, the Orontes, the Tigris, and the Euphrates. The pattern is copied on smaller scales as well, in the brooks, wadis, and underground aquifers that slide from the Judean hills to the coast.

Canaan as a whole, situated at the junction of three continents, has always been a maelstrom of gene flow. Even today its genetic diversity is dazzling, with flora and fauna of Europe, Africa, and Asia mingling in sometimes unsettling ways. A few thousand years ago, when the region was less bruised by human use, the mix was more dazzling still.

In this matter, too, the uplands have played a special role. During the Pleistocene Ice Age, when the locking up of water in glaciers made the earth as a whole drier and much of the Near East was arid steppe, the mountains gave refuge to species in flight from drought.[5] Among these species were humans as well as some of the trees, grasses, and quadrupeds they would later tame. It was the expansion of these species, at the end of the last Ice Age, from their mountain hideouts to the lower foothills of the Levant that set the stage for domestication.

It was also the slopes themselves. For the play of farming to get started, it was helpful that the stage be slanted. On hillsides a wide range of climates can be collapsed accordion-like within the space of a few acres. This produces a menu of variation in wild plants that fairly begs humans to pick and choose: that is, to select. It also encourages transhumance.

Transhumance, the practice of herding livestock to summer pasture in the hills, then back to the valley for the winter—or the other way around in some dry regions—can be seen as a telescoped form of nomadism. (That is not to say it arose later than nomadism; more likely it came first.) It is made possible by Humboldt's Law, which states that climbing a 100-meter hill yields roughly the same drop in temperature as trekking 110 kilometers (one degree of latitude) away from the equator.

Giving hard-earned grain to animals is a late and luxurious practice. The first domestic animals had to fend for themselves. Their wild forebears had followed the grass, the brush, and the seasons. If more or less settled farmers were able to keep them, it was only because those farmers lived in the hills, where the seasons crept up and down the slopes instead of (or as well as) gliding hundreds of miles north and south.

The same piece of legislation made the hilly flanks of the Fertile Crescent the ideal place for the domestication of grains. Variations in elevation produce variations in climate, which produce variations in plants; these in turn provide the raw material for breeding. Emmer, einkorn, and six-row barley were lining up along isotherms (lines of equal temperature) long before they were lined up by farmers. In effect, natural selection had set out upon the tablelands and in the bowl-like valleys of the Near East a smorgasbord from which human selection could take its pick. So the uplands of the Levant were the ideal setting for the domestication of plants and animals alike.

Myths of the world-pole say that the source of the first human life will be the source that sustains human life. It may seem a paradox that a wild or sparsely settled place should seem to be the point of origin of humankind, that is, Eden. But in fact Holocene humans do seem to have come out of the uplands of the Near East, descended into the valleys to build civilization, then edged up the hills again as their numbers swelled. Outside Africa, anatomically modern humans make their first clear appearance in the archaeological record in the uplands of the Levant, in roughly the same place as the first proto-farmers. Some 90,000 years ago, while Neanderthals had the run of Europe, *Homo sapiens* dwelt in the caves of Mount Carmel.[6]

The Mountain was thus the source of one great wave of human advance—farming—and at least the proximate source of an earlier wave, made up of the first creatures whom, if they sat down next to us at a luncheon counter in modern dress, we would not hesitate to ask to pass the ketchup.

The real lesson of the Mountain, though, has nothing to do

with any particular mountains, or even with mountains as such. It has to do with wilderness.

The point is that manmade landscapes, from the wheat fields and vineyards of ancient Canaan to the strip malls of New Jersey, survive only by the courtesy of the wilderness around them, and the wildness that remains in them. Energy flows, water and nutrients circulate, climate is kept within bounds, the ingredients of the air are kept in balance, the soil is made fertile. All these things are matters of life and death for us. All are done for us free of charge, in ways we do not fully grasp. Even if we knew how these jobs are done, we would be unwise to try and take them over. For we would then spend most of our time trying desperately to manage what used to be managed for us.

As the postmodernists never tire of telling us, wilderness is a myth. What they fail to tell us, because they do not comprehend it, is that it is a necessary myth—necessary because, on a biological level that mutely resists deconstruction, it is deeply and urgently real.

True: few wildernesses are certifiably pure. True: all wilderness has a history, in which humans have generally played a part. True: the idea of wilderness has been used as an excuse for elitism, imperialism, and sheer complacency. But the trendy debunking of wilderness may breed even greater mischief. Advanced in the name of the people, it has been seized upon by corporate and political elements whose only interest in people or nature is to squeeze them dry. Even in the best hands, it leads us toward a slippery slope whose final declension we cannot measure.

Wilderness is a social construction. So is the guardrail at the edge of a precipice: and I would not gladly see either dismantled.

THE MESOPOTAMIANS

When farmers first wandered down from the hills of Iran or the Syrian steppe, or wandered up the shore of the Persian Gulf, and gazed on the vast flood plain of the two rivers, they must have been intrigued but not altogether pleased.[7] They knew that rivers were arteries of life, and here were the two biggest rivers they had ever seen. Yet the land before them was no well-watered paradise, but a patchwork of swamp and desert. Swept in summer by a wind like the blowback of a kiln, the dunes shifted irritably under a sparse cover of artemisia (a cousin of sagebrush) and other shrubs, while the remnants of the spring annuals dried up and blew away. What was a farmer to make of this? His wheat and barley would not tolerate either the wet or the dry. His livestock would founder in the marshes or go thirsty among the dunes.

The first signs of permanent settlement on the flood plain date to the sixth millennium BCE. Two thousand years later—the length of an afternoon nap in prehistory—Mesopotamia was a paradise. It was a manmade paradise, a thing without precedent on earth. Although there were still marshes in the south, and plenty of semidesert in which seminomads as well as villagers and cityfolk grazed their herds, a wide tract of land on either side of the Euphrates was generously spangled with grain fields, date plantations, fish ponds, and gardens of lettuce, onions, lentils, garlic, and cress. Cities of sunbaked or kilnbaked mud brick sprawled like lions amid these spoils, outwardly reposeful but inwardly (like the lion of Samson's riddle) buzzing.

The magnitude of this achievement can stun us even now if we stop to think about it. These people—the Sumerians and their predecessors in the region, the Ubaidians—gave us wheeled vehicles, yokes and harnesses so that animals could pull them, animal-drawn plows, sailboats, metalworking (casting, riveting, brazing, soldering, inlay, and engraving in copper and bronze), the potter's wheel, the arch, the vault, the dome, surveying, mapping, and a rough-and-ready mathematics. Above all they gave us the process in which you and I are now engaged, even if we no longer use hensfoot marks on soft clay. On the debit side of the ledger (another Sumerian invention) we might place large professional armies, siege engines, war chariots, a rigid division of labor and status, imperialism, and bureaucracy.

All this is the more remarkable in that hardly any of the raw materials of civilization, apart from the clay to make bricks and tablets, was to be found in the place where civilization began. Metal, wood, stone, and other things needful the Mesopotamians got in exchange for their agricultural surplus and the finished products of their craftsmanship. (By "Mesopotamians" I mean all the civilized peoples who lived in the valley of the Tigris and Euphrates in ancient times: in chronological order, the Sumerians, the Akkadians, and the Babylonians. For the most part they were the same people under different rulers.)

What made it all possible was a series of trenches running alongside the rivers in a pattern like a chain, or like the braids of a young girl.[8] (Later the pattern would be dendritic, sharing the efficient layout of a tree's branching or a leaf's veins.) The sandy soil, with its patchy drainage, had made a mess of the job of distributing the groundwater that seeped from the riverbeds. The canals took over that job. What had looked like desert now proved to be soil far richer than anything wheat or barley had known in their native hills.

In a sense, though, this was the soil they had known in their native hills. Each winter for millennia the rains had gouged the hillsides of Syria and Anatolia. In recent millennia the gouging had been especially cruel, egged on by axes and hoes. Periodic floods had spread the deducted soil over the Mesopotamian plain. Wheat, barley, and humans followed the soil downstream.

But the floods had not spread the soil evenly. When the rivers overflowed their banks, they dropped coarse particles first, fine particles last. As the rivers wound, unwound, and changed their courses, they laid down a patchwork of coarse and fine soils: the former draining too quickly, the latter too slowly. So the humans who now showed up to claim the humus they had lost found it less immediately usable than they might have hoped. The answer was irrigation.

In Sumerian, a single word denotes both rivers and canals. Both were supposed to be the work of the gods, which humans merely maintained. Many ostensible canals were in fact natural channels in which the Euphrates had sometimes run. Unlike the Tigris, whose short course and swift current let it cut a deeper and straighter path, the Euphrates—sluggish as a pasha, and luxuriously indecisive—would flow now here, now there, now both ways at once. As it dropped sediment it made its bed ever higher, like a princess piling up mattresses. In fact, it flowed above the surface of the plain and was kept from overflowing only by the natural levee it built up on either side. But then at some point it would break through the levee and find a new channel. So the river took on a braided look. Although the first settlers on the plain had some experience of small-scale irrigation, by and large they took their cue from the river itself. Some canals were made by adapting the existing side channels, others by mimicking the process by which they were formed.

THE TOWER OF BABEL

At the heart of every Mesopotamian city was a sacred precinct, and at the heart of every sacred precinct was a ziggurat, a stepped pyramid of mud brick. Unimposing by our standards—the great ziggurat of Ur was about seventy feet high—they were by far the tallest objects, natural or manmade, to be found on the Mesopotamian plain. Oddly, some ziggurats seem to have imitated mountains in a fairly literal way. One of the first, in Uruk, stood on an artificial hill about forty feet high. Although in most later temples the hill was replaced by a platform, the tower itself was often called a "cedar-scented mountain." It is not clear whether this was a bare-faced metaphor or whether some planting was done to buttress the claim. Most likely cedar and cypress oils were used as air fresheners within the temple. In the reborn Babylon of the sixth century BCE, the fabled Hanging Gardens were planted in the steps or terraces of a ziggurat. Legend has it that Nebuchadnezzar planted them for his Persian bride, who pined for the hills of Ecbatana.

Every great temple claimed to stand on the axis mundi or elevator shaft of the cosmos, offering the gods a way station between the upper and lower worlds. The creation epic *Enuma Elish* assigns to Babylon the role of divine motel and convention center, a role that seems to have been competed for and claimed by other cities at other times. For the Mesopotamian gods are city slickers. If one or another has his or her "throne-seat" or "abode" on the Cedar Mountain, it is evidently used for ceremonial purposes, or as a summer place. Compared to the city, the countryside is godforsaken.

It is a sign of the Mesopotamians' pride that they drew the gods—and paradise itself—down from the mountains and into their own cities. If the source of life is upstream, downstream is where the fat collects: the rich bottomlands, the canals, the cities, the good life. While the mountains may give life, in these matters it is better to receive.

In preferring the plain to the hills, the river valley to the headwaters as a place to lay out fields and build cities—in noting that the fat collects downstream—the Mesopotamians had a point. They were in fact recipients of the hills' largesse. Their mistake was to forget that fact.

Giddy with prosperity and progress, they came to think they had done it all themselves. Instead of recipients, they came to think of themselves as the source of life and plenty. They controlled the waters, tapped the great rivers like kegs of beer. It was easy to forget that the water came from somewhere. They had agriculture down to a science. It was easy to forget that it had arisen among the savages of the hills. The storehouses spat out grain; the markets were littered with dates and slippery with oil. Surely the city was the source of all life.[9]

One can hardly blame the Mesopotamians for wanting a world-pole closer to home than the distant and (to most of them) invisible mountains. They might have chosen some flatter but still natural world-pole to match the world they knew. They might have embedded the gods in the rivers, or in the salt marshes at the rivers' mouths, which were great dispensaries of wildness and of natural wealth. Maybe they did, at first: Enki, for instance, seems to have spent a lot of time among the canebrakes. But by historical times Enki, like the other great gods, is safely installed in a city.

For some peoples, religious feeling is the feeling that some things are beyond society's control, that the sources of good and bad are unplumbable and can easily drown the flimsy channels we make to contain them. For others, the manmade order is so firmly established that it seems godmade. Awe is stripped from nature and affixed to the social and technical order. On the whole the Canaanites were a culture of the first type, the Mesopotamians of the second.

Today southern Mesopotamia is once again the patchwork of swamp and desert it was when the first settlers arrived. The main difference (apart from the fact that the wildlife is gone) is that much of the soil is no longer even potentially fertile.

In arid climates, the groundwater is often brackish. As long as it stays below the level to which the roots of crops penetrate, it is no problem; but when a field has been used for a while, irrigation without proper drainage can raise the water table. Crops can filter out some of the salt when they drink, but in so doing they make the remaining water that much saltier. Eventually it catches up with them. Falling yields are the first sign of trouble. Then, when the saline groundwater has nudged within a few feet of the surface, capillary action starts to lift it the rest of the way. At the surface the water evaporates while the salt "blossoms out in mockingly beautiful floral patterns."[10] The Mesopotamian idea that a spiteful Tiamat was rising up was not far wrong.

Having a general sense of what the problem was, farmers would fallow a field or else try to flush out the salts with more water. Fallowing might work for a while, because salt-tolerant weeds would move in, suck up some water, and lower the water table. Flushing would work very briefly and then backfire, by raising the water table and with it the salt.

Among the many favors that pots do for archaeologists is to retain, under certain conditions, marks of the kernels of grain that were stored in them. Pots dug up in southern Mesopotamia suggest that from 3500 BCE onward the ratio of wheat to barley in the harvest steadily shrank. By 1700 no wheat was grown at all. In an age before advertising, tastes in food were very stable, so barring a major rise in beer consumption it seems likely that the shift to barley was a matter of necessity rather than choice. One factor may have been the growing importance of wool textiles for export, which meant that more barley had to be grown for fodder. But the evidence points to a necessity a good deal more dire.

As befits a poor cousin, barley is on the whole less finicky than wheat about where and how it grows. In particular, it is far more tolerant of salt. Given the crust of salt that covers so much of Mesopotamia today, and the half-comprehending references to the problem that can be found in ancient texts, it has been suggested that salt must have caused failures of the wheat crop, forcing a shift to barley.[11] Estate records from the period show a steady decline in yields of wheat and a lesser but vexing drop in yields of barley. As the soil turned to salt, the economic base of Sumer fissured and slowly crumbled. This helped make it vulnerable to the growing power of its northern neighbor, Akkad.

In modern times, farmers north of Baghdad grow nine times as much wheat as barley, while farmers near the Gulf grow nine times as much barley as wheat. For both crops, yields are far lower than they were in ancient times.

No one can say "I told you so" to the Mesopotamians. No one told them so. What they did was done for the first time on earth. It seemed a good idea at the time, and in many ways it was. Then the edge of civilization moved on, leaving a desert behind it.[12]

The Hill Farmers

There were, I said, two broad types of culture in the ancient Near East, broadly matched to two types of agriculture: that of the irrigated river valleys and that of the hills. The first is typified by the Mesopotamians, the second by the Canaanites, including the Israelites.

Let us not be deceived by the Bible's polemics against the Canaanites. As anyone who follows radical politics knows, the sharpest barbs are always reserved for those closest to one's own position: the group one schism away. In ecological terms, it's the species one has just split off from that one must compete with for a niche.

The more we know about the Israelites, the clearer it is that they were Canaanite hill farmers who practiced a sophisticated and fairly sustainable mixed husbandry of grains, vines, livestock, and trees yielding fruit, nuts, and oil.[13] They were neither desert nomads mistrustful of nature nor proud hydraulic despots lording it over nature. They were good farmers living frugally on the margins and using the best stewardship they knew. They were dependent on rain and groundwater, neither of which was overabundant, and on thin and rock-strewn soil, and had to use their wits to conserve both. They were not so different from present-day farmers of the Andes or of Szechuan. They were not so different, perhaps, from other peasants of the Mediterranean basin, past and present.

When archaeology first finds the Israelites—about 1100 BCE—they are pioneers in the hills of Judea and Samaria, part of the central range that runs like a spine down the length of Canaan (its Apennines, one might say). There is no evidence that this pioneering was prelude to a "conquest" of the valleys and the coastal plain ("destruction layers" of ash and debris are mostly absent from the relevant strata of the Canaanite sites mentioned in the Bible). Nor is there much evidence of a flight from Egypt. Yet it is true that these settlers had just escaped the pharaoh's yoke. They were not so much settling as resettling the uplands, which had been depopulated during the four centuries when Egyptian rule ravaged Canaan.

Having known both the ax and the torch in earlier times, and getting at the best of times only modest rainfall, the hills of Judea and Samaria were not clothed in what we would call "forest primeval." Where least disturbed, the landscape was the sort of open Mediterranean woodland known as high maquis, with evergreen oak, Aleppo pine, and pistachio (known in the Bible as terebinth) the most common trees. Elsewhere this would dwindle to low maquis, a mix of shrubs and herbs such as rosemary, sage, summer savory, rock rose, and thorny burnet. The settlers cleared a good deal of this forest for pasture and cropland, knowing that beneath lay the red soil now called terra rossa, the richest of all mountain soils. (In Hebrew the words for "earth," "human," "red," and "blood" sound alike and may have a common derivation.) Of this process the Book of Joshua (17:14f) preserves a hint:

> And the children of Joseph spoke unto Joshua, saying: "Why has thou given me but one lot and one part for an inheritance, seeing I am a great people, forasmuch as the Lord hath blessed me thus?" And Joshua said unto them: "If thou be a great people, get thee up to the forest, and cut down for thyself there in the land of the Perizzites and of the Rephaim; since the hill-country of Ephraim is too narrow for thee."

This new round of deforestation promised to be the worst yet. Besides the usual sheep and shoot-nibbling goats, these settlers had big animal-drawn plows with bronze shares, a loan from Mesopotamia. Although still only scratch plows, which did not turn the soil upside-down as mouldboard plows do, these could still be lethal to the soil of any slope steeper than a wheelchair-accessible entrance ramp. The red soil was rich but rarely more than a foot deep.

As the slopes began to lose their thin layer of rich red soil— and as population growth made land dearer and labor somewhat more plentiful—the Israelites began to build terraces. Whether this was their own invention is unclear; a word appearing in the Ugaritic epics may refer to the same device. Either way, there is a good chance that some group or other of Canaanites came up with the idea. As the first farmers of the Mediterranean basin, they devised many of the methods that its peasants use to this day.

To make a terrace was no small matter. Remaking a ramp as

a series of steps meant moving a lot of earth and rock, though the naturally blocky Karst limestone of some regions helped somewhat. (Today in the vicinity of Jerusalem it is hard to tell offhand whether a particular hill got its staircase shape from ancient man or more ancient nature.) Pillars made of large boulders would be erected and the gaps between filled in with smaller stones. Behind these walls, it would not do just to pile up dirt any which way. Above the bedrock would be a layer of soil, on top of that a layer of gravel, and on top of the gravel another layer of soil. In this way water would percolate from one terrace to the next one down. Some of the soil in the terraces seems to have been hauled up from the valley floor, perhaps because erosion was already well along.

For all this effort, farmers got a number of benefits. They got a nice, nearly level surface to plow with ox and ard. They got the soil to stay put, at least for a while. And they got rainwater to tarry far longer than it would usually care to do on a denuded slope. (The same could be done with spring water: in Roman times, if not earlier, a system of channels might distribute the water of a spring near the top of a hill among the terraces below.)

This last was the main reason they took the trouble, for water is the limiting factor in almost all farming in the Near East. Another way farmers tried to control this variable was by catching runoff from the rains in cisterns dug in the bedrock. To make the limestone watertight, they cemented the pits with lime: another technique that the Israelites or Canaanites may have pioneered. Evidently it worked, for the Talmud (*Pirke Avot* 2:11) compares the prodigious memory of Rabbi Eliezer ben Hyrcanus to "a cemented cistern, which loses not a drop."

In general, the way the hill farmers dealt with the whims and capers of nature was by hedging their bets. While they did not exactly have hedges they did have plenty of borders between plots of different crops. The hills were full of nooks and crannies, of micro-climates and microenvironments. As their natural flora and fauna were diverse, so (up to a point) were the flora and fauna the settlers put in their place. A single household might have fields of wheat and barley as well as lentils, peas, and other legumes; a vineyard enclosed by a wall of thorns or of stone, with the vines trailing on the ground or trained to form arbors; and orchards of fig, apricot, almond, and pomegranate. Any patch of hillside that was left would be planted with olive trees, whose fruit was not eaten (the art of curing being unknown) but pressed for the oil used in cooking, lighting, and grooming. A household would also have herds of sheep, goats, and cattle that would winter in dry areas, grazing on rain-primed seasonal growth, or in the upper hills, where they would help to degrade the maquis to the lower and sparser mix of shrubs and herbs known as garigue. In summer the livestock would stay closer to the village, nibbling on stubble and fallow weeds and paying the check with manure.

Nor was husbandry the only source of food. The women might forage for pistachios, acorns, herbs, and other wild foods, the men hunt the gazelles and wild goats that still roamed the hills. To the hearers of the legends from this period collected in the Book of Judges, it apparently did not seem odd that Samson should run into a lion among the vineyards (14:5). Even the poet of the Song of Songs, who lived some centuries later, knew a world in which wild and manmade mingled, not least in the imagery of the human body itself.

When I say that a single household might do all these things, I mean a *bet av*, an extended family of perhaps ten to thirty persons led by a patriarch and living in a cluster of stone or mud brick dwellings. Such a household shielded itself from nature's whims by sharing labor (at harvest, for instance) and food (at times of scarcity) with an even more extended family called a *mishpahah,* a kind of clan or tribe that might take the form of a village. (What is called a tribe in the Bible was a still more fluid grouping in which political allegiance was thicker than blood.) The command to "be fruitful and multiply" (Genesis 1:28), while common to most farming peoples, must have had double force in this frontier setting, where two new hands added far more food than one new mouth subtracted.

Land seems to have been held communally within the *mishpahah,* at least in the sense that a piece of land, even if "sold" to an outsider, would eventually revert to the clan. In contrast to the plantations that sprawled across the great river valleys of the Near East, the hills nurtured a world of small holdings, painstakingly husbanded. When in a larger Israel the royal houses and others began to amass great estates, the prophets were outraged: "Woe unto them that join house to house, that lay field to field . . . " (Isaiah 5:8).

In this respect the Israelites out-Canaanized the Canaanites, who were somewhat more prone to plantation farming and cashcropping. The Phoenicians (as the Canaanites came to be called when, squeezed by Israelites on one flank and Philistines on the other, they bunched up in the cities of the Syrian coast and increasingly took to the sea) were both crackerjack farmers and peerless merchants. Though it is hard to know which role came first, farm produce—in particular, olive oil and wine—was among their primary wares. (This became true of the Israelites during the monarchy, when the kings wanted cash crops for export.)

MOUNT EDEN

Being Canaanites—if Canaanites of a rather peculiar sort—the children of Israel might be expected to have some notion of a World Mountain. So they did. It took several forms, some of which we will deal with later; but foremost among them was Eden.[14]

Today it is not common to think of Eden as a mountain. But in earlier times—from at least the sixth century BCE, when Ezekiel prophesied, to the seventeenth century CE, when Milton wrote *Paradise Lost*—it was very common.

Although the Bible never specifies Eden's elevation, the fact that it is the source of four great rivers speaks for itself. Armed with the knowledge that water does not flow uphill, scholars from Philo's time to the present have placed Eden in the mountains of Armenia, or other mountains vaguely north of Mesopotamia.[15]

These same mountains are vaguely north of Canaan, too. The Tigris and Euphrates arise in the mountains of Turkish Armenia. While the Tigris runs straight into Mesopotamia, the lordly Euphrates adopts a more leisured route, taking in the sights and waters of eastern Syria. Some affluents of the Upper Euphrates start within 70 km—a god's spitting range—of the Ammanus mountains. The closest thing in Canaan to what we would call a river, the Jordan, has its ultimate source in the mountains of Syria.

No wonder, then, that the peoples of the Fertile Crescent shared a firm if somewhat cloudy feeling that life flowed from the north. (As great dams go up, that feeling gets less cloudy and more anxious. An open secret of Near Eastern politics—closed until recently to the publics of the West—is the fact that many struggles in the region, from the fight over the Golan Heights and West Bank to the tussles between Syria, Iraq, and Turkey, have less to do with oil or blood than with water.)[16]

To be the Mountain, it is not enough to be a mountain. But Eden has other qualifications. It is the source of life, in several ways. First, it is the source of water not only for the Near East, but for the known world. That is the import of the four rivers, two real and two mythic (or semimythic), whose hydrologically improbable courses extend to the ends of the earth. Two of these are labeled clearly as the Tigris and the Euphrates; the other two are identified by the rabbis with the Nile and the Ganges.[17] The two rivers that run from El's mountain have been doubled—perhaps under Mesopotamian influence, perhaps in sheer one-upsmanship—so that they may reach and refresh the very corners of the world, dividing it neatly in four quarters.

Like many world-poles, Eden crowns its mountain with a Tree of Life. According to the Midrash (*Bereshit Rabbah* 15:6), this means "a tree that spread its canopy over all living things. . . . All the primeval waters branched out beneath it." To walk around its trunk would take a man five hundred years.

Eden is the source of life in another sense, too. It is the navel of the world—the first home of all creatures, both human and nonhuman. It is even a home of sorts for God, who walks in the garden in the cool of the day. But while God and plants and animals get to stay in Eden, humans get the boot. And this, too, is a hint that what we are dealing with is nothing less than the Mountain of God.

Modern scholars tend to picture Eden as a formal garden in the Mesopotamian style, irrigated to a fare-thee-well. But while some of the sources of the Eden story may have had that squared-off and straight-laced shape, others were a good deal wilder and woolier. In the Mountain of God, even the Garden of God, we have a vision of paradise as a forested peak—the summa and last resort of wildness in a region chock-a-block with cities, fields, canals, herds, and armies. While the Hebrew word *gan* usually means an enclosed vegetable garden or fruit orchard, the phrase *gan Elohim,* "garden of God," seems to be meant as a kind of analogy: just as we might call the prairie "God's lawn," so the ancients saw the wooded mountain as God's private garden.[18]

Such wild places were not paradises for humans, but for gods. They were not meant for humans at all.

The cosmic center is not always thought of as a nice place for humans to live or even to visit. Nevertheless it is the source of life. "All the world is watered with the dregs of Eden," the Talmud says (*Taanit* 10a); and the dregs are as much as it can take. Humans cannot see God's face and live.

If God is the heart of nature, then to say that we cannot stand pure godhead is to say that we cannot stand pure wildness, except in small doses. We can stand (if sometimes just barely) the electric blue of the sky, the buzz of bees, the jolt of sex. Uncut, nature is too much for us. The main lines of wildness make us jumpy—and rightly, for an instantaneous surge can kill.

To think of living in Eden is to deny the primal sundering of heaven and earth, of god and animal and human. The world-pole is the one place where the sundering has not happened, or has been repaired. We must revere it, draw sustenance from it, keep it alive, keep the channels of wildness open. But to think of living in it— why, it's like wanting to live in the sun.

In a Bushman story of beginnings, the sun was on earth and hid its light in its armpit. It was so close, it was useless—darkening with excessive light.[19] Hunter-gatherers agree that division is necessary, that you can't have heaven smothering earth. It follows that you can't live on the world-pole. In fact, even shamans can only climb it once in a while, and soon slip off. It is slippery—wet with the water of life, greasy with the fat of offerings, alive with energy of all kinds.

The peak of the World Mountain is like the head of a pin on which only angels and animals can dance. It is the vanishing point of the trophic pyramid. There is room at the top, but not for us.

Nowadays most people (as opposed to scholars) like to imagine Eden as a wild place: a rainforest rife with orchids and lianas, a savanna rumbling with game. Conversely, they like to stick the words "Eden" and "garden," like Sierra Club stamps, on any wilderness that is not unlivably frigid or arid, especially if they have never been in it themselves. And while they are right to imagine Eden as a wild place, they are wrong to think that such places are still paradises for us. A brief backpacking trip is about as much of real wilderness as most of us can stand, and even that will seem like paradise only if nothing goes wrong: no rain, no grizzlies, no marmots eating our boots. After a week or two, we are glad to be expelled. And if we were to stay—to become settlers, pioneers—we would soon transform the place, or at least our immediate patch of it, into something wildly different.

The World Mountain is a paradise only when seen from a distance, or with the moist eye of memory. Once, wilderness was our home. Looking back, we endow it with all the longed-for comforts of home. We see a garden: a place wholly benign, a place of harmony and plenty. We forget that the harmony, such as it was, was possible only because we were still animals, and the plenty only because we were scarce. As soon as we become fully human, we begin to "fill the earth and subdue it." We begin to destroy Eden, and thereby expel ourselves.

Wheat and the Fall of Man

The myth of the Fall, like that of the World Mountain itself, is based on ecological fact.[20] In fact, of course, the Fall was not a single event. It was a gradual slipping that, by degrees, snowballed into a full-speed charge downhill. Humans began to change their surroundings in a drastic way as soon as they mastered fire, but it was the second great wave of human expansion—based on the alliance with annual grasses, which came to be known as grains—that sealed our self-expulsion. We and our allies moved outward, driving Eden before us. We stripped forests, troubled the soil, uprooted whole ecosystems.

On this point the Bible is clear. "Cursed is the ground for thy sake; in sorrow shalt thou eat of it all the days of thy life. Thorns also and thistles shall it bring forth to thee; and thou shalt eat the herb [grass] of the field. In the sweat of thy brow shalt thou eat bread, till thou return unto the ground; for out of it wast thou taken: for dust thou art, and unto dust shalt thou return" (Genesis 3:17–19). Agriculture as we know it: the earth is tilled, grain (a kind of grass) is planted, weeds interfere.

The Hebrew word *lehem* means food in general, bread in particular. In place of the herbs and fruits of paradise, man will eat bread. As we have said, the culture of barley and wheat—first for beer and toasted seedheads, then for bread—did apparently begin in the uplands of the Near East, some ten thousand years ago. That it was woman, not man, who surely began it—being the foremost gatherer, she must have been the first farmer—may be dimly recalled in the story that it was Eve who first tasted the forbidden fruit, then handed it on to Adam.

What was the forbidden fruit? In the Midrash (*Bereshit Rabbah* 15:7), a rabbi of the second century CE gives a remarkable answer:

Rabbi Meir said: It was wheat, for when a person lacks knowledge people say, "That creature has never eaten bread of wheat." Rabbi Samuel ben Isaac came to Rabbi Ze'ira and asked: "Is it possible that it was wheat?" "Yes," he said. "But is not 'tree' written?" he asked. "It rose high as the cedars of Lebanon," he replied.

If Rabbi Meir is half joking—for this is a typical midrashic game of competitive whimsy, with other rabbis one-upping him by proving that the forbidden fruit was the grape or the fig—his half-joke has deep roots in the Near Eastern mind. Wheat is the premise of civilized life. Whoever has not eaten bread made of wheat is a savage, at best a Bedouin. The Sumerians had a similar gibe for the nomads at the fringe of their world: "The Martu eat bread, but they don't know what it's made of."

Rabbi Meir's notion sounds less odd in Hebrew than in English, for the word translated "fruit" can mean any kind of produce. And if the forbidden fruit is indeed wheat, the role of the snake becomes clear: in ancient times, snakes were used to protect granaries from rodents.

If grains meant knowledge, they also meant hard work, and it was work man had not previously evolved to do. Man was born to labor, as the Book of Proverbs says, but not to labor like this. For five million years we had foraged, scavenged, hunted, gardened a little, which was hard work at times, but desultory, even leisurely. Adam's punishment, like Eve's, was a wrenching departure from the path of primate evolution. Eve was sentenced to pain in childbirth— outrageous pain by any reasonable mammalian standard—because infants were being selected for bigger brains than the pelvis of a bipedal female could accommodate. To be sure, Eve's penance began long before Adam's, millions of years before the start of farming. But farming, by raising the birthrate, made it necessary for her to bear that penance more often. Farming meant more children; children meant more farming. Adam's and Eve's punishments fed each other.

They fed other things, too. With time, with irrigation, mountains of grain became the foundations of cities. To protect the grain from marauding nomads, armies arose and enslaved those whose grain they protected. To dig the great irrigation canals and keep them clear, slaves were called for, and bureaucrats, and despots. (The first great emperor in history, Sargon the Great of Akkad, began his career as a gardener, so it is fitting that the last great emperor, Pu Yi of China, ended his career that way.) Humans were winnowed like grain, separated by function, wealth, power. Civilization arose, and writing, and real estate. All this happened just a few miles down river from Eden.

Adam's fate was to outrun his own nature: to be dragged by his big brain, by his snowballing technology, into regions his body had never known. Like Eve, he was the victim of an overgrown head.

Of course, our big brain is our nature, too. But the fact remains that in eating the forbidden fruit, though we failed to become gods, we ceased to be animals. At that point, Eden could no longer be our home. For whatever place we made our home ceased to be Eden.

The Hebrew phrase usually translated "Cursed is the ground for thy sake" can, with a bit of license, be read to mean, "Cursed is the ground by thy passing over."[21] As the waves of human expansion move across the earth, Eden is trampled underfoot.

Adam was put in the garden "to work it and protect it" (Genesis 2:15).[22] The two jobs are complementary, but they are also contradictory. From what are we to protect Eden, if not from our own work? The more we work the earth—by which I mean not only tilling but the whole spectrum of human meddling, from setting grass fires to splitting the atom—the more we are obliged to protect it. If we fail to do either, we fail to be fully human.

These tasks were set us not just for our brief tenure in Eden, but for the whole span of our stay on earth. Indeed, by setting us the first task God set us up for expulsion. For when we work the earth we work her hard, and the place we work ceases to be Eden. We move outward in waves of work—waves of improvement and devastation, of fruitfulness and waste. By setting us the second task, God set (or tried to set) a limit to the height and reach of those waves.

A HYBRID OF MOUNTAIN AND TOWER

In setting out the contrast between the Canaanites and the Mesopotamians, we have so far placed Israel squarely in the Canaanite camp. Roughly, that is right. But the crucial role of the Hebrew Bible in shaping the Western mind requires us to be more exact.

Israel was not sheltered from the metaphysical winds that blew from the great river valleys. The way of thinking of the Canaanite hillbilly, goatherd, and dirt farmer was altered by Egyptian and Mesopotamian influences. The wild Mountain of God was partly tamed and was crowned with a temple. The result was a vigorous hybrid of Mountain and Tower known as Zion.[23]

The name Zion referred at first to a hill in the southeastern part of Jerusalem, between the Tyropoean and Kidron valleys, on which stood the Jebusite citadel that David seized and made his capital. In the Bible and Talmud the name was used of the Temple Mount, or else of Jerusalem as a whole; nowadays it is wrongly pinned on a hill in the southwest part of the city. Whichever hill one picks, the fact remains that from the geographer's standpoint Mount Zion is no great shakes. At something less than 2,600 feet above sea level, it is overshadowed even by some of its Judaean neighbors. But for the Hebrews it is the navel of the earth.

> *Great is the Lord, and highly to be praised,*
> *In the city of our God, His holy mountain.*
> *Beautiful in height, the joy of the whole earth;*
> *Even Mount Zion, the reaches of Zaphon,*
> *The city of the great King.*
> *God in her palaces*
> *Hath made Himself known for a stronghold.*
>
> (Psalm 48:1–3)

The phrase *yarketei tsaphon,* usually rendered "on the sides of the north" or "the uttermost parts of the north," would be read by an ancient Israelite as a reference to Mount Zaphon, the mountain from which Baal held sway. It is a bald admission of the psalmist's project, which is to make Mount Zion the new cosmic mountain.

Later Ezekiel, an exile in Babylonia, has a vision of the rebuilt Temple. From its east gate runs a trickle of water which, some four thousand cubits downstream, has become an unswimmable torrent with a gigantic tree (or perhaps a large forest) on either side. His guide, a man "with the appearance of brass," explains (47:8–12):

These waters issue forth toward the eastern region, and shall go down into the Arabah; and when they shall enter into the sea, into the sea of the putrid waters, the waters shall be healed. And it shall come to pass, that every living creature wherewith it swarmeth, whithersoever the rivers shall come, shall live; and there shall be a very great multitude of fish . . . And by the river upon the bank thereof, on this side and on that side, shall grow every tree for food, whose leaf shall not wither, neither shall the fruit thereof fail; it shall bring forth new fruit every month, because the waters thereof issue out of the sanctuary; and the fruit thereof shall be for food, and the leaf thereof for healing.

There was, in fact, a spring on the eastern side of Mount Zion, known as the Gihon. While it was neither unswimmably deep nor swarming with fish, it did supply most of Jerusalem's water. And it was holy. It was here that Solomon, at David's behest, was taken to be anointed as king (I Kings 1:33, 38, 45).

Gihon is also the name of one of the four rivers of Eden. Although scholarly opinion has only recently begun to admit it, it is clear that the two Gihons are one and the same. In the book of Genesis the author known as J, who is thought to have lived around 800 BCE under the reign of a descendant of David, links Eden not only to the World Mountain of the north from which the great rivers flow—the Tigris and the Euphrates—but to the new World Mountain, Zion.[24] For the sake of symmetry, and in order to slice the world into four quarters (a plan favored in the Near East as elsewhere), a fourth river is added, the Pishon. Gihon means something like "Gusher," Pishon something like "Bubbler." After the restoration foreseen by Ezekiel has more or less happened, Zechariah (14:8) is emboldened to add an extra stream to Mount Zion itself: "On that day living waters shall issue from Jerusalem, half toward the eastern sea and half toward the western sea, both in summer and in winter." Besides making sure that all of the land of Israel, not just the eastern half, gets a share of the life-giving waters, this mirror trick puts the Mountain of YHWH on a par with the Mountain of El as a "source of the Two Rivers."

The rabbis make YHWH's temple, like El's tent, the springhouse of the world, in which he controls and doles out the primal waters. They call Zion the navel of the universe, the point from which the world was created.[25]

The peoples of the Near East had a strong sense that life flowed from the great mountains of the north. To make it seem to flow, instead, from a skimpy hill on one tattered leg of the Fertile Crescent required oceans of poetry; but this was something the Hebrews had plenty of.

THE MOUNTAIN AND THE DESERT

What has happened to the Canaanite world-pole? Though Baal's mountain, too, had a temple on it, that temple was not shaped by human hands or visible to human eyes. Mount Zion, on the other hand, seems so thoroughly civilized that it might as well be a ziggurat. Has the Mountain been hijacked to serve the needs of priests, kings, and Levites? Are the Hebrews in danger of forgetting the role of wildness?

As if worried that the integrity of the wild Mountain might be at risk, the Hebrews set aside another peak that will perform that role in its unmixed form. Whatever happens to Zion, Sinai remains untamed and untamable.[26] That is partly because it is in the desert; partly because the Israelites were from the outset forbidden to come near it, on pain of death (after Moses, only one man is said to have climbed it, the prophet Elijah); and partly because no one knows where it is. To this day, Sinai upholds fiercely the West Semitic idea of a wild world-pole.

The desert is hardly the source of life, as one expects a world-pole to be. Yet it is the source of what the rabbis called the "tree of life," the Law. The desert was where revelation erupted, where a covenant was welded, where a nation was tempered—plunged hissing into sand, as if into water. If Zion is the eternal city on a hill—"Jerusalem of Gold," as the popular Israeli song has it—then Sinai is the place of rejuvenation.

In all of ancient Near Eastern literature, the Bible is one of the few texts that knows wilderness as a place of majesty, a place where God lets himself be known.[27] And this is wilderness in the modern sense: not only desert but forest, mountain, even (as in the Book of Jonah) the bowels of the sea. Far from rejecting nature, the Hebrews embraced her as a whole, thorns and all. No place is godforsaken, unless it be the cities of men. However bleak, the sand and stones have sermons to preach. Nor do they preach self-mortification or the vanity of this world. What they say is: Go back to your fields. Go back to your vineyards and orchards. Only this time do it right. This time let there be justice and peace. "They shall sit every man under his vine and under his fig tree, and none shall make them afraid; for the mouth of the Lord of hosts hath spoken" (Micah 4:4).

The prophets, it has been said, voice a nomadic nostalgia of sorts, an urge to abandon the stink and swank of the cities, the oily wealth and sweat of the plantations, and head out into the desert. If they seek God in the desert, it is not because they think he is absent from the fields or the vineyards. God is everywhere; what is useful about the desert is that there, there is nothing but God.

When the writers of the Bible adopt the viewpoint of nomads it is not because they are nomads, but because they are not. It is an alienation device, like Brecht's in his plays or the guises of Swift and Montesquieu, and has a similar moral intent. The desert is a corrective. It is an astringent or desiccant applied to the overripe smugness of settled peoples, and above all to the decadence and greed of their rulers.

This is not to say that there were no seminomads among the Israelites. There were such clans in the federation, most of them in the arid south. But the distinction between peasants and seminomads was rarely hard and fast. In the Levant as elsewhere in the Near East, seminomadism was an escape hatch. When a peasant household found itself so beset by tax collectors or armed ruffians (often one and the same) that the game was no longer worth the candle, it could leave its fields, take its flocks, and head for the steppe. In a sense, that is the story of the Exodus.

A nomad bends the knee to no prince. Even a tribal chieftain or sheikh rules only at the sufferance of his tribesmen, any one of whom can vote with his feet, or his camel's hooves. A nomad depends only on God: which is to say, on nature.

The jubilee year prescribed in Leviticus 25 can be seen as a momentary return to the (legendary) nomadic condition of the tribes when they entered Canaan. Every forty-nine years—seven times seven—the Israelites shall "proclaim liberty throughout the land unto all the inhabitants thereof." Slaves are manumitted, debts forgiven, fields returned to their original owners. We might look at it this way: For a split second, ownership of the land reverts to God. Then the assignment of land to tribes and families is repeated, no jot or tittle misplaced. Every stone, tree, and square inch of turf lost to sloth or greed goes back to its hereditary owner. We do not know if the jubilee was ever observed, but the mere idea is revolutionary. The trumpet blast of jubilee is like a burst of music in a game of musical chairs. The portly and comfortably settled are forced to get up. For a while, everyone is on an equal footing. The world melts into primal chaos for an instant and then is re-created—and reapportioned.

The same basic principle recurs on several scales: every seventh day, every seventh year, every seventh seventh year. On the

Sabbath, both humans and animals are freed from the grind of domestication; all technology, right down to the kindling of fire, is taboo. In the sabbatical year, the land itself is allowed to revert to a state of wildness.[28] Sabbath, sabbatical, and jubilee are all eruptions of wildness into the humdrum of the technical and economic order. Earth, plants, animals—even humans—are free to do as they will. So the rivers flowing from Eden leave puddles of paradise in time as well as in space.

Far from forgetting the role of wildness, then, the Israelites expanded that role. They gave the wild Mountain, and wilderness in its most unfriendly form, a social and spiritual function that the Canaanites had barely hinted at. This reverence for wildness, though often submerged by other tendencies in Western culture, would bob up again and again in one odd form or another. Some of our greatest ecological prophets, from St. Francis to John Muir, Bob Marshall, and Edward Abbey, have been heirs of Moses in the wilderness, even if the modern vision is of a bush that *is* being consumed.[29]

THE STILL SMALL VOICE

One of the things that has kept the Bible fresh, while most of ancient Near Eastern literature withered or was embalmed, is the gust of country air that hits the reader the moment he opens the book— the smell of cedar, sheep dung, sun-baked wheat, and olives bruised beneath one's sandals. There are passages in Sumerian wedding songs for Inanna and Egyptian love poetry that have the heady, spicy odor of the Song of Songs, but most of them reek of decadence. They are city boys' vegetable wet dreams. The Song of Songs, despite their manifest influence upon it and its own royal trappings, has an innocence they lack. There are Mesopotamian laws and proverbs that deal sagely with agricultural problems but do so in a language dried out on the desks of scribes and administrators. In all the ancient Near East, only the Hebrew writers have dirt under their fingernails. Amos drove goats ("a herdsman and a piercer of figs," he called himself, referring to the gashing of sycamore figs to hasten their ripening). David was tending sheep when Samuel discovered him. One can almost believe that the trend toward universal literacy, which would make the Jews peculiar among nations (the sort of thing that would later impress Crèvecoeur about the farmers of New England), began, if haltingly, in the time of the First Temple. Indeed, prophets such as Amos may present some of the few cases in the ancient world of an honest-to-God rural point of view finding its way into writing.

In looking at the Hebrew view of nature, it is a common mistake to pay more attention to the form—the bare idea of a single transcendent God—than to the content, both legal and poetic. The content of the Bible shows, as the great nineteenth-century naturalist Alexander von Humboldt noted, a greater and more sweeping sense of the grandeur of nature than is found among the Greeks, even at their most "pagan."

In the second volume of his great work *Cosmos,* Humboldt gives a conspectus of sentiments displayed toward nature by the great cultures of the world, past and present. Having chided some Greek and Roman writers for skimping on descriptions of nature, he goes on to praise the "profound sentiment of love for nature" to be found in the Hebrew Bible. "It is a characteristic of the poetry of the Hebrews, that as a reflex of monotheism it always embraces the universe in its unity, comprising both terrestrial life and the luminous realms of space." Hebrew lyrical poetry "develops a rich and animated conception of the life of nature. It might almost be said that one single psalm (the 104th) represents the image of the whole Cosmos:—'Who coverest thyself with light as with a garment . . . '"30

Humboldt's testimony to the love of nature evinced by the Hebrew scriptures is not just anybody's testimony. Evidently the spirit that drove the first ecologists was not new or exotic, but had lived all along (if partly dormant) in their own culture's central book. Nor was it only the profusely detailed love of nature that inspired them, but the very monotheism of which that love was (as Humboldt says) a "reflex." Monotheism, with its faith in nature's harmony, sustained such Christian pioneers of ecology as Humboldt, Gilbert White, Louis Agassiz, and George Perkins Marsh— until they were sent reeling by Darwin's bloody polytheism. Although Darwin considered himself a Christian, his view of a world shaped by sex and strife, eros and eris, is deeply pagan.

The odd thing is that these two opposing ways of looking at nature pioneered in the nineteenth century—evolutionism and ecology—both turned out to be right. One saw harmony, the other conflict, and between them they saw reality in depth. The same may prove to be true of such older and murkier pairs as monotheism and polytheism, or earth cult and sky cult. Some sense of this resolution can be seen already in Darwin. In fact, it can be seen in Homer. The role Darwin assigns to divine providence is the role Homer assigns it: at the end of the day, after the battle-royal of gods, demigods, and humans, "the plan of Zeus is accomplished."31

On balance there is little reason, either logical or historical, to think that monotheism is less friendly to nature than is polytheism. One underlines the unity of nature, the other its diversity. Both are right. As for transcendence, that is a concept of more interest to theologians than to tinkers or tailors. To the man in the city street, a nature god is more transcendent than a city god, for whatever is outside the city gates transcends his daily experience. For the peasant, just the reverse is true. The schoolbook definition of a transcendent God—one who is beyond nature rather than part of nature—is at once too abstract and too simpleminded to match up with the religious experience of real people. To get a sense of the kind of transcendence the Hebrews knew, the best place to look is Elijah's vision from the mouth of the cave at Horeb, "the mount of God"— Horeb being another name for Sinai:

> And, behold, the Lord passed by, and a great and strong wind rent the mountains, and broke in pieces the rocks before the Lord; but the Lord was not in the wind; and after the wind an earthquake; but the Lord was not in the earthquake; and after the earthquake a fire; but the Lord was not in the fire; and after the fire a still small voice. (I Kings 19:11–12)

This sequence sums up the Jewish understanding of God, man, and nature. It is the keystone of an arch that reaches from the Jahwist to Buber and beyond. The still, small voice makes the best case that can be made for a God that is not in nature. Yet nature is not diminished. God is not absent from nature, any more than Shakespeare is absent from *The Tempest* (any more than Prospero is, for that matter). God is not outside nature so much as unfathomably deep within it: the essence of nature.

Forced into an abstract form of transcendence by later rationalists (themselves influenced by Greek thought), this protean God would escape his cage and burst back into nature time after time in Jewish thought: in Kabbalism, in Hasidism, in the pantheism of Spinoza. Even those among the rabbis and philosophers who insisted on a strict division between God and nature often regarded the earth itself as a living being.[32]

ECOLOGY IN A BIBLICAL PERSPECTIVE

Tikva Frymer-Kensky

W e have become accustomed, in both Judaism and Christianity, to attribute to the Bible the origin of everything good and everything evil. Needless to say, such an attitude has no basis in fact: the world was not a barren wasteland before the writing of the Bible. Nevertheless, it has become the conceit of the Western religious tradition to imagine that the Bible came to bring light to those in utter darkness and to write God's word on the *tabula rasa* of humankind.

Tikva Frymer-Kensky is professor of Hebrew Bible at the University of Chicago Divinity School. She has been the director of biblical studies at the Reconstructionist Rabbinical College and visiting professor at both the Jewish Theological Seminary and Hebrew Union College. She is the author of *In the Wake of the Goddesses* and *Motherprayer* and the English translator of *From Jerusalem to the Edge of Heaven* by Ari Elon (from the Hebrew Alma Dee). She is completing a book on women in the Bible and writing a commentary on the Book of Ruth.

It should therefore not be surprising that ever since Lynn White, Jr.'s, seminal article,[1] the Bible, in particular the Hebrew Bible, has stood accused of teaching us to kill the earth. White's article has been refuted hundreds of times on many different grounds, not the least of which are the many articles showing that the Bible simply doesn't support the "conquest of nature" theology that was imposed upon it a few hundred years ago.[2] Despite all the refutation, it remains constantly cited whenever people once again discover that there is an earth and that the Bible has given us some problems with it.

THE BABYLONIAN CREATION STORY

I would like to take a different path, and tell a story from pre-biblical ancient Babylonia that gives us a good indication of what a pre-biblical Near Eastern view of the relationship of God and the earth was like. The story has a long history. Our copy was written around 1550 BCE. This copy is probably not the original composition, for the copyist tells us that he is a junior scribe.[3] The story had at least a thousand-year history and we find tablets from a thousand years later that contain parts or all of this text, which we call the *Atrahasis Epic,* and they called, "When the gods as humans."

The story begins when there was an earth, but before the creation of humankind. It is a primordial history of humankind, and tells us of the defining characteristics of that pre-human world: the gods had to work. They had to work because they had to eat, and since this text was written in Iraq, the work that they engaged in was digging irrigation ditches. Seven gods seized power and became the administrators, and everybody else worked backbreaking labor for a very long time. They were, of course, gods: the irrigation ditches that they produced were the Tigris and Euphrates Rivers, and the dirt from the excavation piled up as the mountains of Iran. But even for gods, this was a lot of work, and they got very tired of it.

One day, one of the gods (whose name is not given)[4] instigates the others and calls them to strike, and the gods decide they do not want to work anymore; they are going to create a disturbance. In the middle of the night, they set fire to their pickaxes and their spades, and they march to surround the palace of the chief administrator, the god Enlil. The watchman sees them and rouses the vizier; the vizier rouses Enlil, and he immediately wants to set the defense and defeat these rabble-rousers. The vizier halts him, reminding him that "these are your sons." They call a council of the seven power wielders. Anu, the god of heaven, comes down and the god of the subterranean world, the wise god Enki, comes up, and they decide that they need to find out what is happening and why the gods are doing this.

One can imagine this story as an early D. W. Griffith movie, or, better, a Pete Seeger song, because when the council tells Enlil to find out what is happening, he directs his servant to find out who started it. But when the servant goes and asks who proclaimed this rebellion, who started this revolt, then (to the strains of "Solidarity Forever ") all the gods answer, "We all did, every one of us declared rebellion." When this word is brought back, Enlil, the very personification of power, says, in effect, "Well, we gotta break the strike, let's just go in and mash a few heads and set an example of our power." The heaven god, Anu, admonishes that the council has been hearing the worker gods groaning and muttering in the pits for a long time and that they should find a solution to the workers' hard labor.

At this point the wisest of all the gods, the friend of humanity, the god Enki (or Ea, depending on whether you name him in Sumerian or Akkadian) has a brilliant idea: that the gods need a substitute work force, a permanent underclass. Enki proposes a procedure: the gods should purify themselves in a ritual immersion, should moisten the clay that Enki provides with their spittle, and the mother goddess should create a worker person.

The mother goddess, Mami, mixes the clay with the blood of a god slain for this purpose,[5] a god whose name has never been heard of before, in this text or any other myth. His name is We-ilum, which is a play on the word for humankind, *awilum*. Moreover, We-ilum is said to be a god *sa-isu temu,* a god who has sense. Once again, this is a wordplay on the word *etimmu,* the ghost that we have when our body is dead.[6] By infusing the clay of the earth with this god's blood, they give this new creature rationality and create a being who can remember that it has been created. Mami creates seven pairs of this *lullu,* the primitive worker-human, and they create seven pairs of men and women.

The gods then load upon this creature the tasks of the gods. A break on the tablet obscures a long speech about the duties of humankind and when the text picks up again, we hear about an unexpected problem: "twelve hundred years had not yet passed when the lands extended and the earth multiplied, the land was roaring like a bull." The god Enlil cannot sleep from the noise, calls his council, and they send a plague on humankind.

This devastating plague continues until the god Enki, our friend the wisest of all the gods, tells his human devotee, Atrahasis (literally "supersage" or "megabrain") that all human beings should stop worshipping any gods or goddesses except Nambar, the god of the plague. They should devote themselves to him, build him a temple, and bribe him into lifting the plague. Once they do so and the plague stops, then the text continues: "twelve hundred years had not yet passed when the earth extended and the land multiplied, the earth was bellowing like a bull."

Once again, the god Enlil cannot sleep. The problem has recurred, and this time Enlil gets the gods to agree to send a drought. When the drought comes and decimates humankind, once again Enki tells Atrahasis that people should worship only Adad the god of rain, once again humans respond and the drought lifts. But the problem recurs yet again: the text is broken, but it is clear that the gods now pollute the earth and make the soil saline. Once again, Enki saves humankind. The gods then gather to try to find a final solution to the problem, an ending, a *gamirtam*. They decide to bring a flood, and they bind Enki by an oath that he will not inform humankind of this flood. They are determined to end the problem that humans pose.

Needless to say, Enki is not so dumb, and neither is Megabrain—Atrahasis. The next time Atrahasis comes to the Temple on a vision quest, he overhears Enki talking to the walls, saying "Wall, listen to me: reed, but attend my words. Break down your house, build a boat, leave your possessions and save your life." Atrahasis, realizing that this message might have something to do with him, builds a boat, and loads animals and humans on it. The flood comes and destroys all of the earth except for this one boat in which Atrahasis and his family and animals survive.

The gods soon realize what they have done in destroying humanity. To quote the text, "Their hearts were broken and they thirsted for beer." Nobody is feeding them—and their hunger brings them to a realization of the enormous consequences of their actions. Ishtar gets up and articulates the issue, lamenting that they have destroyed their own creation, and the gods turn angry at Enlil who moved them to take such an action.

Once they are truly upset that humanity has been destroyed, Enki has Atrahasis come out of the ark and offer a sacrifice from his animals. The gods are so hungry that they swarm over the sacrifice "like flies." While they are eating, Enlil, the god who instigated the flood, comes and is dismayed that humanity has been saved. But the gods will no longer listen, and wise Enki presents a permanent solution to the problem:

> Let there be a third class among people,
> the women who bear and women who do not bear;
> Let there be a pashittu-demon to snatch babies away
> from the women who bear them;
> Let there be Entu, Ugbabtu and Igisitu women
> who are taboo, and thus stop childbirth, . . .

Here, still in the middle of Enki's solution to the human problem, the text gets very broken, but clearly another innovation is death, or timely death. No longer, after the flood, do people live for thousands of years.[7] After this broken speech comes the poet's summation, "I shall sing of the flood to all people; listen!"

The Atrahasis story is a primeval history that seeks to tell us that the great danger in creation is overpopulation, that the gods try "nature's" methods of controlling population (drought, pestilence, famine), and that when none of these prove anything more than temporary solutions, they are ready to destroy the whole world. In nonmythological language: if overpopulation is not controlled, then the world will be destroyed.

The story then depicts a new order in which the universe is changed so as to contain built-in population safeguards that should prevent a recurrence of overpopulation. These safeguards are perinatal death, barrenness (natural and social), and a shortened lifespan of at most 120 years.[8] The myth thus provides a framework for viewing personal tragedies as cosmic necessities. It also contains a reassuring note about humanity's place in the cosmos, for it turns out that the gods, who are able to destroy humankind, ultimately discover how much they need humanity. To be the workers of the god may imply subservience and dependence on the gods' good will, but it also makes humans indispensable and assures our continued existence. The world of gods and humans is thus interdependent.

The myth does not have such a happy message for the earth itself. The gods are willing to sacrifice the soil and the environment. They send droughts and pollution on the earth in order to decimate humankind. Of course, from our nonmythological perspective, droughts, famine and pestilence are a direct consequence of overpopulation, but the myth does not see it that way. Instead, the mutilation of the earth is the weapon that the gods use against humanity.

The myth does not present an integrated view of nature, humanity, and the gods; on the contrary, the purpose of the soil is to nourish humans, and the purpose of humans is to nourish the gods. This tale presents a clearly defined hierarchical order gods–humans–earth in a mythological setting of a definitely nonmonotheist religion.

THE GENESIS CREATION STORY

When we look at biblical mythology, the situation is much more complicated. I will concentrate on the much-discussed creation story in Genesis, Chapter 1, in order to point out one facet that has been overlooked.

In this chapter, the priestly celebration of creation, God creates by introducing distinctions, divisions, and hierarchies: the very essence of creation is the bringing of order to the formless mass of chaos, depicted as the featureless deep. On the first day, God creates light and declares it good. On the second day God creates the firmament and declares it good. On both days there has been a one-step process and one thing has been created, making one distinction: light/dark, waters above/below, and pronouncing this new creation good. On the third day, God creates the division between the seas and the dry land and pronounces it good, but the third day doesn't end with the creation of earth. On that very same day, God has the earth bring forth vegetation, which is self-perpetuating and seed-bearing and will maintain its own distinct varieties. Only then does the third day end.

This compositional strategy has a significant implication: there is not one moment in cosmic time that the earth exists barren. The earth is created as a fertile, self-sustaining unit. In Genesis 1, there is no need for fertility rituals and no need for humanity to produce a fertile earth: this is the way that earth was created and this is the way it remains if it is not interfered with.[9] By doubling the creations of the third day, Genesis 1 conveys an important theological point. The cult neither has to produce fertility nor even to offer thanksgiving for the fertility because a good universe is fertile, and God created a well-ordered universe.

Genesis 1 uses a similar technique on the sixth day. Both humans and animals are created on the sixth day. The earth did not have animals without humans; the two are interconnected, and humans administrate. The essential position of humankind in the cosmos is not the farmer, but the executive. This is spelled out: humans are to be the *tzelem elohim,* the image of God. *Salmu* (cognate of *tzelem*) is a term we know from Mesopotamian inscriptions, where the king is the "image" of the god. It means the avatar of God on earth, the one who keeps everything going properly. This is humanity's proper human role in the cosmos.

The following chapters, the primeval history of Genesis 2–11, show (among other things) a progressive diminution in the fertility of the world; the world is created fertile, say the priests, but Chapters 2–11 show us that every time humans do something, the world becomes that much less fertile. From the garden that at most has to be tended, humans go out to the world, which has to be tilled by difficult agriculture. After the murder of Abel, that land is no longer fertile and can no longer be successfully planted: the blood of a murdered victim has ended the life of that soil and Cain is told that if he tills it, it will not answer. By the time of the birth of Noah, Noah is named Noah because, the text says, "this one will give us consolation"[10] "from the ground which God had cursed" (Genesis 5:29). The world has become a very infertile place.

In Chapter 6, God looks at the world and sees that it has become contaminated, *nishatah*. *Nishatah* is also used to describe the rotten cloth that Jeremiah first buries and then digs up (Jeremiah 13:7–9). God sees that this earth, which was created fertile and beautiful (Chapter 1) or which humans were supposed to guard and cultivate (Chapter 2), this earth has instead become rotten and full of stains. In this context, the flood comes as a response to this problem. Unlike in Mesopotamia, the problem is not too many people and the post-flood solution is not to build in population safeguards. In Israel the problem is the undirected and lawless activity of humankind and the pollution that results, and the post-flood solution is the giving of law.[11]

After the flood collapsed the old creation by undoing the separation of the waters, then God reasons that God no longer wants to curse the earth because of the deeds of humans. God creates a regular order of nature: summer and winter, cold and heat, so that nature will not constantly fluctuate according to human acts. God also seeks to bring order to human activity; in Chapter 9, by declaring that humans must guard and avenge human life. A clear hierarchy is made very explicit—humans are in control of nature, and their authority reaches over all the animals. Moreover, both animals or humans will forfeit their lives if they kill a human. Humans can kill animals for their own use (without eating the blood), but no one can kill a human being, the avatar of God.

There are three specific regulations in Chapter 9. In the first, humans are told to be fruitful and multiply and fill the earth, probably the only command of God that we've ever fully obeyed. Next, they are told to refrain from eating blood because that is the life: hierarchy does not imply total domination. The third regulation emphasizes that no one (human or animal) can kill human beings, those responsible for the earth, and demands the death penalty for that terrible crime. These laws do not eliminate violence, indeed they include violence, the violence of the law. Violence is ordered and sanctioned as the antidote to violence: "whoever sheds the blood of a human, by a human his blood will be shed" (Genesis 9:6). The blood of the murder is not expurgated except with the blood of the murderer.

These laws do not prevent violence. However, they do protect the earth from being polluted by lawless behavior. The laws are meant to protect the earth. God makes it very clear that God no longer wants to have the earth cursed because of human deeds. Why God wants an earth, we have no idea; for God has no need to eat food. Chapter 2 links the creation of humans with the earth: they are to tend it; but it never tells us why God wants an earth. Chapter 9, a priestly text, explains that God gives the whole legal structure of the world to protect the earth from suffering, but once again it doesn't tell us why God wants the earth. The entire creation is an act of absolute divine desire ("grace"); we don't know what motivates it.

BIBLICAL PROPHECY:
THE LAND AND PEOPLE OF ISRAEL

After Genesis 1–11, the biblical discourse of the Pentateuch and the Prophets is not about humanity and the cosmos, but specifically about the people and the land of Israel. These books talk about the responsibility of Israel and the protection of the sacred land of Israel. As modern readers, we extrapolate and restore a universalist sense to the text. The universalism may have always been there, but the text expresses itself in the immediate terms of its audience, the people of Israel.

In the Pentateuch, the sense that human behavior is responsible for the condition of the earth is very strong. Moral misdeeds pollute the earth: Israel is told to refrain from murder because it will contaminate the land; to refrain from allowing killers to go free because it will contaminate the land (Numbers 35); to refrain from acts of sexual abomination in order to keep the land pure (Leviticus 18, 20).

The book of Deuteronomy, produced by the teachers, makes this explicit. Deuteronomy 11 states the responsibility of humanity starkly: if you do good, God brings rain and abundance and you live a long time on the land; if you do wrong, then skies dry up, the earth will not produce, and you lose the land.

In such a text, we get a strong sense that humans are the intermediary between God and nature, and that God's behavior towards the earth is very reactive to human deeds. In this tradition, unlike in the priestly tradition of Numbers 35 and Leviticus 18, God does not show any more allegiance to the earth than did the gods of Mesopotamia who were prepared to send a drought to decimate humanity. Not only do human misdeeds immediately pollute the earth, but God adds to the earth's suffering by stopping up the skies.

In Israel's prophetic books, particularly Hosea, Jeremiah, and

Ezekiel, the contamination of the land of Israel will lead to disaster. The most extreme formulation of this idea is found in Jeremiah's vision in Chapter 4: here, because of the deeds of Israel, Jeremiah sees the entire collapse of creation. The skies go dark, and no Adam can be found. So, too, Isaiah sees the very earth broken and falling apart (Isaiah 24:19–23).

In all these passages, the Bible presents a very strong statement of human responsibility. The centrality of humanity means that human beings are the intermediaries who influence the condition of the earth both directly, by the immediate polluting impact of their misdeeds, and indirectly by causing a divine reaction that ends the rain and further pollutes the earth.[12] Humanity has long run away from facing this responsibility, but it has become hard to ignore now that technology increasingly gives us the power to impact on the environment and really create destruction by our social misdeeds. At this point a statement that what humans do determines whether the earth continues or not is a simple statement of fact.

Of course, a statement that human actions determine whether the world continues is only a statement of fact if our definition of the world includes humanity. However, even if (horrors to contemplate) we thoroughly pollute the soil or deplete the ozone; even if we bring a nuclear disaster (God and humanity forbid), it may be that the earth will stand and the cockroaches will still survive as they have survived since the age of the dinosaurs, and so in a sense the world will still continue. We will not have destroyed it utterly: we will only have eradicated it as a habitable place for humanity. The earth, Gaia, the ecosystem, existed before us and will continue after us. Somehow, such thinking, characteristic of the Gaia-thinkers, is supposed to make us feel better.

We should note that this approach is almost totally unbiblical. The late biblical prophetic tradition does consider the question. The prophet Zephaniah's terrible prediction of doom might envision earth remaining even though life has gone: "I will utterly sweep away everything from the face of the earth, I will sweep away humans and beasts, I will sweep away the birds of the air and the fish of the sea. . . . I will cut off humankind from the face of the earth" (Zephaniah 1:2–3). But this is not a prophecy that Zephaniah utters with any consolation. Deutero-Isaiah constantly emphasizes the importance of human life in the creation scheme: "[God] who creates heavens and stretches them out, who hammers out the sky and its teeming life, who gives breath to humankind and life-spirit to those who walk upon it" (Isaiah 42:5). Isaiah further tells us that when God created the world, God didn't create it to be unformed *(tohu)* but to be inhabited and inhabitable *(la-shevet)* (Isaiah 45:18). God's ultimate purpose for the earth, whatever it may be, includes a functioning human and animal community.

THE PRIESTLY VOICE: AN AWESOME EARTH

I would also like to praise another voice in the Bible, one which is very often maligned in all contexts, including the ecological discussion: P, the priestly tradition of ancient Israel. It is in priestly writings and in temple writings that we find a profound sense of the awesomeness of nature, of the revelation of God through the beauty of nature, and of the place of humanity as a creature within nature. This love of nature is explicit in such Psalms as 104 and 98. It also underlies priestly legislation, where it is concerned with the land of Israel.

To these priests, the land of Israel is sacred and primary.

Leviticus 18 and 20 explain that when the peoples before Israel polluted the earth, the land vomited out these people. This land belongs to God, and God will protect it. Israel's tenure includes a mandate to protect the land of Israel from becoming polluted by the performance of abominable acts. In this priestly sense of the sacredness of the very soil of Israel, no less than in the prophetic tradition of Hosea, Jeremiah, and Ezekiel, Israel loses its right to the land if it doesn't protect it; the forced exile of the people separates the land from this contaminating force. This exile does not mean that God abandons Israel: the priests hold that God has great allegiance to Israel that goes beyond the land, and present the covenant of circumcision as the sign that land or no land, the relationship with Israel continues forever.

But the land itself is holy, and Israel may be separated from the land and sent far off to a land unknown. In priestly theology, two elements, the land of Israel and the people of Israel, are both extremely vital to God, and neither will be sacrificed for the other.

Interestingly enough, with all the priestly purification rituals, there is no ritual to purify the land.[13] Pollution must be prevented; once it settles in, it cannot be remedied by religious action or petition. The cult helps purify the people and the temple, not the land itself. But the priestly cult did not ignore the land; in fact, the *tamid* sacrifices, offered according to the calendar, were directed towards the whole cosmos to help keep the entire system going.

As we apply the priestly concept of the two independent foci to our current understanding, we must hold both elements, humanity and the ecosystem, in equilibrium. For whatever reason God created the cosmos, God has great allegiance to it. Humanity cannot continue to damage the earth for its own benefit. But, in the biblical viewpoints, humanity also has independent and equal importance.

In biblical theology, the earth must be a place where human ideals of harmony can be fulfilled, a place where humans behave well towards each other, so that the earth is both fertile and inhabited. Forms of deep ecology that place the earth above humanity are not biblical theologies, for the biblical ideal of *shalom* includes the presence of humanity.

This ancient language does not tell us whether, if humans continue on their current disharmonious path, the whole world will be destroyed, or just the people removed and the land preserved for the cockroaches. But it does bring home the recognition that we cannot escape the consequences of the human impact on the world. It further insists that today, now that we have technology that greatly magnifies our powers of destruction, if we do not make and obey rules of harmony and equity, then our connection with the earth will somehow be broken, and whether the cockroaches survive or not, the end of human history will have come, and with it the end of the divine plan.

Earth, Social Justice, and Social Transformation: The Spirals of Sabbatical Release

Arthur Waskow

O ne of the most important aspects of Jewish tradition and practice is that time is seen as a spiral.

Not as a circle, spinning endlessly in the same groove and returning always to the same sacred place in the past, as some traditional societies see time.

Not as a straight line, marching always forward to triumph or oblivion, making yesterday outdated and tomorrow crucial, as modernity sees time.

Rabbi Arthur Waskow founded and is director of The Shalom Center and is a Pathfinder of ALEPH: Alliance for Jewish Renewal. He is co-editor of *Trees, Earth, and Torah: A Tu B'Shvat Anthology* (Jewish Publication Society). His other books include *The Freedom Seder; Godwrestling; Seasons of Our Joy; Down-to-Earth Judaism: Food, Money, Sex, and the Rest of Life;* and *Godwrestling—Round Two: Ancient Wisdom, Future Paths* (Jewish Lights), winner of the Benjamin Franklin Award.

But as a spiral, in which we are always drawing on the past in order to move into the future.

In the world of thought, this spiral approach is encoded into the process and practice of midrash, through which an ancient text is turned in unexpected directions to cast new light upon the present and the future.

In the world of communal relationships and relationships between the human community and the earth, this practice is encoded in the several forms of Sabbath. For the teaching and practice of *Shabbat* (the Sabbath day), the *shmitah* or sabbatical year, and the *yovel* or Jubilee ("Home-bringing") year provided times for rest, reflection, and renewal between periods of working, making, doing.

This provision for reflective time is what made it possible not to run in an endless circle, simply repeating the week, or the year, or the generation that had gone before, but to learn from and digest them so as neither to forget them nor be imprisoned by them.

And it made it possible for the society not to be captured by an obsession with the future, always racing forward to do, to make, to work, but to pause to draw on some wisdom from a longer, deeper history.

Spirals.

In this essay I want to explore two aspects or levels of this sabbatical, spiral pattern: first, its direct effect as an expression of the Israelite relationship with the earth; and second, the possibility that this approach to the earth and human society was itself rooted in a crisis of Israelite society when it was put under the pressure of a sudden leap forward in doing, working, making—the crisis of imperial agriculture, perfected by Babylon.

By looking at these teachings in both these ways, I hope to make it possible for the Jewish people of today to learn from both the content and process of this biblical sabbatical/spiral practice. To learn from its content, what we might draw on and renew from this rhythmic way of rest and renewal; to learn from its process, what we ourselves might do in the midst of our own crisis, confronted as we are by the empires of globalization and ultratechnology, the equivalents in our own day of ancient imperial agriculture.

To begin, then, with the direct meaning of the sabbatical spiral:

Every seventh day, every seventh year, and the year after every seventh cycle of seven years (the fiftieth year), the human community is to pause from work. Not merely to rest from physical labor but also to renew itself, to achieve "release" or "self-reflection" or "detachment" or "holiness." And as the community rests, so does the earth—animals and vegetation are also released.

Before we focus on the implications of this whirling spiral of Shabbats for *adamah,* the earth, let us look at how it affects *adam,* the human race. The Bible connects this rhythm to human freedom and equality. The Shabbat of the seventh day comes first into human ken just after the liberation of the Israelites from slavery. It comes along with the manna, the food that the earth gives freely, so that eating it barely requires any work at all (Exod. 16:14–30). With the manna comes the information that on the morning of each sixth day, the manna will come in a double portion so that no one will have to do even the light work of gathering it on the seventh day, Shabbat.

It is as if the first realization of a people newly freed—even before they have their Great Encounter with God at Sinai—is that there must be time to rest and reflect, for otherwise they are still in slavery.

Indeed, one of the recitations of the Ten Utterances at Sinai focuses on Shabbat as the way of making sure that even in a society where some become indentured servants, "your male and female servants may rest as one-like-yourself." In this version of the Sinai

Encounter (in Deut. 5:12–15), the main reason for the existence of Shabbat is said to be as a reminder of liberation from slavery in the Narrow Place, *Mitzraiim,* Egypt.

In the larger spiral of the seventh year, the Hebrew Bible insists that the sabbatical year be one not only of release from work but release from debt (Deut. 15:1–11). And for the fiftieth year, the year of Jubilee, the Bible makes its most radical demand for political, social, and economic change:

> You shall count off seven sabbaths of years, seven times seven years. . . . Then you shall make proclamation with the blast of the *shofar* [ram's horn]. . . . On the Day of Atonement you shall make proclamation with the horn throughout all your land. And you shall make holy the fiftieth year, and proclaim release throughout the land to all the inhabitants thereof.
>
> It shall be to you a Jubilee [or "a Home-bringing," says the translation by Everett Fox in *The Five Books of Moses,* drawing on the Hebrew roots beneath the word *yovel*].
>
> So you—every one of you—shall return to your own ancestral holding; every one of you, to your family. . . . You shall not sow, nor reap what grows, nor gather the grapes of the unpruned vines. . . . And the land shall not be permanently sold—
>
> *For the land is Mine. You are strangers and visitors with Me.*
> (Lev. 25:8–23)

A radical social transformation! Not only are debts periodically annulled, but once in every generation the rich give up whatever extra land they have acquired, the poor who have lost their family plot return to it.

Yet in proclaiming this series of radical acts of what we would call social justice, the Bible never uses the words *tzedek* ("upright justice") or *mishpat* ("fair judgment"). Instead (Lev. 25), it uses the language of restfulness, detachment, release: *dror* and *shmitah* and *shabbat*. It expands on the sacred rhythm of sabbatical time, and calls for the Home-bringing to begin with the mystic ceremony of blowing the ram's horn at that most sacred time in all the year, the day when the high priest entered the Holy of Holies to purge the community of all its misdeeds and came out to breathe aloud the sacred Name of God in the ears of all the people.

In Leviticus 25 and its sister passage, Deuteronomy 15, what we might call the political emerges organically and inevitably from what we might call the spiritual. Indeed, for the Bible they are one and the same.

And inextricably interwoven with them, perhaps indeed one and the same thing, is what we would call the ecological.

Let us look back at Shabbat with questions of the earth in mind. Shabbat comes into human awareness with the manna. This is the food that comes without the need for war against the earth. For many of us today this may not seem surprising, for we are so divorced from raising crops and pruning trees and guarding sheep that our food may seem to drop like gentle rain from Heaven.

But of course that is not so. To win our food requires a constant struggle with the earth. And ancient Israelites were conscious of that reality. Indeed, they tell a story of its truth: the story of Eden.

In that story human beings who can freely eat of every herb and seed in the Garden of Delight alienate themselves from the Breath of Life by eating wrongly, rebelliously. This may be a necessary part of growing up. (Leaving the womb, going through "the terrible twos," becoming an adolescent may all involve rebellion, as one grows less dependent, more mature.) But one major consequence of this rebellion is that eating will come hard. The earth will bring forth thorns and thistles, and only with sweat pouring down our faces will human beings get to eat. *Every day of our lives,* the story goes out of its way to say.

Until the manna. Until the coming of Shabbat. And the sabbatical year. And Jubilee.

On that day, and in those years, *adam* and *adamah* live in peace with each other. The forty years of manna are Edenic time. The earth pours food upon its people, and the people eat without sweating it. This is when Shabbat comes. Of course! Yet Shabbat outlasts the manna, and continues as the Israelites move into a settled land.

For one-seventh of the time, the troublesome result of troubling Eden is smoothed over. Indeed, if we calculate eight years of every fifty as sabbatical time and add that to one-seventh of the forty-two work years, for almost *two*-sevenths of our days *adam* and *adamah* can live in peace. And if the question arises, In the seventh year, what will we eat? then the Torah teaches, God will bestow blessing *because* we pause from sweating. The earth will give us more, not less, abundance.

Shabbat is the aftertaste of Eden and a foretaste of messianic time.

For Christians, Jesus the Christ is the "new Adam," one harmonious human being come to reverse the sin of Eden. For Jews, Shabbat is the entire Garden once again, the actual living practice in community of both Eden and *Mashiach* (Messiah). And therefore, as Sinai tells us, the sign of continuing covenant between the Breath of Life and the Godwrestling people.

Or—taking into account the biblical report that a "mixed multitude" left Egypt and stood at Sinai, a "mixed multitude" *became* the people of Israel—perhaps the logic must be reversed, to get it right: All those, of any people, who take and celebrate the time for restful reflection and renewal for *adam* and *adamah* enter a covenant with God, YHWH, the inward/outward Breathing of all Life.

And all those who reject this sacred rhythm, who become addicted to making, doing, producing, consuming without cease, have cut themselves off from the Life-Breath and are in deadly danger.

What is more, this danger threatens not only themselves as individuals but the whole society and the earth itself.

For Shabbat is not only a blessing for *adam*. Says Leviticus, "But in the seventh year there shall be a Sabbath of Sabbath-ceasing *for the land,* a Sabbath of YHWH" (25:4). Not for the sake of humanity alone comes restfulness but for the earth as well, in direct relationship with YHWH.

What is the content of this restful time? "Your field you are not to sow, your vineyard you are not to prune, the aftergrowth of your harvest you are not to harvest. . . . It shall be a Sabbath of Sabbath-ceasing for the land. You may eat whatever the land during its Sabbath will freely produce—you, your male and female servants, your hired hand, resident-settlers who sojourn with you, and your domestic-cattle and the wild-beasts in your land may eat all its yield" (25:4–7).

Now here perhaps we may be puzzled. In one breath, no harvest; in the next breath, we may eat what the land gives freely. Is this not a contradiction? How can the Israelites gather if they may not harvest?

And the puzzle is repeated in the passage on the fiftieth-year Shabbat: "That fiftieth year shall be a Home-bringing/Jubilee for you: you shall not sow, neither shall you reap the aftergrowth or harvest the untrimmed vines, for it is a Home-bringing/Jubilee. It shall be holy to you: you may only eat the growth direct from the field" (25:11–12).

To solve the puzzle, think "gatherers."

Think: A people whose earliest legends are of being shepherds, whose closest relatives according to those legends (Esau and Ishmael) are hunters—such a people, called *Ivrim* ("Hebrews "), the Cross-over folk, the Boundary-jumpers, the Wanderers, the Nomads—perhaps this people remembers with a complex nostalgia being food-gatherers.

And, as Evan Eisenberg and Leonard Angel suggest in their contributions in this book, perhaps with this story the people remembers the transformational, troublesome moment when agriculture comes into their ken. If the emergence of the wandering, gathering humans from amidst our cousin primates was a kind of collective birthing of *adam* from the womb of *adamah,* then agriculture was the next step in growing up and growing away from the earth.

No longer fed so easily by earth, human beings choose to bring about a great deal more food to eat, at the cost of being tied to space and property, to harder working, to bosses and to serfs, to great empires built from the abundance of great plantations and built to protect the ownership of those plantations.

Faced with the more efficient economics of organized agriculture, with the more powerful polity of an imperial state and army, what should a pastoral/gathering people do? The Israelites adopted agriculture, but with a difference. For one day of every seven, for one year of every seven, they would renew their ancient roots in an earlier relationship with earth. And if they failed to do this, what would happen? According to Leviticus,

> But if you do not obey Me and do not observe all these commandments, if you reject My laws and spurn My rules, so that you do not observe all My commandments and you break My covenant . . . (26:14–16)
>
> Then I will make-desolate, I Myself, the land, so that your enemies who settle in it will be appalled at the desolation in it. And you I will scatter among the nations; I will unsheathe the

sword against you, so that your land becomes a desolation and your cities become a wasteland.

Then shall the land make up for its sabbath years throughout the time that it is desolate and you are in the land of your enemies; then shall the land rest and make up for its sabbath years.

Throughout the time that it is desolate, it shall observe the rest that it did not observe in your sabbath years while you were dwelling upon it. (26:32–35)

For the land shall be forsaken of them, making up for its sabbath years by being desolate of them, while they atone for their iniquity; because—yes, because!—they rejected My rules and spurned My laws. (26:43)

According to the ecological theory and experience of ancient Israel, the need for Sabbath restfulness, for a rhythm of Doing and Being, is not merely a superficial wistfulness. It is a law of gravity: The earth does rest. If you rest with it, celebrating joyfully, then all is joyful. But if you try to prevent it from resting, it will rest anyway—upon your head. Through famine, drought, exile, desolation, it *will* rest.

And the very last chapter of the Hebrew Scriptures, II Chronicles 36:20, claims to report:

Those who survived the sword, he [Nebuchadnezzar] exiled to Babylon, and they became his and his sons' servants till the rise of the Persian kingdom, in fulfillment of the word of YHWH spoken by Jeremiah, until the land paid back its sabbaths; as long as it lay desolate it kept sabbath, till seventy years were completed.

The cycle of Shabbat, sabbatical year, and Jubilee is not static. It does not imagine that the earth can be renewed, the land can be shared, and justice can be achieved once and for all. And it does not imagine that a little change, year after year, can make for real renewal. The Bible says that for six years of every seven it is all right for some to accumulate wealth and some to lose it, and for the earth to be forced to work under human command, but that once every seventh year there must be a major healing and once every generation there must be a great transformation. And that each generation must know it will have to be done again, in the next generation.

How does the cycle feel when the Jubilee itself comes round at last? There stands the land untilled as it stood the year before, the seventh seventh year. Two years in a row untilled. Imagine how strange (and how anciently familiar) the land would look: more than a touch of wilderness. More than a touch of the land that nomads remember.

Everyone would learn that the biggest action of all is to not act.

Not acting! How fearful the farmers who tried to live by this teaching! The farmer might fear that waiting two years in a row would bring ruin. But the Bible asserts, and modern science confirms, that letting the land lie fallow is a crucial part of its restoration. What looks like a famine in the short run is necessary to prosperity in the long run. Trusting in God and practicing science are not contradictory.

The Jubilee stands beyond the politics of guilt and rage. It does not ask for the rich to give their land away in fear or guilt; it does not ask the wretched of the earth and the prisoners of starvation to rise in rage to take back the land from the swollen rich.

Instead, the Jubilee proclaims a "release," a Shabbat, for everyone. A release for the rich as well as the poor. The rich are released from working, bossing, increasing production—and from others' envy of them. The poor are released from working, from hunger, from humiliation and despair—and from others' pity of them. Both the rich and the poor are seen as fully human, as counterparts to be encountered, not as enemies or victims to be feared or hated.

Perhaps that is why the Jubilee year begins not at the New Moon of the seventh month, not on Rosh Hashanah, when the fiftieth year itself begins, but ten days later—on Yom Kippur, the Day of Atonement, when the community has already purged itself of guilt and rage. Thus Jubilee is both the final healing gift of the people to God to complete the old cycle and God's first blessing to the people and the earth in the new cycle.

But the sabbatical year, with its annulment of debt, and the Jubilee, with its redistribution of land, were not based only on recognizing God's image in every human being and in the breathing earth. They may also have appealed to the class interests of a large group of independent small farmers who wanted to prevent the emergence of a permanent, ever-fattening class of large landholders who could lord it over them and a class of permanent slaves or debtors who would undercut their income.

What is the Torah's economic/ecological vision? We might call it a pulsating rather than an expanding or exploding system. It bears a family resemblance to what some economists and ecologists today call sustainable economies, which can meet their peoples' needs year after year, generation after generation, by restoring the earth to the same degree that they deplete it. Not the same as economic growth.

And the great sabbatical spiral renews human community as well. Here we see the Torah's vision of social justice focus on resting, not only from the physical work of tilling the land but from the political and social work of building institutions and concentrating capital. Stop work for even just one day, and for that day hierarchy dissolves: no boss, no employee. Stop work for an entire year, and the institutions of society, normally so useful, periodically dissolve. People are freed up, the imagination is freed up, the Breathing-Spirit of the world blows where it likes.

For the "eco-Judaism" of the Bible, spiritual enrichment is profoundly connected with limiting the society's exploitation of the earth, and both of these are intimately intertwined with limiting the mastery of the rich and powerful over the poor. And the energy flows in all directions through this organic whole. In one direction, only the spiritually well-fed can ease their hunger for land, for wealth, and for power. In another direction, only those who rest from working the earth and from amassing wealth can get in deepest touch with God. In still another direction, the greed and envy that pushes people toward overworking the land cannot end unless everyone knows there is no point to envy: debts will be annulled and the land will be redistributed.

At another level, the sabbatical process shapes time into a spiral. For the Jews, the cycles of the earth, the moon, and the sun became not endlessly repetitive circles, unchanging, year after year after year. Nor did Jewish time ignore these cycles and turn time into a straight line always going forward, defined simply by historical and social change.

What the Shabbats of the seventh day and the seventh year accomplished was making a turn possible from one level to another of the repetition of the days and years. Taking time for reflection, for digestion of the last six days or years, made it possible to "repeat" them in a new key, at a new level. To learn from them so as not to have to repeat them. To integrate the forward reach of historical, personal, and social change into the rhythms of forever. As in a spiral, Jewish time went backward in order to go forward.

If this theory of the origins and intentions of biblical "eco-Judaism" is correct, it teaches us a still deeper truth, one of method as well as content. We know that when, two thousand years ago, the Jewish people faced a great economic, political, and scientific transformation in the form of Greco-Roman Hellenistic civilization and its shattering of biblical society, their response was the creation of Talmudic/Rabbinic Judaism (and their help in the creation of Christianity and Islam). They responded by adopting some of the approaches of this new Hellenistic ability to control the earth and human beings, and by infusing them with the more ancient wisdom of the Torah—the wisdom of Being as well as Doing, Loving as well as Controlling.

Now we may begin to see that this kind of transformation—the classic Jewish strategy of midrash, of going back to an older practice and an older text in order to go forward—this kind of transformation may have been at the heart of the Bible itself. The struggles of history cannot be reduced to mere antiquarian and academic footnotes, for in these struggles are the Godwrestlings that bring spiritual wisdom into the lives of the people.

What are the turning-moments that inscribe the grand spiral of Jewish history?

Shepherds struggling to find glimmers of God in the triumph of imperial agriculture without abandoning the spiritual wisdom of the nomad.

Rabbis struggling to find glimmers of God in the triumph of

Hellenistic commerce without abandoning the spiritual wisdom of the local farmer.

And perhaps Jews struggling to find glimmers of God in the triumph of Modern global technology without abandoning the spiritual wisdom of the shtetl, the neighborhood, the kibbutz, the havurah.

In each era, struggling under new conditions to renew a sacred relationship between *adam* and *adamah*.

PART 2

Rabbinic Judaism: One People, Many Lands

For most of the past two thousand years, the Jewish people lived in a world profoundly different from that of the Bible. By 140 of the Common Era, the Temple in Jerusalem had been destroyed and the Jewish community of the land of Israel had been shattered by the legions of imperial Rome. The relationship between the people and land was severed.

The Jewish people no longer had even a foothold in the small land on the eastern edge of the Mediterranean Sea that had been its intimate partner in relationship with God. No longer were the foods that sprouted from that land brought to its center at the Holy Temple, there to be offered as "near-bringings" to connect the people with their God. No longer could the sabbatical rhythm of the seventh year bring an intimate pause for the people and the land to converse with each other.

During these two thousand years, most Jews have walked a life-path we call Rabbinic Judaism. This transformation did not happen all at once, though it was given its final seal after Rome smashed the Jewish revolt of 132–135 CE. During several centuries of turmoil, as Hellenistic-Roman civilization gained sway over the Jews of the Mediterranean Basin, Jews debated how to shape their future. One group, whom we now call the Rabbis, wove an intricate mesh of stories, philosophies, legal decisions, flights of imagination, debates, and midrashic reinterpretations of the biblical texts. Most of these teachings were inscribed in two enormous texts called the Talmud—one based chiefly on teachings from the Babylonian Diaspora, the other on teachings from the land of Israel.

Most Jews chose to follow the life-path described in the Talmud, in law codes that evolved from it, and in continuing midrashic unfolding of the ancient texts, according to patterns defined by the Rabbis. Thus Rabbinic Judaism became the life-map of most Jews until late in the nineteenth century.

As they had to rethink the relationship between the Jewish people and the far-flung *adamah,* the Rabbis taught that as the Altar had been the collective dinner table of the Jewish people—its most intimate connection with the earth—so every dinner-table in all the scattered Jewish spaces would now be an Altar for that household.

But this meant a profound change in how the Jewish people could address issues of the earth. Jews no longer had the power to define an economic/ecological policy over a single land, and they lived in the nooks and crannies of civilizations where others held that power. What was left that could be called a Jewish ethic of the earth?

Two possibilities: the personal, individual spirituality of a relationship to the world of rivers, trees, and mountains; and a household ethics focused on consumption of goods more than on their production.

In regard to the first (embodied in aggadic texts, what we might call spiritual, emotional, philosophical teachings), the Rabbis were far more ambivalent about celebrating earth than the writers of the Psalms had been, with their outpourings of awe and love. They talked of Torah study in the way the Psalms and the Song of Songs had spoken of intertwining with the earth. Indeed, they transferred nature imagery to the world of yeshiva study. Not only did they call the Torah a Tree of Life; they said the study of Torah was as erotically delightful as sex with a "doe of the dawn." Perhaps we should see these metaphors as mute testimony to their continuing but repressed love affair with the earth; but repressed it certainly was.

So in the Talmudic sources we find ambivalence about celebration of the earth: to greet it with unbounded joy, or to limit celebration whenever that might interfere with Torah study. In this book several texts show this ambivalence. Then a much later text from Nachmanides (Ramban), a thirteenth-century commentator and philosopher with a Kabbalistic orientation, speaks aggadically of the importance of protecting all species from extinction.

As for the second aspect (in the world of *halakhah*, the details of a lawful Jewish life-path), the Rabbis sought to create a household ethics that limited the (mis)use of the earth. In a silent irony, the Rabbis drew on a Torah text—quintessentially about the power of a national community to make war—in an effort to set limits to the use of the earth by Jewish communities that had no power to make war or to govern a land. The Rabbinic doctrine of *bal tashchit*, "Do not destroy," emerged from reinterpretation of a passage in Deuteronomy (20:19) that forbade destruction of the enemy's fruit trees during a war. The Rabbis enormously expanded the domain where *bal tashchit* applied and then limited its force within that larger domain.

Over the centuries, most Rabbinic authorities ruled that *bal tashchit* forbade wasting natural resources and human-made objects. As they balanced ecological concerns with economic needs, they rarely interfered with the use of the earth to meet human needs.

This section opens with a series of talmudic and later rabbinic texts (most of them translated by David E. Sulomm Stein) that set the boundaries of this centuries-long evolution. (These texts are presented with their full contexts, not shorn to bare eco-relevant comment. In this way, we can understand the truth that environmental matters were not the Rabbis' central concern.) The texts reveal a concern not to destroy needlessly and a sense of economic calculation in deciding what is needful. We look at some texts from the twelfth-century philosopher and halakhist Maimonides (Rambam), who summed up in his halakhic code the cautiously balanced conclusions of Rabbinic tradition about *bal tashchit.*

On the other hand, there is a much more recent interpretation of *bal tashchit* by Rabbi Samson Raphael Hirsch, about whom Fred Dobb writes in Part I of Volume 2 of this book. Writing a century ago, Hirsch was already sounding alarms about the impact of modernity upon the earth; he gives a much stronger earth-protective orientation to *bal tashchit.*

We turn from these texts, taken from the classical sources of Rabbinic Judaism, to writings that analyze the Rabbinic tradition's attitude toward the earth. These were all written during the past generation, as concern arose over a possible global ecological crisis and as some argued that various religious traditions were responsible either for getting the planet into this crisis or for now taking action to get it out (or both).

Among these recent articles, Norman Lamm's magisterial essay on ecology in Judaism begins its overview before the Rabbinic era. But Lamm is mostly concerned with presenting the perspectives of different times and flavors of Rabbinic Judaism. A major part of his article follows the long career of *bal tashchit.* Then Lamm shows us how two divergent currents of rabbinic thought—the more ecstatic Hasidic and the more intellectual Mitnagdic currents—reassessed

Jewish attitudes toward nature, as Modernity increasingly enforced human control over nature in the eighteenth and nineteenth centuries.

Lamm's article is followed by a series of essays that address more specific questions about earth-related activity that arise in the Rabbinic worldview. To some extent, these authors also look beyond the Rabbinic context in an effort to defend it or draw new wisdom from it.

Jonathan Helfand focuses on the aggadic/philosophic question of the degree to which God has delegated control over the earth to human beings.

David Ehrenfeld and Philip Bentley look at the tradition of stewardship as the role of humanity toward the earth.

Fred Dobb takes a step beyond in mining Rabbinic tradition for a "usable past." He does this by explicitly using as a framework some of the major thought categories of contemporary ecologists and asking how the Rabbis addressed those issues. For those who want to root contemporary environmentalist Judaism in Rabbinic thought, he gathers the strongest evidence from a many-voiced tradition.

Jeremy Benstein takes up one of the texts with which this section opens: the one denouncing those who interrupt their Torah study in order to enjoy nature. He traces the ways in which various generations of Rabbis addressed this text, how they balanced (or did not balance) love of Torah with love of nature and the earth. In the process, Benstein reminds us that the Rabbis did not think in our contemporary ecological categories and often took positions not consonant with them. From the last sections of his article, we can anticipate the next two parts of this anthology (Volume 2), which look at the ways in which recent Jewish thought—Zionism and Eco-Judaism—view this question.

Reading these articles, we begin to see the possibility and the importance of others that are not yet written. A number of aspects of the Rabbinic approach to *adam/adamah* issues remain to be explored. For example, What is the role of the earth in Rabbinic liturgy—in the language of the prayer book, in the understanding and practice of the festival cycle, in the Rabbis' choice of particular prophetic passages and psalms for use in the liturgy?

In understanding these articles—these, and others yet unwritten—we must keep in mind that their authors are more concerned with Rabbinic attitudes toward *adam/adamah* than over the centuries the Rabbis themselves had been. All these studies emerge from an effort to understand what Rabbinic insights were into questions the Rabbis did not ask in quite the ways we would.

In this way, the wave of articles on views of the environment in Rabbinic Judaism share an intellectual stance with recent studies of Rabbinic thought on other questions, for example, the role of women in prayer, the status of homosexuality, the responsibilities of a secular Jewish state, the relationships between the Jewish people and other peoples living in the land of Israel. All of them emerge from a sense of needing to deal with a new world that the Rabbis did not live in and turning to Rabbinic traditions for hints on how to do this.

By looking for such hints, these writings are exploring the ocean of tradition for pools of a usable past. "Usable" in the sense that this makes it possible for contemporary Jews to put our own spin on the hints we find. This is part of the process of making "macro-midrash"—not merely gleaning new insights into the meaning of a particular phrase from an ancient text, but seeing the texts as a whole in a new light in order to help us deal Jewishly with new problems.

Some people expect that seeing the texts this way may make it possible to continue living in an evolving version of Rabbinic Judaism. Others think that the Jewish people may need to shape a quite different worldview and life-practice, as different as Rabbinic Judaism was from Biblical Israel. In either case, we may find that these assessments of Rabbinic thought may point the way to new questions we might ask:

- Is there a contradiction between, or can we integrate, celebration of nature and celebration of Torah?
- Can we balance or integrate the protection and healing of the earth with concern for social justice and the needs of society?
- What role should the cycles of earth, moon, and sun have in our understanding and observance of the festival cycles?
- Does the history (rather than the explicit texts) of the Rabbinic transformation of Biblical Judaism teach a spiritual path for transformation of Rabbinic Judaism under present circumstances, or does it point toward gradual change within rabbinic practice?

The essays assembled here emerge from concern for how Rabbinic Judaism dealt with issues that have become urgent in a new world quite different from the Jewish past. Two major aspects of this new world are the subjects of Volume 2: the creation of the State of Israel, in which the Jewish people has come back in direct physical relationship to the land of Israel, and the realization of an epochal crisis in the planetary *adam/adamah* relationship, which by affecting all humanity affects Jews who live everywhere.

RABBINIC TEXTS

A. *AGGADAH:*
CELEBRATION AND AVOIDANCE

W hen the Holy One, Blessed Be, created *Adam Harishon,* God took Adam and led [him/her/it/them] around all the trees of the Garden of Eden. And God said to Adam:

"Look at My works! How beautiful and praiseworthy they are! And everything I made, I created for you. Be careful, [though,] that you don't spoil or destroy My world—because if you spoil it, there's nobody after you to fix it." (*Kohelet Rabbah* 7:13)

Rabbi Ya'akov says: One, who while walking along the way, reviewing his studies, breaks off from his study and says, "How beautiful is that tree! How beautiful is that plowed field!" Scripture regards him as if he has forfeited his soul. (*Pirkei Avot/Ethics of the Fathers* 3:9)

Heaven and earth were finished—all their array.[1] (Genesis 2:1)

Our Rabbis said: "Even those things that you may see as super-fluous to Creation—such as flies, fleas, and mosquitoes—even they too were inherent in Creation; for through it all is God's purpose carried out—even through a snake, a mosquito, or a frog."

Midrash Genesis Rabbah § 10:7

Land of Israel, c. 400 CE

[trans. David E. Sulomm Stein]

Do not take the mother bird together with her young. (Deuteronomy 22:6)

Do not slaughter [for food] both a (domesticated) sheep, goat, or cow and its offspring on the same day [even though you worked hard and raised them for this very purpose] (Leviticus 22:28). *Do not take [for food] both a [wild] mother bird and her [helpless] offspring [that you might happen upon, even though it seems like a free lunch]* (Deuteronomy 22:6)—The reason behind both of these precepts is: [on the one hand, focusing on *Adam*] that we should not be cruel and merciless; or [on the other hand, focusing on *Adamah*] that Scripture would not permit destructive acts that risk wiping out the whole species—even though it permits the slaughter [for food] of [some members of] that species. In the latter sense, killing both mother and [helpless] offspring on the same day, or [even] taking the [mother with all of the] young once they have fledged, [while probably not a literal threat,] is [on a symbolic level] like exterminating that species.

Rabbi Moses Nahmanides

Commentary on the Torah, Deuteronomy 22:6 (c. 1260 CE)

[trans. David E. Sulomm Stein]

---

[1] The Hebrew *tza-va* (array, hosts) connotes "rendering service" (in this case, to God), which implies that all aspects of Creation were made for a purpose.

The quality of urban air
compared to the air in the deserts and forests
is like thick and turbulent water compared to pure and light water...
In the cities with their tall buildings and narrow roads,
the pollution that comes from their residents, their waste,
... makes their entire air reeking ... and thick, ...
although no one is aware of it. ...
Because we grow up in cities and become used to them,
we can at least choose a city with an open horizon ...
And if you ... cannot move out of the city,
try at least to ... let the house be tall and the court wide enough
to permit the northern wind and the sun to come through,
because the sun thins out the pollution of the air ...

Rabbi Moses Maimonides
Fostat, Egypt, 1135–1204 CE
"The Preservation of Youth"

B. *Halakhah:* The Law of *Bal Tashchit* (Do Not Destroy)

Translated by David E. Sulomm Stein

*O**nly trees that you know*[1] (this means a food tree [past its prime]) *are not food-bearing* (this means a barren[2] tree) *you may destroy and cut down. . . .* (Deuteronomy 20:19).

But if in the end we include both kinds of trees [as eligible to be cut down], why did the Torah explicitly say, *not food-bearing*?

When given a choice, [cut down] a barren tree instead of a food tree.

---

[1] The Hebrew connotes "have experience with."

[2] Any species that does not produce edible fruit or nuts.

Rabbi David E. Sulomm Stein is a Reconstructionist rabbi who edited *A Garden of Choice Fruit: 200 Classic Jewish Quotes on Human Beings and the Environment.* Now a project editor for the Jewish Publication Society, he lives in Redondo Beach, California.

And when does this rule apply? You might infer that [the Torah meant for us *always* to cut down a barren tree first], even if [when left standing] it would have a higher market value [than the fruit tree's future yield]; but the Torah text says [to cut the barren tree first] *only* [when the market value for the two types of trees is *equal*. (In general, relative market values should be used to decide which tree to cut down first.)]

Midrash Sifre to Deuteronomy 20 *(Shofetim)*

Land of Israel, c. 400 CE;

Talmud of Babylonia, *Baba Kamma* 91b–92a

Rav said, "A date palm that yields a *kav*[3] of fruit—it is forbidden to chop it down. [If it yields less, you may chop it down. The deciding factor is the yield.]"

But [Mishnah *Shevi'it* 4:10 seems to contradict that claim:] "How much must an olive tree [yield] that it not be chopped down? A quarter [of a *kav*]." [So which volume of fruit is the correct minimal yield?]

[Resolution:] Olives are different in that they are more valuable. [A quarter-*kav* of olives is thus worth the same as a *kav* of dates. What counts is not volume but rather market value.]

Rabbi Hanina said, "My son Shivhat passed away for the sole reason that he cut down a fig tree before its time."[4]

Ravina said, "If [his tree] would have been worth more [when chopped down, as compared to the value of its fruit yield, then cutting it down] would have been permitted. [The proper decision procedure is to assess the net benefit based on market values.]"

Talmud of Babylonia, *Baba Kamma* 91b

c. 200–c. 600 CE

---

[3] A measure of volume, like a bushel.

[4] Illustrates literally . . . *the trees of the field equal human lives* . . . (Deut. 20:19).

Whenever Rav Hisda had to pass through prickly shrubs and this-tles, he used to lift up his garment, saying, "If that [i.e., my body] is scratched, it will heal itself; but if that [i.e., my garment] is torn, it will not heal itself."

Talmud of Babylonia, *Baba Kamma* 91b

c. 200–c. 600 CE

[With regard to the adjustment of lamps, we have] an ancient, au-thoritative statement [from Tosefta *Shabbat,* ch. 2; focusing on the needs of *Adam*]: "[Even on Shabbat,] a lump of salt may be placed in a lamp in order that it burns more brightly [in contrast to trimming the wick, which is not done on Shabbat];[5] conversely, mud or clay may be placed under the lamp so that it burns more slowly."[6] [From the complementary perspective, focusing on the needs of *Adamah,*] Rabbi Zutra said: "One who covers an oil lamp [so that it burns less efficiently], or uncovers a naphtha lamp [so that it burns less effi-ciently], breaks the rule against needless waste [derived from Deuteronomy 20:19]."

Talmud of Babylonia, *Shabbat* 67b

c. 200–c. 600 CE

Rav Huna once ripped some silk garments in front of his [grown] son Rabbah, thinking, "Let me see whether or not he gets upset."[7]

Objection: But perhaps [his son] indeed would have gotten upset [and reacted angrily]—then [Rav Huna] would have broken the rule, *Do not place a stumbling block before the blind* (Leviticus 19:14)

---

[5] Salt clears the oil of suspended particles, so that the wick absorbs the oil more readily.

[6] Their mass absorbs heat, keeping the oil cooler and hence thicker.

[7] At issue in the Talmud at this point is what it means to "honor" one's parents. The text has granted that it would be reasonable for one to be concerned about the bizarre ac-tions of one's parents where the value of one's potential inheritance was at stake. Then it relates this anecdote, in which a parent appears to have put that idea to the test.

[by inciting Rabbah to dishonor him—which would have been a most serious offense]!

Reply: [No,] he was willing to forgo his honor for his son's sake.

Objection: But it broke [the spirit of] the rule against needless waste (Deuteronomy 20:19)!

Reply: [No,] he ripped each garment along the seam with its border [so that no real damage was done].

Objection: But [if so,] perhaps that would obviate any need for Rabbah to get upset [thus making the test meaningless]!

Reply: [No,] he tested him when he was already [too] upset [about something else to notice this subtle ploy].

Talmud of Babylonia, *Kiddushin* 32a

c. 200–c. 600 CE

Rav Hiyya bar Avin said: Samuel said, "When someone gets chills [on Shabbat] after bloodletting,[8] we may make a fire [to warm that person and/or to prepare warm food, because the high risk of death overrides the normal prohibition against lighting fires on Shabbat] . . . " [Yes, but it's Shabbat—a tough time to find or purchase firewood; and it's Babylonia—located on a dry, artificially irrigated flood plain with few trees. So how does one get ready fuel for such a fire?] For Samuel himself, they chopped up an expensive, drum-shaped stool made of teak. For Rav Judah, they chopped up a juniper-wood table. For Rabbah they chopped up a [wooden] chair. At which point Abbaye said to Rabbah, "[They're destroying your perfectly good furniture merely for kindling!] Aren't you breaking the rule against needless waste (Deuteronomy

---

[8] The Talmud mentions bloodletting frequently both as therapy to treat disease and as a regular wellness practice to prevent disease. Indeed, bloodletting seems to have been a commonplace practice throughout the Near East in ancient times.

20:19)?" He replied, "[Avoiding the] 'needless waste' of my body takes priority for me."[9]

Talmud of Babylonia, *Shabbat* 129a

c. 200–c. 600 CE

[Focusing on the needs of *Adamah,* the wealthy] Rav Hisda [who could certainly afford to eat the finest foods] said: "One who has the opportunity to eat barley bread but instead eats wheat bread is violating [the spirit of] the rule against needless waste (Deuteronomy 20:19)."[10] [Likewise, the wealthy] Rav Papa said: "One who has the opportunity to drink beer but instead drinks wine is violating [the spirit of] the rule against needless waste (Deuteronomy 20:19)."[11] [Focusing on the needs of *Adam,* the anonymous editor notes:] But this is not what matters most! [Avoiding the] "needless waste" of one's own body takes priority.[12]

Talmud of Babylonia, *Shabbat* 140b

c. 200–c. 600 CE

---

[9] Because the one who is responsible for my well-being is me alone, God has charged me with that responsibility above all.

[10] Both barley and wheat were staple grains in the Near East. Barley could grow in poorer soil and was half the price. But the point here seems to be that barley did not deplete the soil as much as wheat did.

[11] In Babylonia, vineyards were rare; beer (usually made from barley) was the plentiful national beverage. But the point here seems to be that in Babylonia, the ingredients for beer used natural resources more effectively than vineyards did.

[12] The editor may be seen as adding an explicit qualifcation that presumably the foregoing sages would have agreed with. The editor claims that what Rav Hisda meant was "One should eat barley bread rather than wheat bread so long as one does not neglect one's own body in so doing." (The two grains were not seen as equivalent; wheat was considered to have twice the nutritive value of barley [*Mishnah Pe'ah* 8.5].)

In accord with the verse, *Do not destroy its trees!* (Deuteronomy 20:19), we do not cut down [the enemy's] food trees[13] outside a [besieged] city. [Might you think it still acceptable to kill such trees by a different means? The Talmud therefore notes that, for example,] we [also] do not withhold irrigation from them so that they wither. And [do you think that this rule applies only in war? On the contrary, it applies] not only during a siege. [That was merely a case when one might mistakenly imagine that, under the extreme circumstances, destroying a food tree would surely be justified.] Rather, the Torah's rule is broken whenever a food tree is cut down just to be destructive. ¶ On the other hand, [according to the Talmud's examples,] we may cut down a food tree whenever it is damaging other [food] trees, or damaging another person's field, or its [economic] value for other purposes is greater [than that of its food yield]. In short, the Torah forbids only senseless destruction [of food trees]. ¶ At the same time, this principle applies not only to trees. [It was extended by the Talmud to other cases:] Whenever someone destroys a useful artifact, or rips clothing, demolishes a building, plugs up a spring, or senselessly destroys food, it violates the spirit of the Torah's "do not destroy" rule. Such actions are disgraceful.

Rabbi Moses Maimonides
Mishneh Torah, Book of Judges,
Lore of Kings and Wars §§ 6:8, 6:10
c. 1178 CE

This prohibition of purposeless destruction of food trees around a besieged city is only to be taken as an example of general wastefulness.

Under the concept of *bal tashchit (You must not destroy!),* the purposeless destruction of anything at all is taken to be forbidden so

---

[13] Trees that bear fruit or nuts.

that our text becomes the most comprehensive warning to human beings not to misuse the position that God has given them as masters of the world and its matter to capricious, passionate, or merely thoughtless wasteful destruction of anything on earth. Only for *wise use* has God laid the world at our feet when God said to humankind, . . . *fill the earth and master it; and rule* . . . ! (Genesis 1:28)

Rabbi Samson Raphael Hirsch

Germany, 1808–1888

The Pentateuch: Translated and Explained [German] (1878), comment on Deuteronomy 20:20 (Trans. adapted from Isaac Levy by Shomrei Adamah for *Garden of Choice Fruits*) Cf. *Horeb: Essays on Israel's "Duties" in the Diaspora* 56 (1837)

ECOLOGY IN JEWISH LAW AND THEOLOGY

Norman Lamm

The unprecedented growth of science and technology, which has become one of the chief characteristics of Western civilization, is today the subject of profound and trenchant criticism. The very success of technology threatens to become its undoing. Students of ecology now alarm us to the dangers that an unrestrained technology pose for the delicate balance of nature on which the survival of the biosphere depends.

Ever since the publication of Rachel Carson's *The Silent Spring*, the public has become more and more concerned about the possible consequences of man's unthinking interference in and disruption of the natural processes that make life possible on earth. Polluted air,

Rabbi Norman Lamm is president of Yeshiva University and the author of *Faith and Doubt*. He was the founding editor of *Tradition: A Journal of Orthodox Jewish Thought*.

dirty water, littered landscape, an environment contaminated with impurities from radioactive strontium to waste detergents—all of these place in jeopardy not only the quality of life, but the very survival of many or all species including the human. Sheer necessity has caused ecology to emerge from its ivory tower of pure science to pronounce a great moral imperative incumbent upon all mankind—to curb its arrogant and mindless devastation of nature.

The case for the ecological movement is obvious and beyond dispute. One point, of the many cogent ones made in the growing literature on the subject, is worth repeating here. René Dubos has reminded us that we still know precious little about pollution. Seventy percent of all the precipitate contaminants in urban air are still unidentified and, twenty to thirty years hence, those who are today below the age of three will undoubtedly show varying signs of chronic and permanent malfunction. Man is clever enough to conquer nature—and stupid enough to wreck it and thereby destroy himself.

THE THEOLOGIANS' MASOCHISM

Unfortunately, the ecology issue has itself inspired a new pollution problem—a fallout of silliness in the theological environment. It has now become almost a dogma of the avant-garde *cognoscenti,* who only a short while ago were telling us that the Bible is an impediment to the search for knowledge and the advancement of science, that the cultural provenance of man's technological rapacity and extravagant exploitation of nature is the biblical mandate to man to "subdue" the earth. Ecclesiastical endorsement has been granted to this accusation, in an altogether predictable theological conference on the subject. Under the crisp title of a symposium on "The Theology of Survival," a group of Protestant clergymen met at the School of Theology in Claremont, California, and "virtually all of the scholars agreed that the traditional Christian attitude toward nature had given sanction to exploitation of the environment by science and technology and thus contributed to air and water pollution, overpopulation, and other ecological threats."[1] In truth, such public theological self-flagellation should occasion no surprise. After experiencing the convulsions of Radical Theology in the 1960s and the attempt to write the obituary for The Deity and debunk His best seller, there is nothing particularly startling about His deputies and interpreters asserting in the 1970s that religion (and in this context "Christianity" is intended to be synonymous with Judaism, since the culprit is identified as the Bible and the "Judeo-Christian tradition") is responsible for our dirty planet, and that the solution requires another one of those "major modifications" of current religious values. Such exhibitions of moral masochism have, regretfully, become commonplace.

Were it not for the uncritical acceptance granted to these ideas, and the prominence of the organs in which they were disseminated (from *Science* to *The New York Times*), it would have been best to treat these comments with studied neglect. However, since they were given wide currency, they may at least serve as a convenient excuse to examine the sources of the Jewish tradition—biblical and midrashic, halakhic and theological—to discover whether these sources possess any resonance for the ecological values that will in all likelihood, and with justification, become part of the culture of Western man.

THE BIBLICAL PERSPECTIVE

The starting point for a religious consideration of man's relations with his natural environment is the divine blessing to man in Genesis 1:28: " . . . be fruitful and multiply and replenish the earth and subdue it; and have dominion over the fish of the sea and over the fowl of the air and over every creeping thing that creepeth on the earth." This is the passage that, it is asserted, is the sanction for the excesses of science and technology, the new ecological villains. "And subdue it" is proclaimed by theologians as the source of man's insensitivity and brutality to the subhuman world, as "dominion . . . over the fowl of the air" is equated with the right to foul the air.

It does not take much scholarship to recognize the emptiness of this charge against the Bible, particularly as it is interpreted in the Jewish tradition. The Torah's respect for nonhuman nature is evident in the restrictions that follow immediately upon the "subdue" commandment: man is permitted only to *eat* herbs and greens, not to abuse the resources of nature.[2] Furthermore, this mastery over nature is limited to vegetables for the first ten generations. Vegetarianism yields to carnivorousness only after the Flood when, as a concession, God permits the eating of meat to the sons of Noah. Even then, the right to devour flesh is circumscribed with a number of protective prohibitions, such as the warnings against eating blood and taking human life.[3] The laws of *kashrut,* the biblical and Rabbinic dietary rules, preserve the kernel of that primeval vegetarianism by placing selective restrictions on man's appetite for meat. His right to "subdue" nature is by no means unlimited.

Man's commanding role in the world brings with it a commensurate responsibility for the natural order. He may rule over nature, not ruin it. Adam is punished for his sin by the diminution of nature's potencies: thorns and thistles, sweat of the brow, enmity between the species, complications in the relations between the sexes, the ultimate victory of earth over man.[4] The upsetting of the balance of nature, man included, is a curse. Cain, too, is punished by alienation from nature. The blood of his slain brother is soaked up by the earth, corrupting it and disturbing its peace, and the retribution is in kind: "When thou tillest the ground, it shall not henceforth yield unto thee its strength; a fugitive and wanderer shalt thou be in the earth."[5] Ten generations later the world is filled with "violence" *(hamas)*, "for all flesh has corrupted their way on the earth," and, hence, "behold, I will destroy them with the earth."[6] And in the eschatological vision of Isaiah, the restoration of man to primordial harmony in and with nature is the prophet's most powerful metaphor for the felicity of the Messianic redemption. "And the wolf shall dwell with the lamb . . . and a little child shall lead them. . . . They shall not hurt nor destroy in all My holy mountain."[7]

Biblical concern for the ecological balance in territory from which a large population had been banished because of warfare is evidenced in the following passage in which the Israelites are told of their eventual inheritance of the Land of Canaan from its original inhabitants: "I will not drive them out from before thee in one year, lest the land become desolate, and the beasts of the field multiply against thee. Little by little will I drive them out from before thee, until thou be increased and inherit the land."[8] We find biblical legislation to enforce pollution abatement in the commandment to dispose of sewage and waste by burial in the ground, rather than by dumping into streams or littering the countryside.[9]

Perhaps the most powerful expression of the Bible's concern for man's respect for the integrity of nature as the possession of its Creator, rather than his own preserve, is the Sabbath. This institution was never understood by Judaism as solely a matter of rest and refreshment.[10] It pointed primarily to the relationships between man, world, and God. The six workdays were given to man in which to carry out the commission to "subdue" the world, to impose on nature his creative talents. But the seventh day is a Sabbath; man must cease his creative interference in the natural order (the Halakhah's definition of *melakhah* or work), and by this act of renunciation demonstrate his awareness that the earth is the Lord's and that man therefore bears a moral responsibility to give an accounting to its Owner for how he has disposed of it during the days he "subdued" it. The same principle underlies the institutions of the Sabbatical and Jubilee years. The Sages of the Mishnah[11] interpreted the words of the Psalmist, "a song for the Sabbath day" (Ps. 92), as "a song for the hereafter, for the day which will be all Sabbath." Thus, for the Rabbis the weekly renunciation of man's role as interloper and manipulator, and his symbolic gesture of regard for nature, was extended into a perpetual Sabbath; hence, a new insight into Jewish eschatology: not a progressively growing technology and rising GNP, but a peaceful and mutually respectful coexistence between man and his environment.

This respect for the inviolability of nature extends not only to nature as a whole but to its major segments as well. The original identity of species must be protected against artificial distortion and obliteration. This confirmation of the separateness and noninterchangeability of its various parts may be said to lie at the heart of some of the less rationally appreciated Pentateuchal commandments—those prohibiting the mixing of different seeds in a field, of interbreeding diverse species of animals, of wearing garments of mixed wool and linen.[12] Here the Bible demands a symbolic affirmation of nature's original order in defiance of man's manipulative interference. Perhaps never before have these laws been as meaningful as in our times when the ecology of the entire planet is in such danger, when entire species are threatened with extinction, when man has become capable of "ecocide."

Interestingly, one of the major biblical sources of the laws forbidding such intermingling of species is immediately preceded by the famous commandment, "Thou shalt love thy neighbor as thyself."[13] Reverence for the integrity of identity is common to both laws. Respect for the wholeness of a fellow man's autonomy must lead to respect for the wholeness of all the Creator's works, mute nature included. This autonomy of nature is known in Rabbinic literature as *sidrei bereshit,* the "order of creation." The Rabbinic attitude to these "orders of creation" is manifest in the following passage:

> Our Rabbis taught: once there was a man whose wife died and left him with a nursing child. He had no money to pay a wet-nurse. A miracle happened, and he developed two breasts like a woman and he nursed his child. Said R. Joseph: "Come and see, how great is this man that such a miracle should have been performed for him." Said Abaye to him: "On the contrary, how lowly is this man that for his sake the orders of creation should have been altered."[14]

The "orders of creation" are the manifestations of the act of creation, the juridical warrant for divine ownership of the universe, and whosoever interferes with them is "a lowly person."

THOU SHALT NOT DESTROY

The biblical norm which most directly addresses itself to the ecological situation is that known as *bal tashchit,* "thou shalt not destroy." The passage reads:

When thou shalt besiege a city a long time, in making war against it to take it, thou shalt not destroy the trees thereof by wielding an ax against them; for thou mayest eat of them but thou shalt not cut them down; for is the tree of the field man that it should be besieged of thee? Only the trees of which thou knowest that they are not trees for food, them thou mayest destroy and cut down that thou mayest build bulwarks against the city that maketh war with thee until it fall.[15]

These two verses are not altogether clear and admit of a variety of interpretations; we shall return to them shortly in elaborating the Halakhah of *bal tashchit*. But this much is obvious: that the Torah forbids wanton destruction. Vandalism against nature entails the violation of a Biblical prohibition. According to one medieval authority, the purpose of the commandment is to train man to love the good by abstaining from all destructiveness. "For this is the way of the pious . . . they who love peace are happy when they can do good to others and bring them close to Torah and will not cause even a grain of mustard to be lost from the world. . . . "[16] A more modern author provides a somewhat more metaphysical explanation: the fruit tree was created to prolong man's life and this purpose may therefore not be subverted by using the tree to make war and destroy life.[17] Those few cases in Scriptural history in which this norm was violated are special cases. Thus when Hezekiah stopped all the fountains in Jerusalem in the war against Sennacherib,[18] which Sifre regards as a violation of the biblical commandment equal to chopping down a fruit tree, he was taken to task for it by the talmudic Sages.[19] In another incident Elisha counseled such a scorched earth policy;[20] Maimonides considered this a temporary suspension of the law for emergency purposes *(horaat shaah)*, a tactic permitted to a prophet but an act that is not normative.[21]

The talmudic and midrashic traditions continue this implicit assumption of man's obligation to, and responsibility for, nature's integrity: Nothing that the Lord created in the world was superfluous or in vain;[22]—hence all must be sustained. An aggadah, often repeated in the literature, says that God created the world by looking into the Torah as an architect into a blueprint. Creation, the Rabbis were saying, is contingent upon the Torah—or, the survival of the world depends upon human acceptance of moral responsibility.

THE HALAKHIC PERSPECTIVE

Let us now return to the commandment of *bal tashhit* to see how the biblical passage is interpreted in the halakhic tradition. At first blush it would seem that the biblical prohibition covers only acts of vandalism performed during wartime. The Halakhah, however, considers the law to cover all situations, in peacetime as well as in war;[23] apparently the Bible merely formulated the principle in terms of a situation in which such vandalism is most likely to occur and in a most blatant fashion. Indeed while Maimonides forbids the destruction of fruit trees for use in warfare,[24] other authorities such as Rashi[25] and Nahmanides[26] specifically exempt the use of fruit trees for such purposes as bulwarks from the prohibition; what the Torah proscribed is not the use of trees to win in a battle, which may often be a matter of life and death, but the wanton devastation of embattled areas so as to render them useless to the enemy should he win, e.g., a "scorched earth" policy.[27]

The specific mention in the biblical passage of destroying by "wielding an ax" is not taken by the Halakhah as the exclusive means of destruction. Any form of despoliation is forbidden by biblical law, even diverting the irrigation without which the tree will wither and die.[28] Again it was assumed that the Torah was enunciating a general principle in the form of a specific and extreme case.

Similarly, the mention of "fruit trees" was expanded to include almost everything else: "And not only trees but whoever breaks vessels, tears clothing, wrecks that which is built up, stops fountains, or wastes food in a destructive manner transgresses the commandment of *bal tashchit* ("thou shalt not destroy"), but his punishment is only flogging by rabbinic edict."[29] Likewise is it forbidden to kill an animal needlessly or to offer exposed water (presumed to be polluted or poisoned) to livestock.[30]

In order to understand the relevance of the Halakhah on *bal tashchit* to the problem of ecology, it is important to test certain underlying assumptions of the halakhic conception. First, then, it should be pointed out that there is present no indication of any fetishistic attitude, any worship of natural objects for and of themselves. This is obvious from the passage just cited, wherein other objects, including artifacts, are covered in the prohibition. Furthermore, nonfruit-bearing trees are exempt from the law of *bal tashhit,* as are fruit trees that have aged and whose crop is not worth the value of the trees as lumber.[31] Also, fruit trees of inferior quality, growing amidst and damaging to those that are better and more expensive, may be uprooted.[32]

What must be determined is whether the Halakhah here is concerned only with commercial values, perhaps based upon an economy of scarcity, and possibly, even more exclusively, on property rights; or whether there are other considerations beyond the pecuniary that, although they are formulated in characteristic halakhic fashion *sui generis* and without reference to any external values, nevertheless may point indirectly to ecological concerns.

It is at once obvious that commercial values do play a central role in the law. Thus the fruit tree may be destroyed if the value of the crop is less than its value as lumber, as mentioned above, or if the place of the tree is needed to build a house thereon.[33] Such permission is not granted according to the later authorities for reasons of esthetics or convenience, such as landscaping. [34] However, the economic interest is not overriding, it must yield to considerations of health so that in case of illness and when no other means are available to obtain heat, fruit trees may be cut down and used for firewood.[35] Even when the criterion is a commercial one, it is clear that it is the waste of an object of economic value per se that the Halakhah considers unlawful; it is not concerned with property rights nor does it seek, in these instances, to protect private property. Thus in a complicated case concerning a levirate marriage, the Mishnah counsels one to act so that he does not needlessly disqualify the woman from later marrying a priest.[36] The Gemara quotes R. Joseph, who avers that Rabbi, redactor of the Mishnah, thereby intended a broader principle which R. Joseph phrases as, "One should not spill water out of his pool at a time when others need it," i.e., one should never spoil an object or an opportunity even where the gain or loss refers completely to another individual and not to himself. [37] We previously quoted the author of the *Hinnukh,* who explains all of *bal tashchit* as teaching the ideal of social utility of the world rather than of purely private economic interest: the pious will not suffer the loss of a single seed "in the world" whereas the wicked rejoice at the destruction of the world."[38] In his summary of the laws included in the rubric of *bal tashchit,* the author mentions that it certainly is proper to cut down a fruit tree if it causes damage to the fields of others. [39]

A most cogent point is made in this respect by the late R. Abraham Isaiah Karelitz, of blessed memory, author of *Hazon Ish.* Maimonides, codifying the law of the Sifre,[40] decides that *bal tashchit* includes the prohibition to divert an irrigation ditch that waters a fruit tree. What, however, if the tree were watered manually by filling a pail with water and carrying it to the tree: is the passive failure to do so considered a breach of *bal tashchit*? *Hazon Ish* decides that it is not in violation of the law, because all sources indicate that the commandment of *bal tashchit* is directed not at the owner of the tree or object but at all Israelites. Were the law addressed to individual proprietors, one could then demand of them that they continue to irrigate their trees in any manner necessary, and the failure to do so would constitute a transgression. However, the law is addressed to all Israel, and hence it is negative in nature, prohibiting an outright act of vandalism such as diverting a stream from a tree but not making it incumbent upon one actively to sustain every tree.[41] What we may derive from this is that the prohibition is not essentially a financial law dealing with property *(mammon),* but religious or ritual law *(issur),* which happens to deal with the avoidance of vandalism against objects of economic worth. As such, *bal tashchit* is based on a religio-moral principle that is far broader than a prudential commercial rule per se, and its wider applications may well be said to include ecological considerations.

Support for this interpretation may be found in the decision codified by R. Shneur Zalman of Ladi, applying the law of *bal tashchit* even to ownerless property *(hefker).* His reasoning is that if the Torah disallowed needless destruction of property of an enemy in wartime, it certainly forbids destruction of ownerless property.[42] Here again we find that we are dealing with a religio-moral injunction concerning economic value (not property), rather than an economic law which has religious sanction.

That this is so may be seen, too, from the special seriousness with which the Talmud approaches the subject, and from aggadic and quasi-halakhic sources dealing with it. Thus, the Talmud relates that R. Hanina attributed the untimely death of his son to the latter's cutting down a fruit tree prematurely.[43] The Rabbis hesitated to pay a social call to a dying scholar who, for medicinal purposes, kept a goat in his house in order to drink its milk; the goat despoils the grazing land and hence is to be banished from such pastures.[44] The Tabernacle was built of acacia wood[45] to teach man that if he wishes to build a house for himself he should not despoil fruit trees for this purpose.[46] Even though one is halakhically permitted to destroy a fruit tree if he wishes to build his home on its place,[47] nevertheless he should refrain from doing so.[48]

THE THEOLOGICAL PERSPECTIVE

In moving now from the Halakhah, with its specific proscriptions focused upon man's empirical conduct, to the larger theological formulations of man's relationship with nature, it is best perhaps to begin with a ludicrously extreme view taken by a professor of history in an article in *Science*,[49] where he avers that the verse in Genesis ("subdue it"), coupled with the "Judeo-Christian" rejection of pagan beliefs in the divinity of nature, has made possible Western man's exploitation of nature "in a mood of indifference to the feelings (*sic!*) of natural objects." We shall be saved only by a return to the deification of nature and the acceptance of the theology of ancient paganism. A rather extravagant price to pay for correcting a fallible professor's misbegotten exegesis and his faulty interpretation of the biblical view of man in relation to his environment!

Unquestionably, Judaism, in contradistinction to paganism, refuses to ascribe the quality of holiness to nature and natural objects as such. Nature is profane. Harvey Cox was correct when, in his *The Secular City*, he wrote of the "disenchantment with nature" as one of the major contributions of biblical faith. The God of the Bible is beyond, not within, nature: "In the beginning God created heaven and earth."

Nevertheless, upon further examination one does notice the development of a view affirming the holiness of nature in a certain period of the history of Jewish thought—but in a form and a significance utterly different from that of pagan thought. Beshtian Hasidism emphasized the immanence of God in the world. The dictum *melo kol ha-aretz kevodo* ("the world is full of His glory"[50]) and the Zoharian phrase *let atar panuy mineih* ("there is no place empty of Him") were adopted as major and most meaningful expressions of Hasidic immanentism. The spirit of the Creator is present in the creation. Hasidism continued the Kabbalistic tradition of viewing the world as a symbol of God. Nature was considered a garment of the Shekhinah. Without the immanence of God in nature and all its parts, even the most lowly, all of creation would return to primordial chaos; it would simply cease to exist. The Holy One is *memalé kol almin* ("fills all the world"), according to the formula of the Zohar, to greater or lesser extent, depending upon the level of each object in the chain of being. R. Isaac Luria taught that "even the most mute objects, such as stones and dust and water, possess *nefesh* (the lowest soul or spiritual dimension) and spiritual vitality."[51]

From the above one might be led to conclude, although the masters of Hasidism never did so explicitly, that Hasidism attributes to nature the dimension of holiness. Moreover, once the door has been opened to the theory that nature possesses inherent sanctity, the next step follows: all of nature is uniformly holy, thus denying the pluralistic judgment of Halakhah as to the hierarchy of holiness in the world—ten levels of holiness, one higher that the other.[52] Of course, there is a fundamental difference between the halakhic category of *kedushah* as applied to places (the Land of Israel, Jerusalem, the Temple courtyard, the inner sanctum, etc.), and the immanentistic ascription of holiness to natural places and objects. For the Halakhah, such holiness is not innate, a quality of the object by virtue of its God-withinness, but superimposed on it by an external act of sanctification and, therefore, capable of desacralization. But the immanentistic view of the holiness of nature, tending towards a sense of uniform sanctity, inclines towards a displacement of the hierarchical structure as conceived by the Halakhah. The danger inherent in such a theology is obvious: the denial of the Halakhah, which is based on a value pluralism (ten levels of holiness, sacred and profane, pure and impure, permitted and forbidden, guilty and innocent, etc.), and the homogenization of all value distinctions in an antinomian monism. And from here it is only one short step to pantheism—and the common denominator of pantheism and paganism is the ascription of divinity to nature.

As we mentioned above, Hasidic thinkers never came to such strange and perilous conclusions, which would have placed the movement outside the pale of Judaism. There were some Maskilim, Ephraim Deinard[53] among them, who did indeed categorize Hasidism as pantheistic, but there is no doubt that their conclusions are absurd and the result of dilettantism instead of scholarship. The emphasis on the closeness of God to man, His immanence, and hence the feeling of respect for the natural order and the readiness to discover in it the opportunities for *devekut*—these Hasidic principles do not at all require or imply at bottom a Spinozistic pantheism. At most, one can say that, as opposed to classical theism, Hasidism may be characterized as panentheistic, to use Professor Charles Hartshorne's felicitous term. God includes the world within Himself, but is not limited to or by it. He is immanent, but also remains transcendent to it. "He is the place of the world, but the world is not His place."[54]

The task of exposing the latent antinomianism in Hasidic im-manentism was undertaken with greatest thoroughness by R. Hayyim of Volozhin, the chief theoretician of the Mitnagidim. In Part 3 of his *Nefesh ha-Hayyim,* R. Hayyim points to a number of anti-halakhic practices that had begun to appear in the early Ha-sidic movement. As a Kabbalist himself—the school of the Gaon of Vilna was firmly anchored in the Jewish mystical tradition—R. Hayyim could not very well deny the omnipresence of God, in-deed, His immanence, as implied in the Zohar's *let atar panuy mineih.* But R. Hayyim showed that, taken to its logical conclusion and adopted in practice, this view leads to a denial of all existence and a thorough acosmism. Therefore, R. Hayyim accepts this acos-mic, monistic immanentism as being true from God's point of view ("from His side") alone. Man, however, from the point of view of his religious experience and obligation and his own exis-tential condition ("from our side"), must accept God and world as separate from each other. In effect, this is a form of "kicking radi-cal immanentism upstairs" and, for all practical purposes, embrac-ing a non-immanentistic view which posits an abyss between God and world and thus leaves the latter totally devoid of holiness. Na-ture is thus left completely profane.[55]

In truth, R. Hayyim was logically and philosophically correct anticipating apprehensively the antinomian results of Hasidic imma-nentism. History, however, as so often happens, marches along in majestic disdain of logic and philosophy. Not only did Hasidism re-main within mainstream Halakhic Judaism—this might at least be partially attributed, paradoxically, to R. Hayyim's vigorous criti-cism—but the signs of incipient antinomianism R. Hayyim noticed were insignificant and infrequent and, for the most, were folk aber-rations that did not receive the approval of the leaders of the move-ment.[56] Despite these early symptoms, Hasidism kept itself in check, restrained its latent potential antinomianism from playing itself out to its logical bitter end, remained within the boundaries of traditional Judaism, and never concluded that nature is holy. Nevertheless, the awareness of *kirvat Elohim* (the closeness of God) predisposed it to searching within the natural order for an undeveloped seed of holiness, for the spirit of God deeply hidden and concealed and rich in spiritual possibilities once it is revealed. Thus, R. Nahman of Bratzlav declared that the world is full of idols and abominations; it is utterly and disgustingly profane. Yet when man begins to ask, *ayeh mekom kevodo?* ("Where is the place of His glory?"—from the *Kedushah* prayer of the Sabbath *Musaf* service), when man quests for God in this impure and corrupt world, he may yet find Him and succeed in exposing the holiness so very deeply embedded within the world, thus returning this holiness to its supernal source.[57] The world may not be holy, but it contains the possibilities of holiness and God-consciousness.

Hence, while Hasidism does not directly declare nature holy, it finds in it sufficient potentialities for the sacred to allow for a greater respect for and closeness to the natural world while the Mitnagdic dualism ("from His side"/"from our side") so completely desacralizes nature as to leave it completely neutral and irrelevant religiously, to be viewed totally objectively and without any feeling of relationship whatever. The sense of human relationship with nature is evident in a saying of the Baal Shem Tov, founder of Hasidism, according to a disciple's notes: "A man should consider himself as a worm, and all other small animals should be regarded *as his friends in the world,* for all of them (i.e., man and the other species) are all created."[58] For Hasidism, which is immanentistic and panentheistic, man has a kinship with other created beings, a symbiotic relationship with nature, and hence should maintain a sense of respect, if not reverence, for the natural world, which is infused with the presence of God. The Mitnagdic view, emphasizing divine transcendence, leaves no place for such feelings and conceives the Man-Nature relation as completely one of subject-to-object, thus allowing for the exploitation of nature by science and technology and—were it not for the halakhic restraints that issue from revelation and not from theology—the ecological abuse of the natural world as well.

Taking the Hasidic and Mitnagdic positions as the two poles defining the limits of the Jewish attitude towards man's relationship with his natural environment, we may conclude that Judaism avoided either extreme—the deification and worship of nature on the one hand, and contempt for the world on the other. Hasidism taught respect, possibly even awe, for nature as the habitat of the Shekhinah, but it fell short of ascribing to it the inherent quality of sanctity. Rabbinic Judaism, in the Mitnagdic version, completely and unequivocally denied to nature the dimension of holiness but conceded that from the divine perspective of reality ("from His side") there cannot be conceived a world not utterly suffused with the Presence. This theological tension is resolved, or at least committed to practice, with the aid of the Halakhah: Nature is not to be considered holy, but neither is one permitted to act ruthlessly towards it, needlessly to ravage it and disturb its integrity.

Within this framework, it is important further to elaborate on the relation of man to nature in order to provide the value foundation for the moral imperatives that issue from ecology. "And subdue it" certainly implies a mandate to man to exercise his technological talents and genius in the upbuilding of the world and the exploitation of nature's resources. From the days of R. Saadia Gaon and R. Sabbatai Donnola, a tradition of interpretation has understood the biblical term "the image of God" to include, if not primarily to signify, man's capacity for creativity: just as the Creator is creative, so has His imaging creation been endowed with the same propensity.

This creative urge is man's glory, his very God-likeness. In a remarkable passage we read that Turnus Rufus, a pagan Roman general, asked R. Akiva which was more beautiful (or useful): the works of God or the works of man. Holding some stalks of grain in one hand, and loaves of bread in the other, R. Akiva showed the astounded pagan that the products of technology are more suited for man than the results of the natural process alone. So did R. Akiva proceed to explain the commandment of circumcision; both world and man were created incomplete, God having left it to man to perfect both his environment and his body. Similarly, the commandments, in general, were given in order that man thereby purify his character, that he attain spiritual perfection.[59] Man, the created creator, must, in imitation of his Maker, apply his creative abilities to all life: his natural environment, his body, his soul.

When R. Shelomoh Eger, a distinguished Talmudist, became a Hasid, he was asked what he learned from R. Menahem Mendel of Kotzk after his first visit. He answered that the first thing he learned in Kotzk was, "In the beginning God created." But did a renowned scholar have to travel to a Hasidic Rebbe to learn the first verse in the Bible? He answered: "I learned that God created only the beginning; everything else is up to man."

However, this doctrine, which teaches man's discontinuity with and superiority to the rest of the natural order, must not be misconstrued as a sanction for man to despoil the world. First, while he is beyond the merely natural, he also participates in it; he is an intersection of the natural and the divine (or supernatural).

The plurals in the verse "And God said, Let us make man in our image," are explained by R. Joseph Kimhi as addressed by God to the earth, or nature. Man remains inextricably tied to nature even while he is urged to transcend it. Man is a creature, and the denial of his creatureliness turns his creative powers to satanic and destructive ends. Second, the very nature of the concept of the imagehood of man implies the warning that he must never overreach in arrogance. He may build, change, produce, create, but he does not hold title to the world, he is not the "King of the world," an appellation reserved for the Deity, because the original all-inclusive creation was exclusively that of God, and mortal man has no part in it. His subordinate role in the cosmic scheme means that nature was given to him to enjoy but not to ruin—a concept reinforced by the law that before deriving any benefit or pleasure from the natural world, such as eating or drinking, one must recite a blessing to the "King of the world": an acknowledgment that it is God, not man, who holds ultimate title to the universe. Hence, without this blessing-acknowledgment, it is as if one stole from God."[60]

That man's role as co-creator with God must not be exaggerated we learn from the following Talmudic passage: "The Rabbis taught: man was created on the eve of the Sabbath. Why? So that the Sadducees (i.e., heretics) should not say that God had a partner in the act of creation of the world."[61] This statement does not contradict that of R. Akiva, who declared man's actions more beautiful, or suitable, than those of God, hence emphasizing the religious sanction of man's creative office. Man remains a partner of God in the ongoing creative process. However, here we must distinguish between two Hebrew synonyms for creation: *beriah* and *yetzirah*. The former refers to *creatio ex nihilo* and hence can only be used of God. The latter describes creation out of some preexistent substance, and hence may be used both of God (after the initial act of genesis) and man.[62] God has no "partners" in the one-time act of *beriah* with which He called the universe into being, and the world is, in an ultimate sense, exclusively His. He does invite man to join

Him, as a co-creator, in the ongoing process of *yetzirah*. Hence, man receives from God the commission to "subdue" nature by means of his *yetzirah* functions; but, because he is incapable of *beriah,* man remains responsible to the Creator for how he has disposed of the world.

A Halakhic Parable

The relations between God the Master, man the *yetzirah* creator, and nature may be clarified further by referring to the halakhah concerning the relationships between owner, material, and artisan. The Mishnah[63] discusses the case of a man (owner) who gave some material to an artisan to fashion it. The artisan, instead of repairing, spoiled the object. The law is that the artisan must pay the amount of the damages to the owner. The question then arises in the Gemara: What is this object that the owner gave over to the artisan, and the damages for which the latter must compensate the owner? Clearly, if it was a finished vessel, and the artisan broke it, the latter must pay the difference in value. But if the owner gave raw material to the worker, asking that he fashion it into a complete vessel, and the artisan did so but then broke the very vessel he made, is the artisan obligated, in such a case, too, to compensate the owner for the difference in value between a perfect vessel and a broken one, or is he free of obligation since the broken vessel is no less in value than the raw material with which he began? The question was in controversy amongst both Tannaim and Amoraim. Some held that *uman koneh bi'shevah kelim,* that the artisan has a monetary right in the vessel by virtue of the improvement he effected in it in transforming it from, for instance, mere planks into a table. If the table belongs, then, to the artisan, he cannot be held responsible to pay the owner of the planks for damages to that table if he should later break it. Others disagree: the improvement in the material is the property of the original owner, and if the artisan later destroyed the completed object, he injured the owner and must compensate him. Most authorities[64] decide the law in favor of the latter opinion: it is the original owner of the raw material who has proprietary rights in the completed artifact, not the artisan who invested his fabricative talents. The explanation for the artisan's legal responsibility for the finished product is contained in a Tannaitic source: The artisan is to be considered a *shomer sakhar* or paid trustee for the article he fashioned, and that belongs to the original owner, and as such he must pay for the object if he damaged it.[65]

What we learn from this, then, is that the artisan is paid by the owner for two functions: for improving the material by fashioning a vessel out of it, and for watching over and protecting that vessel once it is completed. This artifact which he created with his own hands, over which he labored with the sweat of his brow, into which he put his remarkable talents, this vessel must now be guarded by him for the owner from any damage it sustains in the course of his trusteeship over it. This is so because, the Halakhah decides, the artisan has no proprietary right in the article he created. It simply does not belong to him.

Let us now project this specific case onto the cosmic scene. God is the Owner, man the artisan, and the raw material is all the wealth of this world: nature, life, culture, society, intellect, family. Man was charged with applying to them his *yetzirah* creative talents. He was commissioned to improve the world, build it up, transform it, "subdue" it. If he does so, he is "paid" for his labors. But man never has title over his own creations, he has no mastery over the world. Despite his investment of labor and talent, the world, even as perfected by him, belongs to the original Owner. No matter how extensive and ingenious man's scientific and technological achievements in the transformation, conquest, and improvement of nature, he cannot displace the rightful Owner who provided the material in the first place. And not only does man not have proprietorship over raw nature, but he is not even the absolute master of his own creations, the results of his magnificent *yetzirah*. He may not undo what he himself did, for once having done it, it belongs to the Owner and not to the artisan. Man must never entertain the notion that because he labored over his creations, he has the right to destroy them, to repeal his creativity.[66] He remains a paid trustee over his very own products and must guard them and watch over them with the greatest care.

Man the *yetzirah*-creator, according to the teaching of Halakhic Judaism, is responsible to God the *beriah*-Creator not only for the raw material of the natural world into which he was placed, but is responsible as well for protecting and enhancing the civilization which he himself created. "Subdue it" is not only not an invitation to ecological irresponsibility; it is a charge to assume additional moral responsibility, not only for the natural world as such, but even for the manmade culture and civilization that we found when we were born into this world.

CONCLUSION

The charge that the despoliation of our natural environment has received its sanction in the Western world in the Bible and the biblical tradition is thus seen, at least from the perspective of Judaism, to be groundless. To appeal to contemporary man to revert, in this twentieth century, to a pagan-like nature worship in order to restrain technology from further encroachment and devastation of the resources of nature is a piece of atavistic nonsense.

Judaism—exegetically, halakhically, and theologically—possesses the values on which an ecological morality may be grounded.

Perhaps the most succinct summary of what we have said concerning the role of man and nature before God is given early in the biblical narrative where we are told of God placing Adam in the Garden of Eden—which, from its description in Scripture, was a model of ecological health. "And the Lord God took the man and put him into the Garden of Eden to work it and watch over it." [67] The undefiled world was given over to man "to work it," to apply to it his creative resources in order that it yield up to him its riches. But alongside the mandate to work and subdue it, he was appointed its watchman: to guard over it, to keep it safe, to protect it even from his own rapacity and greed. Man is not only an *oved,* a worker and fabricator, he is also a *shomer,* a trustee who, according to the Halakhah, is obligated to keep the world whole for its true Owner, and is responsible to return it in no worse condition than he found it.[68]

THE EARTH IS
THE LORD'S: JUDAISM
AND ENVIRONMENTAL ETHICS

Jonathan Helfand

The earth is the Lord's and the fullness thereof. (Psalm 24:1)
The heavens are the Lord's heavens, but the earth He has given
to mankind. (Psalm 115:16)

The apparent contradiction between these two biblical verses
troubled Jewish sages over a thousand years ago, and modern society still seems to be plagued by the dilemma they embody:

Dr. Jonathan Helfand is professor of modern Jewish history at Brooklyn College of
the City University of New York and also has rabbinic ordination from the Isaac
Elchanan Theological Seminary. Professor Helfand has authored numerous works on the
social and religious history of French Jewry, his field of specialization. He was one of the
first Jewish scholars to write extensively and lecture on ecology and the Jewish tradition.

to whom does the earth really belong and what are the consequences of holding such title?

For the past century and more, Western man has acted as master and lord of his environment, paying no heed to the effects of his actions on the environment. In the name of progress, water, land, air, and the wildlife they support have been despoiled and depleted, perhaps beyond reclaim, and in a manner unmatched in the annals of human history. Not all society was blind to this devastation. The outrage over man's rapacity, the demands for the protection and preservation of the environment, became more vocal and vehement as the corruption of nature grew in scope. Attacking this destructiveness, environmentalists sought to discover a cause for it, much as others had sought an excuse. For some, the nemesis of modern man turned out to be the biblical tradition itself.

The argument of these environmentalists was as follows. The pollution of the environment associated with the advance of the industrial revolution and the recklessly extravagant consumption of nature's irreplaceable treasures could all be traced to one cause: the rise of monotheism. The doctrine that placed one God above nature removed the restraints placed on primitive man by his belief that the environment itself was divine. Monotheistic man's impulses were no longer restrained by a pious worship of nature, and the God of Genesis told man to subdue and master the earth, proclaiming man's dominion over the natural world.[1] This approach is baseless, however: in both content and spirit the Jewish tradition negates the arrogant proposal that the earth is man's unqualified dominion.

In presenting a Jewish theology of the environment, I draw on three types of sources: halakhah, aggadah, and tefillah. Halakhah, from the verb meaning "to go," refers figuratively to the rules and statutes by which one is guided. It includes not only the Jewish scriptures, but also their traditional interpretation in the literature of the "Oral Law"—the Mishnah, Talmud, commentaries, codes, and responsa.[2] *Aggadah,* from the verb meaning "to tell," describes the vast non-juristic literature, including biblical exegesis, homilies, parables, and proverbs, whose aim is religious and moral instruction and edification.[3] Finally, *tefillah* is prayer or liturgy. In his seminal work on Judaism in the early Christian era, George Foote Moore observed that "the true nature of a religion is most clearly revealed by what men seek from God in it. The public and private prayers of the Jews thus show not only what they esteemed the best and most satisfying goods, but their beliefs about the character of God and His relation to them, and their responsive feelings toward Him."[4] *Tefillah* also has a didactic dimension. Rooted in the halakhic and aggadic traditions, it embodies their spirit and can be a vehicle for educating the worshipper. Indeed, the verb for prayer, *hitpalel,* is in the reflexive mode, as if in praying the worshipper is also addressing himself.[5] While the first source, *halakhah,* is the obvious guide in practical issues, as *aggadah* and *tefillah* sensitize man, they too offer important guidance and direction in establishing the outlines of a Jewish theology of the environment.

In formulating such a theology, three primary questions must be addressed: To whom does the world belong? What is the plan or purpose of creation? What are the practical consequences of the answers to the above questions? Does the tradition translate the theological dimension into reality? If so, how?

The Proprietorship of the World

The argument that the Bible gave man dominion over nature and with it license to destroy at will, is based on the story of creation. Specifically, it relates to God's placing all of creation in Adam's hands with the directive to "master it" (Genesis 1:28–30). In the same narrative, however, it is apparent that man was not given a license to destroy at will (Genesis 2:15). To the contrary, God never fully relinquishes dominion over the world. In promulgating the laws of the sabbatical year (Leviticus 25:23), He reasserts His proprietorship over creation, stating, "The land is mine."

This principle of divine ownership of nature is enunciated in the *halakhah* and is the basis for several categories of liturgical blessings. According to the *Tosefta,* "Man may not taste anything until he has recited a blessing, as it is written 'The earth is the Lord's and the fullness thereof' (Psalm 24:1). Anyone who derives benefit from this world without a (prior) blessing is guilty of misappropriating sacred property."[6] The list of blessings based on this concept includes numerous specialized and general blessings recited on comestibles and a host of rules and regulations regarding their application and priorities.

For example, there are specialized blessings for bread ("Blessed art Thou, Lord our God, King of the universe, who bringest forth bread from the earth"), for fruit that grows on trees ("Blessed art Thou . . . who creates the fruit of the tree"), for fruit that grows in the soil ("Blessed art Thou . . . who creates the fruit of the earth"), and for nongrowing comestibles ("Blessed art Thou . . . by whose words all things come into being"). In addition, Jewish law prescribes various blessings upon observing or enjoying natural phenomena, for example, smelling spices, seeing the wonders of nature, seeing an electrical storm, seeing a rainbow. In all these instances man speaks not as the master of nature, but by the grace and good-ness of God, as its beneficiary.[7]

The sense that man partakes in a world that is not exclusively his receives expression in an aggadic interpretation of the phrase *yumat ha-met* (Deuteronomy 17:6)—literally, "let the dead one be killed." The implied question, of course, is, How can a person be dead before he is executed? The *Midrash Tanhuma* explains: "An evil person is considered dead, for he sees the sun shining and does not bless 'the Creator of light' (from the morning prayer); he sees the sun setting and does not bless 'He who brings on the evening' (from the evening prayer); he eats and drinks and offers no blessings."[8] Thus, while man is placed on the earth to "master it," he does so in the Jewish tradition as a bailee, responsible and answerable to the will of his Master and obliged to acknowledge God's proprietorship at all times.

THE DIVINE PLAN

The fact that God is Creator endows all of creation with an intrinsic significance and importance. The Talmud observes: "Of all that the Holy One Blessed be He created in His world, He created nothing in vain (superfluous)."[9] Nothing in creation is useless or expendable; everything manifests some divine purpose. It follows, therefore, that there is a divine interest in maintaining the natural order of the universe.

Several expressions of this theme are to be found in conjunction with the laws of hybridization and mingling *(kilayim)*. "My statutes you shall keep; you shall not let your cattle mate with a different kind, you shall not sow your field with two kinds of seed, you shall not wear a garment of wool and linen" (Leviticus 19:19). The context within which this law is recorded is of special importance—it is posed between the command to love one's neighbor and laws about forbidden conjugal relations. The laws that surround our text deal with the social order while the laws of crossbreeding deal with the natural order. From their juxtaposition it seems clear that all are part of a broader concern of the Bible to maintain the order of the world—natural and social—as created and envisioned by God.

An exegetical passage in the Palestinian Talmud epitomizes this teaching. Commenting on the opening phrase in this verse, "my statutes you shall keep," the Rabbis define these statutes as *hukkot she-hakakti be-olami,* "the statutes that I have legislated in my world"; that is, you may not disturb or disrupt the natural law.[10]

This theme is developed further in a thirteenth-century study of the commandments called *Sefer Ha-hinukh.* Explaining the roots of this commandment against "mingling," the author says: "The Holy One created this world with wisdom, knowledge, and understanding and formed all creatures in accordance with their needs. . . . He commanded each species to reproduce according to its kind . . . and not to have species intermingle, lest something be lacking in them and His blessings no longer apply to them."[11] Man was therefore enjoined from undermining the work of creation by engaging in acts of hybridization or intermingling. Similarly, the *Sefer Ha-hinukh* explains the injunction against sorcery: "Therefore we were commanded to remove from the world anyone who attempts this (sorcery), for he goes against the wishes of God who desires the settling (of the world) in the natural order that was set from creation and this (sorcerer) comes to change everything."[12]

Judaism's concern with the violation or distortion of nature is demonstrated in a talmudic tale. A poor man's wife died in childbirth and he could not afford to hire a wet nurse. A miracle occurred and he developed breasts and suckled the child himself. Upon hearing this, Rav Yosef commented: "Come and see how great is this man that such a miracle was performed for him." To which his colleague Abaye retorted: "On the contrary, how lowly is this man that the orders of creation were changed on his account."[13] While undoubtedly sharing Rav Yosef's concern for the well-being of the infant, Abaye simply could not countenance such an unthinkable violation of the rules of nature.

OPERATIVE PRINCIPLES

Judaism's genuine concern for maintaining what the rabbis called *sidrei bereshit*—the orders of creation, the plan and intent of the Creator, is expressed in several ways. Juridically we may distinguish two categories: first, injunctions against the despoliation of nature and natural resources and, second, legal imperatives regarding the development and conservation of the God-given environment.

Bal Tashchit

The Bible (Deuteronomy 20:19) forbids the destruction of trees by an army besieging an enemy city. In the *halakhah* this biblical injunction—known as *bal tashchit* (you shall not wantonly destroy)—has been expanded to form a protective legal umbrella encompassing almost the entire realm of ecological concerns. These extensions affect three aspects of the law of *bal tashchit:* the situation, the object, and the method of destruction.[14]

While literally the Bible applies *bal tashchit* only to military tactics, the commentaries observe that the choice of this situation was not intended to limit its applicability; the Bible simply cited the most likely situation in which such destruction might occur.[15] The Talmud applies *bal tashchit* to numerous nonmilitary situations. Maimonides, in his twelfth-century code, declares: "This penalty [flogging, the punishment imposed for violating this biblical rule] is imposed not only for cutting it down during a siege; whenever a fruit-yielding tree is cut down with destructive intent, flogging is incurred."[16]

The *halakhah* extends the compass of *bal tashchit* with regard to the object destroyed, as well. Not only trees but "all things" are included by the Talmud under this rubric.[17] Specifically, the Talmud mentions the destruction of food, clothing, furniture, and even water as being in violation of *bal tashchit*.[18] The nineteenth-century code of Shneur Zalman of Ladi sums up the consensus of Jewish legal opinion when he rules that "the spoiler of all objects from which man may benefit violates this negative commandment [*bal tashchit*]."[19] Similarly, *halakhah* extends the jurisdiction of *bal tashchit* to include indirect and partial destruction as violations of this principle.[20]

The ethical implications of this analysis are clear. Man bears the responsibility for the destruction—complete or incomplete, direct or indirect—of all objects that may be of potential benefit or use to mankind. As part of the divine plan of creation himself, man has the obligation to respect his inanimate and animate counterparts in the world.

Endangered Species

Jewish tradition also addresses itself to the problem of the endangered species. An *aggadah* in the Talmud re-creates the scene from the ark and has the raven rebuke Noah, saying: "You must hate me, for you did not choose [to send a scout] from the species of which there are seven [that is, the clean birds of which Noah was commended to take seven pairs] but from a species of which there are only two. If the power of the sun or the power of the cold overwhelm me, would not the world be lacking a species?"[21] This concern over the destruction of a species is also invoked by the medieval commentator Nachmanides to explain the biblical injunction against slaughtering a cow and her calf on the same day (Leviticus 22:28) and the taking of a bird with her young (Deuteronomy 22:6). "Scripture will not permit a destructive act that will cause the extinction of a species, even though it has permitted the ritual slaughtering of that species (for food). And he who kills mother and sons in one day, or takes them while they are free to fly away, is considered as if he destroyed that species."[22] The *Sefer Ha-hinukh* offers a similar explanation, stating that there is divine providence for each species and that God desires them to be perpetuated.[23]

This theoretical sensitivity for animal life is translated into popular custom in a most touching manner. According to custom, a person wearing new attire is blessed: "May they wear out and may they be renewed [that is, may you get new ones]." According to some authorities, this is not to be recited in the case of shoes or other garments made from animal skins since, by implication, it calls for the killing of yet another animal.[24]

MAINTENANCE AND DEVELOPMENT OF THE ENVIRONMENT

Thus far, we have seen how Jewish tradition views the environment as God's domain and enjoins man from upsetting the *sidrei bereshit* ("orders of creation"). There exists another dimension to man's relationship to the universe: his role as creator, as extender of *sidrei bereshit*.

Several ordinances regulating Jewish life in ancient Israel offer further guidance to our study and introduce a principle of fundamental importance to our topic: *yishuv ha-aretz* ("settling of the land"). The Mishnah states: "One may not raise goats or sheep in the land of Israel," because by grazing they defoliate property and thereby interfere with the process of *yishuv ha-aretz*.[25] The same legal principle is invoked by the Mishnah in ruling that "all trees are suited for piling on the altar except for the vine and olive tree."[26] Since these trees represented the principal products of Israel, the rabbis feared that permitting their use on the altar might lead to the decimation of the groves and vineyards and irreparably damage the Holy Land.[27] The operative principle in these two cases, *yishuv ha-aretz,* calls upon the Jew in his homeland to balance the economic, environmental, and even religious needs of society carefully to assure the proper development and settling of the land.[28] In its active mode it demands that specific actions be taken to promote the maintenance and conservation of the natural environment.

The Jewish Scriptures mandate the establishment of a *migrash,* an open space one thousand cubits wide around the Levitical cities, to be maintained free of all construction and cultivation.[29] According to Maimonides, this applied to all cities in Israel.[30] The reason, as explained by the eleventh-century commentator Rashi, is that the open space is an amenity to the city.[31] The need for such a provision is ultimately based upon the principle of *yishuv ha-aretz*.[32] The implication in this and in other such cases is that *yishuv ha-aretz* requires man to consider the consequences of his creative activities in the world, not merely to clear stones and build cities or to avoid acts of wanton destruction but to maintain a proper balance in the environment, providing the necessary amenities while insuring the mutual security of society and nature.

A striking example of this principle in action may be found in the fourteenth-century code of Jacob ben Asher, known as the *Tur*. In discussing the "rights of preemption" that a farmer has in his neighbor's property, the *Tur* notes that these rights are suspended if the purchaser acquired the land for the purpose of building a house and the owner of the adjacent field wants the land for sowing, since there is a greater *yishuv ha-olam* ("settlement of the world") accomplished by building houses than by sowing. However, if the neighbor wishes to plant trees, he can remove the purchaser, since trees are more important for *yishuv ha-olam* than houses.[33]

An important change has been made in this last case. In explaining the law the *Tur* employs the term *yishuv ha-olam* ("settlement of the world") instead of *yishuv ha-aretz* ("settling the land" of Israel) thereby extending the concept and its legal application beyond the borders of the land of Israel.[34] Nor is Rabbi Jacob ben Asher the only authority to do so. For example, the eighteenth-century scholar Rabbi Jacob Emden applied the concept of *yishuv ha-aretz* to a situation arising in Germany, concluding that even in cases where a destructive act is for sacred purposes and therefore not in violation of *bal tashchit*, considerations of *yishuv ha-aretz*, man's obligation to equitably and ethically continue the process of "settling the world," may render it illegal.[35]

The aforementioned cases are a far cry from the carte blanche desired by some environmentalists in their struggle to protect our natural resources. They do not offer unquestioning protection to the natural environment; nor do they offer an immutable schedule of priorities to guide the actions of man. They do, however, enunciate an important legal and moral principle: the environment, like man, has certain unalienable rights, and these rights are endowed to it by the Creator—and, as a result, they may not be summarily dismissed or violated. It is the obligation of society to respect and protect these rights with the same procedures, institutions, and legislative initiatives that are employed to guarantee and protect the rights of man. And even if it, at times, must be done (as in the case of the *Tur*) at the expense of personal privileges and individual rights.

CONCLUSION

While nature has indeed been, to use Weber's term, "disenchanted" by the biblical creation epic, it is wrong to conclude that by releasing man from primitive constraints monotheism has given him license or incentive to destroy. In the Jewish tradition nature may be disenchanted, but never "despiritualized." For Judaism nature serves as a guide and inspiration. "Bless the Lord, O my soul," cries out the Psalmist as he views the heaven and earth and the wonders of creation. "How great are Thy works, O Lord; in wisdom You have made them all; the earth is full of your possessions" (Psalm 104:1, 24). Even a cursory glance at the daily prayer book reveals the depth to which the Jew must be stirred by nature and recognize in it a profound manifestation of God. The legal and ethical imperatives to preserve and conserve the environment are highlighted as the daily liturgy begins with a blessing for the rooster who distinguishes between day and night. The following blessings and Psalms to God as Creator offer in nature a spiritual sustenance for man's faith.[36]

Similarly, the pilgrimage festivals ordained by the Bible do not just celebrate historic events but mark the agricultural cycle—spring, first fruits, harvest—even for the child who has never seen an orchard or walked in a field of grain. The prayers for dew and rain recited on Passover and Tabernacles, respectively, alert man to the needs of nature and to his own dependence on the vagaries of rain, wind, and sun.

Thus, even in the midst of the concrete urban setting, prayer and ritual keep man in touch with nature, teach him to revere nature, and heighten his sense of dependence on nature. Suffused with the spirit of the Psalms, he comes to view nature as a living testimony to a living God. Says the Talmud: "He who goes out in the spring and views the trees in bloom must recite, 'Blessed is He who left nothing lacking in His world and created beautiful creatures and beautiful trees for mankind to glorify in.'[37] Praying man admires, praises, and is inspired by nature; how can he wantonly destroy it?

The Talmud tells the story of a farmer who was clearing stones from his field and throwing them onto a public thoroughfare. A *hasid* ("pious man") rebuked him, saying, "Worthless one! Why are you clearing stones from land which is *not* yours and depositing them on property which is yours?" The farmer scoffed at him for this strange reversal of the facts. In the course of time the farmer had to sell his field, and as he was walking on the public road, he fell on those same stones he had thoughtlessly deposited there. He then understood the truth of the *hasid's* words: the damage he had wrought in the public domain was ultimately damage to his own property and well-being.[38]

Modern man, like the ancient farmer of our parable, suffers from self-inflicted wounds. The reason for his suffering is perhaps best analyzed by the rabbis in the following passage from *Ethics of the Fathers* (a tractate of the Mishnah). *Ha-kin'ah ve-ha-ta'avah ve-ha-kavod motzi'in et ha-adam min ha-olam.*[39] "Jealousy, desire, and pursuit of glory remove man from this world." Or, in the modern idiom, keeping up with the Joneses, impulse control breakdown, and ego tapping—these are at the root of man's estrangement from nature. In this aphorism and in countless other sources, Judaism calls upon man to control his appetites and respect the rights of others. In the final analysis, this is perhaps the key to all of conservation ethics.

JUDAISM AND THE PRACTICE OF STEWARDSHIP

David Ehrenfeld and Philip J. Bentley

During the past millennium or more of Jewish history, the Jews have become, partly by choice but mostly by force, an increasingly urban people. Hedged in by laws restricting land ownership, occupations, and dwelling places, especially in Christian Europe, they often found themselves living in crowded ghettos out of touch with the natural world.[1] The Hasidic Jews, who more than any other group cling to this European Jewish ghetto culture of

Dr. David Ehrenfeld is a professor at Cook College, Rutgers University, where he teaches courses in ecology at the undergraduate and graduate levels. His books include *The Arrogance of Humanism and Beginning Again: People and Nature in the New Millennium*. He was a scientific organizer of the first World Conference on Sea Turtle Conservation.

Rabbi Philip J. Bentley is rabbi of Temple Sholom in Floral Park (Queens) New York. The author of many articles on justice, peace, the environment and other issues in the Jewish tradition, Rabbi Bentley is honorary president of the Jewish Peace Fellowship.

centuries past, are like the Amish in many respects, yet a people more cut off from nature and the natural world cannot be imagined. When one thinks of Jews one thinks of merchants, financiers, shopkeepers, peddlers, professional people, artists, intellectuals, and craftsmen; one does not usually think of farmers, fishermen, or naturalists, although, of course, there have been exceptions.

Thus it is not surprising that most people, including most Jews, are unaware that Judaism was one of the first great environmental religions—that it speaks of humanity, land, and nature not in vague generalities, but in great depth and detail and with a wisdom that seems to grow more appropriate and profound with each passing decade.

One volume of the Mishnah is entitled *Seeds*. It describes in exacting detail the Jewish legal strictures about every phase of agricultural practice, documenting the originally intimate relationship between Jews and the land. Many of the early Jewish sages were farmers—indeed, by the seventh century, during the first Islamic conquests, it was only their needed agricultural skills that saved some Jews in Arab lands from being put to the sword.[2]

Among the religions that speak profoundly of humanity's need to care for nature, for the rest of God's creation, Judaism stands at one end of a philosophical spectrum—the human-centered end—in which the human role in the world is that of careful steward. At the other end of the spectrum are religions such as Jainism, which emphasize humanity's role in nature as one of absolute nonviolence and noninterference. A Jain monk abstains from eating meat, fasts frequently to avoid hurting plants, walks barefooted so as not to injure the small creatures of the earth, and may even breathe through a mask of seven thicknesses of gauze to avoid inhaling and killing any of the tiny organisms of the air.[3]

Judaism is not at all like this. Jews commonly believe that every live thing on earth must have some human reference and use, even if it is only to remind us of our place in the scheme of things. And Jains believe that every live thing on earth is, or has a right to be, free of human reference.

Both of these attitudes towards nature have great validity and appeal, yet they are extreme positions. On the one hand, it seems to most of us that it is neither possible nor desirable for billions of humans to live in the world without changing it substantially; therefore, wise stewardship is necessary. On the other hand, stewardship is easily corrupted to the belief that we are lords, not caretakers, and that we are capable of managing and resolving all of the technological and social problems that we may have produced in our complex society.[4]

We cannot speak to the objections to Jainist doctrine. It is clear, however, that restraint, noninterference, and humility were an integral part of the original Jewish concept of stewardship, regardless of corruptions that may have taken place subsequently, and that these restraining virtues may yet prevail. This idea is a quiet corollary of the powerful theme running through Jewish teaching that human beings are not to be deified, that we are not true lords of anything except our free will. In the talmudic tractate *Sanhedrin* we find the statement:

> *Our masters taught:*
> *Man was created on the eve of the Sabbath—and for what reason?*
> *So that in case his heart grew proud, one might say to him:*
> *Even the gnat was in creation before you were there.*[5]

Nevertheless, it cannot be denied that while it is almost impossible to pervert the Jain philosophy in a way that leads to widespread environmental damage, the same thing cannot be said of the

Jewish, or, for that matter Christian, ideas of a human-centered world. As Jews and Christians have found, to their sorrow, the practice of stewardship, under the intoxicating influence of the power that comes with science and technology, is easily twisted and distorted so that stewardship becomes subjugation. When this occurs, as it does all around us, the vision of a power higher than humanity, which gave the original sanction and limit to the idea of stewardship, is itself washed away in a flood of collective egomania.

One effect of this humanistic arrogance has been to turn some environmentalists against Judaism and Christianity, the religions of stewardship, as if it were the notion of stewardship rather than its distortion that has caused all of the trouble. Such criticisms are usually supported by the quotation of Genesis 1:26, 28, the familiar injunction to have dominion over the earth and to subdue it, about which we will have more to say.

Christian thought and Christian interpretation of Jewish and Christian Scripture is so pervasive in Western society that even most of the Jews who think about these matters do not realize that the problem of the chasm between humanity and the rest of nature exists more for Christians than for Jews. Christianity has a stronger emphasis on the Other World than on this world, and classical thought has a much stronger hold on Christianity than on Judaism.[6] In the classical view, nature is an entity unto itself and humanity is something apart from it. In Judaism we consider this world of great importance. As for nature, there isn't even a Hebrew word for it, at least not in Rabbinic Hebrew.

HISTORICAL CONTEXT

Before examining the practice of stewardship in Judaism, we must pause a moment for an important caution. It would be a mistake to pretend that the ancient rabbinic sages had any inkling of the extent, or even the possibility, of the kind of global pollution and massive environmental destruction that we are witnessing today. To the ancients the world was a huge place. No one had seen with his own eyes the physical extent of it, nor could he have imagined a worldwide crisis concerning such basic resources as water or air, particularly a crisis caused by man. If we could not control the elements, we could not destroy them either.

So one cannot ask, What does traditional Judaism say about our environmental crisis? It doesn't say anything about it. That doesn't mean, however, that Judaism offers no guidance on the question of humanity's relationship to the environment. We simply have to search the literature properly, phrasing our questions to suit the context of the times, and interpreting the rabbinic "answers" in a restrained and literal way, in order not to interject our own ideas.

When this caution is observed, several critically important ecological ideas can be seen occurring in the Jewish tradition, even apart from the ideas of stewardship and the Lord's dominion.

First is the idea that if *man does evil, nature reacts.* This idea, which was brilliantly explored by Faulkner's *Go Down Moses*, has yet to be grasped by either the majority of people in the industrial world or their leaders, but it is often encountered in the older Jewish literature, including the Torah, itself, e.g., Deuteronomy 11:13–17.

A second ecological concept that is part of the tradition is that *there is a definite order to the world ordained by God as part of creation. Nothing was created for no purpose or in vain.* In our century the best secular statement of this ancient idea was made by Aldo Leopold and it has found its way into nearly every conservationist's philosophy—although, frankly it is easier to defend from a theological than an ecological standpoint.[7]

Third is that most general of ecological principles: *you don't get something for nothing.* This is entrenched in the early Jewish writings and finds one of its best expressions in the accepted Rabbinic belief based on Scripture and the oral tradition that Adam was not allowed to eat in the garden of Eden until he had first worked for his food by tilling and keeping the garden.[8]

And the fourth, embedded deep within Judaism, is the profound ecological idea of *human dependence upon nature;* our work alone does not suffice to keep us alive. In fact, as Richard Hirsch has pointed out, the idea is taken far beyond this. He writes that "our sages formulated a philosophy that could be called 'survival of the sustainers,' succinctly expressed in the [talmudic] saying 'Not only does man sustain man, but all nature does so. The stars and the planets and even the angels sustain each other.'"[9]

Dominion, Creation, and the Hebrew Language

The verses of Genesis 1:26, 28, in which man is given "dominion" over all the animals of the earth, are mistakenly believed by many environmentalists to summarize and represent the entirety of the Jewish and Christian teachings on the subject. We will leave the defense of the Christian tradition to others like Wendell Berry; in the case of the Jewish attitude towards the environment, the attack is easily disposed of regardless of whether one's biblical interpretation is liberal or strictly orthodox and without doing damage to the historical context in which the biblical verses first appeared.[10]

There are two answers to the "dominion" criticism, each of

which would be sufficient to refute the charge. The first is to point out the superficial nature of the interpretation and its lack of content. There is no evidence that we are aware of that these verses of Genesis were ever interpreted by the Rabbis as a license for environmental exploitation. Indeed such an interpretation runs contrary to their teachings and to the whole spirit of the oral law. As Berry has said, to put these verses in their proper context we need go no further than Genesis 2:15, Adam's instructions to "dress" and "keep" the garden, which have always been assumed to have a bearing on how the dominion was to be exercised. In other words, although the "dominion" phrases of Genesis could have been interpreted in the harsh, exploitative way that some critics suggest, they were never in fact interpreted that way within the Rabbinic tradition.

A second answer to the dominion criticism is based on the inadequacy of the English translations of the original Hebrew of the Jewish Scriptures. By chance an excellent example of this inadequacy concerns the word "dominion" itself. A quarter of a century before William the Conqueror invaded England, Rashi had this to say about the "dominion" of Genesis 1:26: "The Hebrew [*yirdu*] connotes both 'dominion' (derived from *radah*) and 'descent' (derived from *yarad*): when man is worthy, he has dominion over the animal kingdom; when he is not he descends below their level and the animals rule over him."[11] Here is a whole dimension of meaning that cannot be conveyed by an English translation.

In the prevailing English translation of the Bible, humankind and its world come in "the beginning," an interpretation that lends itself to arrogance and ego-centeredness. In the original, however, the sense of the Hebrew from the first word of Genesis is that we and our universe were not here in the beginning, if there was a beginning, a thought conducive to humility and God-centeredness. This is an oriental vision of tiny humanity in a vast universe like the Chinese paintings of little human figures set against a background of gigantic waves and mountains, which environmentalists are fond of citing.

More important, perhaps, is the accepted Jewish implication of the word *bereshit,* that creation is an ongoing process; it is not finished. In the morning religious service we find the words "Daily He renews the work of creation." Humanity participates in some aspects of this ongoing act of creation but only when we act in the proper spirit and appreciate the continuing role of the Creator in His creation. This is the background against which we must view the Jewish idea of stewardship and humanity's relationship to the rest of nature.

Stewardship

What is the traditional Jewish notion of stewardship really like? If we search in the Hebrew Bible we find a number of familiar verses that stress God as creator and owner, and humankind as humble caretaker or steward of the earth: "And . . . God . . . put him into the garden of Eden to till it and to keep it" (Genesis 2:15). "The land shall not be sold for ever: for the land is Mine; for you are strangers and sojourners with Me" (Leviticus 25:23). Many other biblical texts can be construed as being relevant, in a more or less direct way, to the idea of stewardship.[12]

Many modern Jews and Christians interpret these statements as a biblical mandate for stewardship. But how did the Jewish sages, who lived in a different world, treat them? If one looks at the Rabbinic commentaries on Psalm 119:19 and I Chronicles 29:15, both of which repeat the idea of our being strangers and sojourners in God's world, we find no mention of the environment. The reference is to the transitory nature of man's life on earth and the necessity of living the good life and keeping the commandments. Moreover, the environmental connotations of Genesis 2:15 are not even alluded to by Rashi in his commentary.

Does this mean that environmental thought and the idea of stewardship are missing from the philosophy of the Rabbis, who first codified Jewish law and gave form to its tradition? No. Again, we must remember the historical context of the times in which they lived. Then, "the environment" was not viewed as set apart from humankind; there was nothing to comment on. Nor did humans have the power to take actions that would quickly lay waste large parts of the natural world.

We do not find teachings that say "a man has a responsibility to the environment"; rather, we discover that the care of the natural world which we do not own was an implicit part of the Rabbinic image of the good person. In this image, the idea of human accountability to a higher authority, the Owner, is always central.

An excellent illustration of this point is provided by a quotation from the writings of the great eleventh-century Spanish rabbi, Jonah ibn Janah of Saragossa, the pioneering Hebrew philologist:

> A man is held responsible for everything he receives in this world, and his children are responsible too. . . . The fact is nothing belongs to him, everything is the Lord's and whatever he received he received only on credit and the Lord will exact payment for it. This may be compared to a person who entered a city and found no one there. He walked into a house and there found a table set with all kinds of food and drink. So he began to eat and drink, thinking, "I deserve all of this, all of it is mine, I shall do with it what I please." He didn't even notice that the owners were watching him from the side! He will yet have to pay for everything he ate and drank, for he is in a spot from which he will not be able to escape.[13]

This quotation deals with humanity's responsibility to God, not with our relationships to nature. Yet it includes the first principle of stewardship: the steward is not owner of the property in his care and will ultimately be held accountable for its condition.[14]

Of course, not all early Jewish references to stewardship of the natural world are indirect or obscure. The following *aggadah* is from *Ecclesiastes Rabbah,* which was redacted in approximately the eighth century:

> *In the hour when the Holy One Blessed Be He created the first*
> *   man,*
> *He took him and let him pass before all of the trees of the garden*
> *   of Eden,*
> *And said to him:*
> *See My works, how fine and excellent they are!*
> *Now all that I am going to create for you I have already created.*
> *Think about this and do not corrupt and desolate My world;*
> *For if you corrupt it, there will be no one to set it right after*
> *   you.*[15]

BAL TASHCHIT AND
ZA'AR BAALEI HAYYIM

Beyond the general principles of ultimate ownership and accountability, the exercise of stewardship has never been left to the imagination of the stewards. There are, in Judaism, a number of specific rules—together constituting a kind of "Steward's Manual"—setting forth humanity's particular responsibilities for its behavior towards natural resources, animals, and other parts of nature. First among these rules is the commandment of *bal tashchit* ["do not destroy"].

In Deuteronomy 20:19 we read: "When you besiege a city a long time, in making war against it to take it, you shall not destroy the trees thereof by wielding an ax against them; you may eat of them, but you shall not cut them down; for is the tree of the field man, that it should be besieged of you?"

From this source is derived the notion of *bal tashchit,* an ancient and sweeping series of Jewish environmental regulations that embrace not only the limited case in question but have been rabbinically extended to a great range of transgressions including the cutting off of water supplies to trees, the overgrazing of the countryside, the unjustified killing of animals or feeding them harmful foods, the hunting of animals for sport, species extinction and the destruction of cultivated plant varieties, pollution of air and water, over-consumption of anything, and the waste of mineral and other resources.[16]

Samson Raphael Hirsch eloquently summarized the meaning of *bal tashchit* for a religious Jew:

"Do not destroy anything!" is the first and most general call of God, which comes to you, man, when you realize yourself as master of the earth. . . . God's call proclaims to you . . . "If you destroy, if you ruin—at that moment you are not a man, you are an animal, and have no right to the things around you. I lent them to you for wise use only; never forget that I lent them to you. As soon as you use them unwisely, be it the greatest or the smallest, you commit treachery against My world, you commit murder and robbery against My property, you sin against Me!" This is what God calls unto you, and with this call does He represent the greatest and smallest against you and grants the smallest, as also the greatest a right against your presumptuousness.[17]

According to Hirsch, even the practice of hoarding property and doing nothing with it, rather than using it wisely and maintaining it, is condemned under *bal tashchit*. This is strikingly similar to contemporary arguments against many current agricultural practices. It is also in accord with the recent ecological awareness that when people abandon or neglect land that has previously been farmed with care and skill, the number of species of native wild plants and animals suffers a sharp decline.[18]

Inhumane conduct towards animals is also powerfully enjoined in Jewish law. The prohibition against inflicting *za'ar baalei hayyim* ("pain of living things") has multiple biblical sources, including Deuteronomy 22:6, which forbids the killing of a bird with her young. According to Jewish tradition, the prohibition against one form of inhumane conduct towards animals is one of the seven commandments given to the children of Noah and, therefore, is binding on all humanity, not just upon Jews. Some kinds of work are even permitted to Jews on the Sabbath, if the purpose is to relieve the suffering of an animal. Kindness to animals is one of the few virtues that the Jewish tradition specifically associates with the promise of heavenly reward.

The ultimate extension of *za'ar baalei hayyim* is to abstain from killing animals at all; the result is vegetarianism, a practice that has been institutionalized in Jainism, Hinduism, and other Eastern religions. Vegetarianism, although not mandated by Jewish law, is a practice that has long appealed to Jews; the sages believed (based in part on Genesis 1:29) that humans were vegetarian until after the Flood, when the eating of meat was permitted. The Jewish dietary laws are much simpler for vegetarians to observe than for those who eat meat, and some authorities see this as deliberately punitive, with the intention of reducing the number of animals killed for food. Jewish law mandates only humane slaughter of healthy animals for food, and there are those who maintain that the consumption of animals that have been "factory"-raised under inhumane conditions violates the spirit of *kashrut* as well as the letter of other *mitzvot*. Jewish vegetarianism is a small but strong movement with its own magazine.[19] Its best-known modern advocate was the late Chief Rabbi of Palestine, Abraham Isaac Kook.

SABBATH AND STEWARDSHIP

When stewardship is corrupted by power in the absence of restraint, it becomes ecological tyranny and exploitation. This is the central problem of stewardship, a problem that has always existed but has become critical only with the rise of modern technology and its side effects, including overpopulation. With technology, humanity has achieved a power and a presence that is utterly subversive of the practice of stewardship. Modern theorists have despaired of finding noncoercive ways of resolving this tragic dilemma,[20] and many environmentalists have condemned stewardship itself as an inherently unworkable concept.

Nevertheless, within Judaism there still exists a mechanism—the original mechanism—for reconciling stewardship's absolute need for human restraint and forbearance with the mundane exercise of power. *Bal tashchit* and *za'ar baalei hayyim* are not enough. For Jews, it is the Sabbath and the idea of the Sabbath that introduces the necessary restraint into stewardship. It is also the Sabbath alone that can reconcile the Jewish attitude towards nature with the attitude of secular environmentalism, of holistic ecology, or of the non-anthropocentric religions such as Jainism.

An hour past sundown on Saturday, at the conclusion of each

Sabbath, we pronounce a blessing which says in part: "Blessed are You, O Lord, who makes a distinction between holy and ordinary, between the seventh day and the six working days." In this blessing there is no implied criticism of either the ordinary or the six working days. The Sabbath needs the six working days, just as they, in turn, need the Sabbath. Stewardship is one function of the six working days and it shares this complementary relationship with the Sabbath. Just as the recollection of wise stewardship enhances the Sabbath and makes it possible, so is stewardship incomplete and imperfect without the complementary recollection and restraining influence of the Sabbath *during the rest of the week.*

On the Sabbath, the traditionally observant Jew does more than rest, pray, and refrain from ordinary work. There are at least three other elements of Sabbath observance that are relevant to stewardship: we create nothing, we destroy nothing, and we enjoy the bounty of the earth. In this way the Sabbath becomes a celebration of our tenancy and stewardship in the world.

Nothing is created, and this reminds us of God's supremacy as Creator and our own comparative inadequacy.[21] Nothing is destroyed, and this reminds us that the creations of this world are not ours to ruin. We enjoy the bounty of the earth, and this reminds us that although our work, if properly done, will uncover for us far more of God's bounty than we would otherwise have enjoyed, nevertheless God, and not human invention, is still the ultimate source of that bounty.

Two tangible environmental applications of the idea of the Sabbath are the sabbatical and Jubilee years, as described in Leviticus 25.[22] Every sabbatical or seventh year the land of Israel is to lie fallow; every fiftieth or Jubilee year not only was the land left untilled, but it reverted to its original ownership, thus (when observed) preventing the kind of concentration of large blocks of land in a few hands that now characterizes the American agricultural system and which is the cause of many of our most intractable environmental difficulties.

That the sabbatical and, presumably, Jubilee years were actually observed in ancient Israel is shown by the fact that Alexander the Great and Julius Caesar both remitted tribute to the Jews every seventh year, and that Tacitus cites the sabbatical year practice as evidence of the inherent laziness of the Jews.[23] Even today, the sabbatical year receives some form of recognition from religious Jews in Israel.

But there is yet a deeper environmental significance to the Jewish Sabbath. Abraham Joshua Heschel wrote,

> Technical civilization is man's conquest of space. It is a triumph frequently achieved by sacrificing an essential ingredient of existence, namely, time. In technical civilization we expend time to gain space. To enhance our power in the world of space is our main objective. . . . The power we attain in the world of space terminates abruptly at the borderline of time. But time is the heart of existence. . . . The more we think the more we realize: we cannot conquer time through space. We can only master time in time. . . . Our intention here is not to deprecate the world of space. To disparage space and the blessing of things of space, is to disparage the works of creation, the works which God beheld and saw "it was good." . . . Time and space are interrelated. To overlook either of them is to be partially blind.[24]

To Heschel, control of space without mastery of time, which is eternal, is a meaningless achievement. It is the Sabbath that gives access to the realm of time. Or, as he put it, the Sabbath "tries to teach us that man stands not only in relation to nature but in a relation also to the creator of nature." In our work with nature and its laws we deal largely with space and things. Yet, as many ecologists perceive, it is always the element of time that eludes the engineers, the agribusinessmen, the planners, and the remodellers of the earth. A desert ecosystem that has been destroyed in seconds by the heedless passage of a few motorized vehicles cannot be restored by us, and will take more than 100 years to restore itself.

Without the influence of the Sabbath, stewardship in practice is corruptible and unstable. For Jews, it is the awareness of the Sabbath during the working days that can bring the realm of time and its accompanying sense of restraint and limit to stewardship. It is the Sabbath that defines the relationship between steward and Ruler. It is the Sabbath, ultimately, that completes and confirms the environmental wisdom of Judaism.

The Rabbis and Expanding Environmental Consciousness

Fred Dobb

The seed of my research was straightforward: Rabbinic texts about trees. As it took root, however, I heard the texts speak more of contemporary environmental issues than of tree species or genres of Rabbinic literature. I knew that my work would branch out beyond the texts themselves by applying Rabbinic teachings to today's ecological issues. The Rabbis (i.e., the authors of Mishnah, Talmud, and early Midrash spanning roughly 100 BCE–500 CE) say that if you turn the entire Torah tradition around and around, you'll

Rabbi Fred Dobb was ordained in 1997 from Philadelphia's Reconstructionist Rabbinical College. Ever since an environmental education walk across the United States ten years ago, he has been writing, teaching, and organizing around ecology and Judaism. He serves on the board of trustees of COEJL and the Teva Learning Center and as rabbi of Adat Shalom Reconstructionist Congregation in Bethesda, Maryland.

find everything contained within it (*Mishnah Avot* 5:25). In that spirit, I hope that the fruits of this study will be ecological inspiration for our day.

The Torah is the Tree of Life (Proverbs 3:18). With reference and deference to the Five Books of the Tree of Life, then, I suggest five modern categories by which we can examine the ecological roots of this Tree:

First, the rabbis understood our obligation to live in "right relation" to the rest of creation; our place in God's universe is a humble one, and we must be responsible tenants of God's Earth.

Second, our awareness of creation should be intensive, as exemplified by today's "bioregionalism," and should compel us to both bless and protect the goodnesses around us.

Third, we must "think like a mountain," practicing "ecosystem management" sustainable over Godly lengths of time—what does the Earth need from us not next quarter, but in a thousand generations?

Fourth, in contrast to the current trend, "environmental regulations" should be embraced as Torah-ordained protections of the public good.

And fifth, all beings are interconnected as parts of a cosmic whole—whether the Gaia hypothesis or God, it calls us to protect the full biodiversity within God's rich creation.

I. RIGHT RELATIONSHIP— HUMANITY'S PLACE IN GOD'S CREATION

The psalmist asks, "What is humanity, that You even bother to know it?" (Psalms 144:3). The traditional response has often been self-congratulatory or anthropocentric: we are little lower than angels;

we have dominion; for our sake was the world created. But another rabbinic answer also emerges, a humbler one. Why was humanity created last? "So that if humanity's mind becomes haughty you can say to it, 'even the mosquito preceded you in the work [order] of creation'" (*B. Sanhedrin* 38a). Similarly, *B. Bava Metzia* 85a speaks not only of the law of compassion for animals *(tza'ar ba'alei hayyim)* but also of the relation between people and other life forms:

> The sufferings of Rabbi Elazar b. Rabbi Shimon . . . came through an incident and left through an incident.
> Came through an incident—what is it? This calf that was being led to slaughter broke away, and hid its head in the folds of [the rabbi's garment], and cried. He said to the calf: "Go— you were created for this." [The heavenly host] said: "Since he has no compassion, let us place sufferings upon him."
> And went through an incident?—One day his maid was sweeping the rabbi's house. There were some young weasels, and she swept them away. He said to her: "Let them go—it's written ,'God's mercy is on all of God's works.'" [The heavenly host] said: "Since he has compassion, we will have compassion for him." (Psalm 145:9)

Divine retribution against someone who supports the veal industry—how radical! While not every Rabbinic voice is an ecological clarion call, they generally understand that humanity is given choices and should choose wisely. Consider this midrash (*Bereshit Rabbah* 8:12) on the controversial commandment in Genesis 1:28 to "subdue" and "have dominion" over the Earth:

> "And have dominion (*u-rdu*) over the fish of the sea," etc. (Genesis 1:28). Rabbi Chanina said: If humanity merits it, *u-rdu* ("it will have dominion"); and if humanity doesn't merit it, *yirdu* ("it will descend/fall"). Rabbi Ya'akov of Kfar Hanan:

That which is "in our image, according to our likeness" (Genesis 1:26), *u-rdu* ("will have dominion"); and that which is not in our image according to our likeness, *yirdu* ("will descend").

If this is so, the question now becomes, How do we best exercise the dominion which is ours, like it or not? This is a critical and humbling recasting of a difficult text. In another, still more famous *midrash*, the Rabbis echo this theme:

> When the Holy One, Blessed Be, created *Adam Harishon,* God took Adam and led [him/her/it/them] around all the trees of the Garden of Eden. And God said to Adam:
> "Look at My works! How beautiful and praiseworthy they are! And everything I made, I created for you. Be careful, [though,] that you don't spoil or destroy My world—because if you spoil it, there's nobody after you to fix it." (*Kohelet Rabbah* 7:13)

So we see that the Rabbis understand our humble place in God's universe. But humility is ethereal. To actualize it, the Rabbis needed laws. *Bal tashchit* ("do not waste"), for one, is the product of the vivid rabbinic imagination applied to Deuteronomy 20:19's wartime prohibition of cutting down an enemy's trees. Here, an early midrash (*Sifrei Shofetim* 203) reads into Deuteronomy's rhetorical question—"For is the tree of the field human?"—a strikingly modern environmental notion: "This teaches us that humanity has no life except that which comes from the tree."

In the Talmud, this law is extended to a variety of areas. Most important for our day, "Rav Zutra said: Whoever covers an oil lamp, or uncovers a naphtha lamp, transgresses the law of *bal tashchit*" (*B. Shabbat* 67b). These two actions, it turns out, cause the lamps to burn less efficiently, thus necessitating the use of more fuel than necessary. Energy conservation dates back not to 1973 but to the Talmud, circa 400 CE!

Moreover, we are forbidden to dump out our well water when another might need it (*B. Yebamot* 11b), and are even told to choose those foods that require the fewest resources to make—barley bread over wheat bread (*B. Shabbat* 140a), for instance. And *B. Bava Kama* 91b extends *bal tashchit* even to the point of asceticism: "Rav Hisda, when he walked among thorns and thistles, lifted up his garments—he said, "This [body] will heal, but this [garment] will not heal.""

Much later, *Sefer Ha-Hinuch*—the *Book of Education,* from Spain circa 1300—offers a radical medieval statement of conservation, and misleadingly labels it classically Rabbinic in origin, though the Rabbis had not forbidden all destructive acts:

> Righteous people of good deeds . . . do not waste in this world even a mustard seed. They become sorrowful with every wasteful and destructive act that they see, and if they can, they use all their strength to save everything possible from destruction. But the wicked are not thus; they are like demons. They rejoice in the destruction of the world, just as they destroy themselves. . . . Generally speaking, the rabbis forbade all destructive acts, and they linked one who destroys anything in anger to one who worships idols.

Finally, humility includes sensitivity to the beauty and goodness around us. From such awareness and awe must also flow concrete actions, both ritual and ethical, turning vague notions into a formula for environmental protection. We consider this aspect of right relationship in the following section.

II. Bioregionalism—Awareness, Blessings, and Protection

Awareness, an essential part of the Rabbinic system, is also the key element of the ecological concept known as bioregionalism. This approach suggests that what works in one place may not work in another. Bioregional awareness has staggering implications from agriculture to pet ownership, industrial siting to eating habits. As Carolyn Merchant explains, bioregionalists "are local caretakers. Dedicated to the concept of living-in-place, they espouse 'watershed consciousness'. . . . Bioregionalism advocates a new ecological politics of place."

A bioregional mentality requires knowledge of one's natural surroundings, and how this region compares with other areas. And the rabbis know! *Mishnah Shvi'it* 9:2 explains, "There are three lands for removal (of third- and sixth-year fruits): Judea, Trans-Jordan, and the Galilee. And there are three regions within each of these [Galilee] lands: the Upper Galilee, the Lower Galilee, and the Valley." These different regions are based on the varying elevations in the land of Israel, where villages and fields just a few kilometers apart can have radically different growing seasons. In *B. Pesahim* 53a, a rabbi even plays field guide, identifying ecosystems by signal species! The same sensitivity is applied to produce:

> "A land of hills and valleys" (Deuteronomy 11:11): This tells us that fruits from the hills do not have the same taste as fruits of the valley, and [vice-versa]. R. Shimon Bar Yochai says: Twelve lands were given, corresponding to twelve tribes of Israel—and the fruits of one land do not have the same taste as the fruits of any other land. (*Sifre Ekev* 39)

To be fair, one could certainly argue that the Rabbis' knowledge and awareness of the natural world is merely agricultural, not ecological. Even so, we stand to gain from emulating our ancestors' closeness to the land. We become aware by developing a sense of place. One Rabbinic euphemism for the Divine is *Makom* ("Place"), and thus a sense of place is also a sense of God! *Tanchuma Berakha 7* is explicit about this dual awareness of God and world:

> The evil person is considered dead even in their life—since they see the sun shine [in the morning] and don't bless *"yotzer or;"* [they see it] set but don't bless *"ma'ariv aravim";* they eat and drink, but don't bless on it. But the righteous bless on every single thing that they eat, or drink, or see, or hear.

The Rabbis make much of expressing gratitude to the Creator of all, who is also the Owner of all. *Mishnah Avot* 3:7 bids us, "Give to God from that which is God's—since you, and all that is yours, is God's." This same depreciation of human ownership underlies the Sabbatical Year (*Sanhedrin* 39a): God said "Sow six [years] and rest [on year] seven, in order that you should know that the land is Mine."

Yet the Rabbis saw a countertendency within Psalms (115:16): "The heavens are God's heavens, but God gave the Earth to humankind." How can the Earth be both God's and ours? The Talmud (*Berakhot* 35a-b), responding to this apparent contradiction, emphasizes awareness:

> Whoever enjoys something from this world without [saying] a blessing—it's like stealing from God's stores, since "The Earth is God's" . . . this verse (Psalms 24:1) applies *before* the blessing is said; that verse (Psalm 115:16) applies *after* it.

Thus one "should not taste anything until they have blessed, as it is said, 'The Earth is God's and all that fills it'" (*Tosefta Berakhot* 4:1). The very act of blessing reminds ourselves of humanity's delimited stewardship of the planet. The language of the blessings can be even more explicitly ecological, as in the *motzi:* "Blessed are you . . . who brings forth bread from the Earth." The last phrase, "from the Earth," seems superfluous, unless it reminds us that bread comes not from stores or kitchens, but from the *adamah*/Earth which gives *adam*/humanity its life. Even the blessing for seeing fine people, animals, or trees reminds us how good things really are: "Blessed is the One who has it like this in God's world!" (*B. Berakhot* 58b).

We bless God in gratitude for the created order, known as the *sidrei bereshit*. Yet if we bless God for creation, which God likes as it is (Genesis 1:31), then who are we to meddle? Through the concept of *sidrei bereshit*, the Rabbis hold that any upsetting of the natural order is improper. Consider Leviticus 19:19, the prohibition against mixing seeds, which opens with "my statutes you shall keep." In the Jerusalem Talmud "The rabbis define these statutes as *hukkot she-hakakti be-olami*, 'the statutes that I have legislated in my world' (*J. Kilayim* 1:7); that is, you may not disturb or disrupt the natural law."

Imagine the consequences for science, industry, and society if we truly did not disrupt nature! It might push us toward the more "organic" lifestyle hinted at in *B. Sanhedrin* 108b: "Jonah said before the Holy One, Blessed Be: Master of the Universe, may my food be bitter like a [raw] olive but provided from Your hand, and may it not be sweet like honey but from the hand of flesh and blood." So much for the pesticide, herbicide, and packaged food industries!

At *B. Shabbat* 53b the Rabbis offer a particularly powerful example of their respect for the *sidrei bereshit*:

Our rabbis taught: It happened that a man's wife died and left him with an infant, and he had no money to give to a wet-nurse. And a miracle happened to him—he developed two breasts, like the two breasts of a woman, and he breast-fed his child!

Rav Yosef said: Come and see how great this man is, that a miracle like this was done for him. Abaye said to him, on the contrary, how disgusting this man is, that the orders of creation were changed for him.

One might think that in the realm of miracles, at least, such considerations as the natural order would be suspended. Yet the rabbis understand miracles not as the *suspension* of the natural order, but as that natural order *itself*. We affirm this daily in the eighteenth paragraph of the Amidah: "And for your miracles which are with us every day, and for your wondrousnesses and goodnesses which are at every moment: evening, and morning, and afternoon."

We conclude this section noting a progression. When aware of the beauty and bounty of the created order, we are inclined to bless the Creator. But it does not end there: once we have blessed the Creator we have sanctified the creation, and our relationship with the latter has changed as well. Blessings lead us not only back to awareness, but forward to action. How better to get people to care about and protect nature than to sacralize it?! Thus Rabbi Meir's suggestion of one hundred blessings a day (*B. Menahot* 43b) is an activist as well as a spiritual discipline.

III. Thinking like a Mountain— Ecosystem Management

Our modern world thinks in thirty-second sound-bites and frets endlessly about the coming fiscal year. Torah, on the other hand, reminds us that evil gets requited to the third and fourth generations even as goodness is passed on to the thousandth (Deuteronomy 30:19).

The mid-century environmentalist Aldo Leopold was also a critic of our disposable, consumerist, short-term society. His response was to advocate "thinking like a mountain," measuring time in eons rather than hours. In their own way, the Rabbis share his concern. Perhaps they advocate "thinking like a tree"—we should recognize the sustaining power and beauty of earthly trees as if they were all the Tree of Life, which is eternal. *Avot de Rabbi Natan* B 31 agrees. "Rabbi Yohanan b. Zakkai says: If you are holding a sapling in your hand, and someone says to you, 'here comes the Messiah!'— come and plant the sapling, and afterwards go and welcome the Messiah." Similarly, we imitate God when we plant trees:

> Rabbi Yehudah b. R. Shimon opened (from Deuteronomy 13:5), "You should walk after the Eternal your God." But can flesh and blood walk after the Holy One, Blessed be God? . . . Rather:
>
> At the beginning of the creation of the world, the Holy One (Blessed be God) only busied Godself with the "initial planting." This accords with what is written, "and the Eternal God planted a garden in Eden" (Genesis 2:8) Even you, when you enter the Land of Israel, should busy yourselves with nothing else besides "initial planting." Thus it is written (Leviticus 19:23), "and when you come into the Land, you should plant all kinds of trees. . . . " (*Vayikrah Rabba* 25:3).

Perhaps the most famous Rabbinic tribute to long-range planning is also Judaism's best-loved story of tree-planting. At *B. Taanit* 23a, Honi Ha-Me'agal, the circle-drawer, turns from sage to student:

> One day Honi was walking down the road, and he saw a man planting a carob tree. Honi said to him: "Since the carob doesn't bear fruit for seventy years, are you so sure that you'll live seventy years and eat from it?!"
>
> The man replied: "I found a world that was full of carob trees. Just like my ancestors planted for me, so I plant for my descendants."

Just as the Rabbis exhort us to plant trees, so they exhort us not to cut them down wantonly. The law of *bal tashhit* addresses this clearly, as do a number of Rabbinic *aggadot* (homilies): "At the moment that people cut off the wood of a tree that bears fruit—its voice carries from one end of the world to the other end, but it is not heard" (*Pirke de Rebbi Eli'ezer* 34). Among the reasons why the celestial lights are weakened are "those who cut down good trees" (*Sukkot* 29a) who because of their actions will "never see a sign of blessing" (*B. Pesahim* 50b). Prefiguring George Washington and his cherry tree, Rabbi Hanina said, "The only reason that my son died is that he cut down a fig tree before its time" (*B. Bava Kama* 91b). Even the devastating Bar Kokhba rebellion of 132–35 CE began, says *B. Gittin* 57a, with the Jews' zealous defense of their local trees.

Recalling the Rabbis' love of trees, we now consider the new forestry school of ecosystem management. This much-discussed idea advocates taking a broad approach, balancing the many human uses of the land with the long-term needs of the ecosystem itself, and thus avoiding the historic sole regard for what can be extracted from it. The spotty results of its early implementation, however, are mixed.

Once again, the Rabbinic parallels are striking. One is *Yishuv Eretz Yisrael,* the settling of the land of Israel—a somewhat parochial model for environmental protection later broadened to the settlement of the world. By this the Mishnah (*Tamid* 2:3) tells us that "all woods were kosher for use on the [Temple's] altar except for that which comes from the vine and from the olive tree." Why, the Gemara asks? "Rav Pappa said, since they have knots. Rav Aha b. Ya'akov said, because of *Yishuv Eretz Yisrael*" (29b). Since vines and olives were particularly important for the economy and the culture, and olive trees grow slowly, they could not be used for their wood.

Another example of "ecosystem management" is the *migrash ha'ir,* the open field around cities, which can be converted neither to city nor farm. The Biblical requirement covers only cities of the Levites; in the Rabbinic and medieval periods, it is extended to all walled cities. Such an institution, itself a defense against urban sprawl, has tremendous ecological implications. By preventing re-zoning, the Talmud reminds us that no one generation "has the right to dispose of its natural resources simply as it deems fit, without handing over to future generations the same possibilities it inherited from the past." (*Tamari* 297)

Again, the ancient Rabbis are "thinking like a mountain."

Lastly, I see two very specific echoes of ecosystem management within the Rabbinic texts. Today clear-cutting is done by lumber interests; then, it was primarily by small cattle such as goats which kill all vegetation by grazing close to the ground (today, the cattle industry is one of the driving forces behind rainforest depletion). *Mishnah Bava Kama* 7:7 orders us to "not raise small cattle in the Land of Israel"; the Gemara (79b) explains that this is "because of *Yishuv Eretz*

Yisrael"; and Rashi (the eleventh-century French commentator) adds, "since they destroy the fields." On the following page, *B. Bava Kama* 80a, comes a powerful story about the seriousness with which this prohibition was treated. Here, even one's personal health cannot override the common good:

> Rabban Gamliel . . . told [his students] that it's permitted [to keep gifts of small cattle from outside of Israel], but only if they don't go out and graze with the herd, but rather are leashed to the legs of the bed.
>
> Our rabbis taught that it happened with a particular *hasid* (good person) who suffered from his heart: and he asked the doctors, and they said his only remedy was to drink fresh milk every morning. And they brought him a goat and tied it to the legs of the bed, and he drank from it every morning.
>
> After a while his friends came in to visit him. When they saw the goat tied up to the legs of the bed, they turned around and said, "Armed robbers are in his house, and we should visit him?!"
>
> They returned and checked [into his life], and found nothing [wrong] about him, except for that one sin of the goat. And even he himself said at the hour of his death: "I know that there is no sin in me, except for the sin of that goat, when I transgressed the words of my friends."

The still-developing science of ecosystem management juggles conflicting priorities for land use, and sometimes must deny individual people's desires or even needs. The Rabbis already faced such a dilemma, and in this story of the goat they too reject personal needs in favor of nature and the public good.

Second, from the same extended discussion (*B. Bava Kama* 81a), the Rabbis place their own, rather stringent, views of "ecosystem management" into the mouth of a biblical character:

Our rabbis taught: Joshua laid down ten stipulations [upon entering Israel]: That they may graze [cattle] in woods, and gather wood in private fields, and gather grasses everywhere except where curly plants grow, and cut off shoots/saplings everywhere except the stumps of olive trees, and . . .

"They may graze in woods:" Rav Pappa said, this only speaks of [small] cattle in large woods. But small cattle in a small forest, or large cattle in a large forest, no—and even more so is large cattle in a small forest prohibited . . .

"Cut off shoots/saplings everywhere except the stumps of olive trees:" R. Tanhum and R. Berias explained in the name of an old man—with olive trees, [the amount of the shoot you must leave is] like an egg; with reeds and vines, [you may cut] from the knot and up; and with all other trees, [you may cut] from a new part that doesn't make fruit, but not from an old part that makes fruit; and not from the trunk of a tree, but from the shoots of a tree.

The old man, cited approvingly by Rabbis Tanhum and Berias, seems to be giving a field biology lesson in how much of a tree must be left standing in order for it to regenerate from its own shoots. And the very notion that we should never cut "from the trunk of a tree, but from the shoots of a tree," if taken seriously, would entail nothing short of a revolution in forestry. Likewise we might offer Rav Papa's sustainability-based grazing criteria to the Bureau of Land Management and other agencies which still offer government-subsidized grazing rights on sensitive public lands. All these are just more applications of the Rabbis' "ecosystem" consciousness.

IV. ENVIRONMENTAL REGULATION— THE RABBINIC LAW OF DAMAGES

The analogy of Earth to a lifeboat, with all of us "in it together," has long been popular in the environmental movement. Adlai Stevenson aptly summed it up in his final public speech:

> We travel together, passengers on a little spaceship, dependent on its vulnerable reserves of air and soil; all committed for our safety to its security and peace; preserved from annihilation only by the care, the work, and the love we give our fragile craft, and, I may say, each other.

As with much of contemporary ecological thought, this idea too was expressed by the Rabbis. According to *Leviticus Rabbah* 4:6,

> Hezekiah taught: It's said, "Israel are scattered sheep" (Jeremiah 50:17). Israel is compared to a lamb: As with a lamb hurt on its head or any of its limbs, and all of its limbs feel it, so it is with Israel—one of them sins, and all of them feel it: "One person sins, and You will be angry with the entire community!" (Numbers 16:22)
>
> Rabbi Shimon b. Yohai taught: This is like people that were sitting on a boat. One of them took a drill and began to drill under his own place. His fellow travelers said to him, "What are you doing?!" He said, "What do you care—aren't I drilling [only] under my own place?!" They said, "The water will rise and cover us [all]."

If our lifeboat sinks, it will be into the boiling seas of a globally warmed Earth. If our spacecraft crashes, it will be because the sun's ultraviolet rays crashed through our denuded ozone layer.

Our sacred texts demonstrate society's right and responsibility to enact and enforce public safeguards. As on the boat above, *kol Yis-rael arevim zeh bazeh*—all of Israel, and now all the world, are responsible for one another (*B. Shavuot* 39a). Rabbinic texts emphasize that communal concerns—pollution, safety, ecology, public health, and so on—are a higher priority than "private property rights" or even "economic growth." This is not a radical position; economy and property are important within the Rabbinic system as they are in modern America. Yet the Rabbis insist that private gain cannot overshadow the public good.

To appreciate the Rabbinic perspective on these issues we must first consider the two important terms *reshut ha-rabim and reshut ha-yahid,* usually translated as "public domain" and "private domain." They recur frequently in the Talmudic "Order of Damages" *(Nezikin).* Although these terms may seem to indicate a strict separation between public and private, in fact the Rabbis clearly understood the fleeting nature of private ownership. Consider *B. Bava Kama* 50b:

> Our rabbis taught: "a person should not remove stones from their private domain to the public domain." It happened that a particular man was removing stones from his field into the public thoroughfare, and a *tzaddik* ("righteous person") found him doing so. He said to him, "Empty one! Why are you removing stones from a place that isn't yours to a place that is yours?!"
>
> After time passed, he was forced to sell his field. As he was walking on that very same public thoroughfare, he tripped on those very stones. He said, "Correctly that *tzaddik* said to me, 'Why are you removing stones from a place that isn't yours to a place that is yours?!'"

Since private ownership is fleeting, we are driven to a deeper sense of communal responsibility—only public lands are truly "ours," and we should protect them. But also, it means that society cares what happens to temporarily "private" lands. The Rabbis unswervingly regulated around both concerns, usually by holding people liable for their actions (shorthand for anything from restitution to flogging to capital punishment). Two such examples concern the proximity of public and private lands:

> The one who digs a pit on private property and opens it into a public area, or [digs a pit] in a public area and opens it into private property, or [digs a pit] on private property and opens it into another's private property—is liable.
>
> The one who digs a pit in a public area, and an ox or donkey falls into it and dies—is liable. (*B. Bava Kama* 5:7)
>
> The one who chops wood in a private area and causes damage in a public area, [or] in a public area and damages a private area, [or] in a private area and damages another private area—is liable (*B. Bava Kama* 3:7)

These proclamations presuppose that what you do on your own land may have adverse impacts beyond the property line, and you are fully responsible for any injury that your actions cause. These injuries, usually physical or fiscal, can in the long run include environmental degradation and lowered quality of life.

Another area of both contemporary and Rabbinic concern is air pollution. Even in preindustrial times dirty air was a public health issue no less than an aesthetic one. The following sources, which regulate necessary though harmful industries, demonstrate that without being "anti-business," the Rabbinic model still embraces zoning and other regulations to minimize the adverse effects of such industries:

> Ten things were said about Jerusalem . . .
> (6) "We can't make garbage/dung piles in it," because of the reptiles [who would thrive in them, and create impurity].

(7) "We can't operate kilns in it," because of the smoke.

(8) "We don't create gardens or orchards in it," because of the odor [of rotting produce] (B. Bava Kama 82b)

We keep a fixed threshing floor 50 cubits away from the town. A person should not make a fixed threshing floor within their property unless they have 50 cubits in every direction, and distance it from the plantings and plowed fields of their neighbor, in order not to do damage. (B. Bava Batra 2:8)

We keep carcasses and graves and tanneries 50 cubits away from the town. We only put a tannery to the east [downwind] of the town. Rabbi Akiva says in any direction except west; and distanced 50 cubits. (B. Bava Batra 2:9)

The legacy and logic of these Rabbinic regulations still need to be defended today against the weakening of environmental laws and against "takings" legislation which would limit their applicability. So too should we cherish the important precedents offered by *Mishnah Bava Kama,* which enacts liability for damages caused by placing injurious objects into the public sphere (3:1); by improper resource extraction, dumping of hazardous wastes, or shoddy construction techniques (3:2); or by improper disposal on, or treatment of, public land (3:3). Again, environmental quality and justice each demand this.

Furthermore, not only are we responsible for the immediate consequences of our actions but for their indirect effects as well. In *B. Bava Batra* 23a we learn of liability for second-generation contamination; even "indirect causality of damage is forbidden." This poses a broad challenge to chemical manufacture, strip mining, cattle ranching, industrial siting, and numerous other practices. The same page of Talmud also offers the no less dramatic ruling that "there is no legal title to things which cause damage."

Though Rabbinic sources around pollution control are impressive, their positive attitude toward environmental regulations hardly stops here. As described earlier, the important law of *bal tashchit,* which prohibits wanton waste and destruction, is an example of the rabbis' willingness to curtail a certain amount of individual autonomy in the name of the greater good. They also established many proactive regulations, as seen in the numerous Rabbinic exhortations to plant trees. The requirement that all cities have greenery in order to be suitable for habitation by scholars (*B. Eruvin* 55b) is another example of proactive regulation, as are the laws of compassion for animals *(tza'ar ba'alei hayyim).* And perhaps most urgent for our day, given current political and environmental discourse, are the "ecosystem management" teachings about forestry and grazing detailed above.

Of course, Rabbinic literature is not universally ecological; we find no contemporary questioning of the need for tanneries and other problematic industries, nor any analysis of the consumer's role. And there are indeed cases where the Rabbis allow economic concerns to take precedence. But by now the thesis should be clear: the rabbis believed in environmental regulations, and so should we. Though they come at a cost, regulations are worth it. Aryeh Carmell paraphrases the end of a story at *Bava Metzia* 101a: "To be able to recognize the overriding importance of ecology against the property rights of the individual—this is greatness." And the modern scholar Meir Tamari offers the clearest summation of this Rabbinic view:

> . . . over and above the economic considerations involved in ecological cost-benefit analysis, there is a moral element involved. By insisting that enterprises that harm the public have to be removed, we are asserting a moral and religious framework that regards such governmental interference as legitimate.

Without this moral context the industrialist will feel that his [*sic*] personal rights are being arbitrarily abridged for the benefit of others. In the Torah scheme of things, the Jew is educated to understand that the public has rights in his property, and therefore his own property rights are necessarily and consistently limited.

V. THE GAIA HYPOTHESIS— THE ETERNAL IS ONE AND GOD'S WORLD IS ONE

The idea of the entire Earth (or at least the biosphere) being one living organism, popularized by James Lovelock as the Gaia hypothesis, informs science with a much-needed and deeply ecological perspective. According to this view, the "biosphere is a self-regulating (cybernetic) system. Gaia as a living earth is more than the mere sum of its parts. Life itself plays an active role in maintaining the conditions necessary for its own continuation." For this, too, we find Rabbinic antecedents:

> Rabbi Shimon b. Yohai said, "Three things are weighed together, and they are land, humanity, and dew (rain)." Rabbi Levi b. Haytah said, "And all three of these are from three letters, to teach you that if there's no land there's no dew, and if there's no dew there's no land—and without either of them, there's no humankind." (*Bereshit Rabbah* 13:3)

As this midrash suggests, the Rabbis saw our place within Earth as integral but not supreme. The related idea that nature exists for its own sake, rather than for ours alone, is an important aspect of

Gaia or any other deep ecology perspective. While the Rabbis are often anthropocentric, still there is a definite Rabbinic sensitivity to nature's existence for itself. According to *Bereshit Rabbah* 13:8, "God causes rain upon the land, even without humanity—it is a covenant inscribed with the land, as it is written, 'To rain on the land without people, the desert that has no one in it'" (Job 38:26).

Since humans are just another species in the web of life, Gaia downplays the differences between people and nature. The Rabbis have already done so by anthropomorphizing the created world, as in *Bereshit Rabbah* 13:2: "'Any shrub *(siah)* of the field'" (Genesis 2:5): It's as if all the trees converse *(masichim)* with one another. It's as if all the trees converse with the created things. All the trees were created for the enjoyment (benefit) of creation."

Lastly, seeing the Earth as one organism means understanding that nothing was created in vain, and that everything on Earth has a role to play. This view, known either as Gaia or as normative Rabbinic Judaism, is critical for the construction of a contemporary Jewish ecological ethic, for it addresses perhaps the single most pressing global threat: the loss of biodiversity, or the short-sighted human actions which are daily annihilating dozens of God's unique species.

Grazing, burning, and logging of forest habitat are among the greatest threats to Divine biodiversity; at Tu B'Shvat we consider the life-saving drug Taxol made from the near-extinct Pacific yew tree, and the unknown riches we daily destroy throughout the world's forests. In rivers, deserts, wetlands, and coral reefs as well, the loss of any species is an affront to the One whose singular creations are "good" and whose interconnected whole is "very good" (Genesis 1:31). Once more, the Rabbis presage our concern. *B. Sanhedrin* 108b relates the midrashic dialogue by which the raven, a nonkosher bird of which there were but two on Noah's ark, suggests that Noah instead send a dove to search for dry land in the wake of the flood:

> The raven said to Noah, "Great is your hatred for me! . . . you withhold [sending a scout] from a species of which there are seven, but send [me] from a species of which there are two. If the power of heat or cold overwhelms me, would not the world be lacking a species?!"

This deserved (and successful) rebuke suggests concern for the continuation of all God's species. There is a Divine purpose behind every aspect of creation, irrespective of our ability to discern it. In that spirit, "Rabbi Yehudah said in the name of Rav: Everything that the Holy One, Blessed Be, created in God's world—God did not create a single thing in vain" (*B. Shabbat* 77b). The capstone of this consciousness is seen in the following Rabbinic midrash from *Exodus Rabbah* 10:1:

> Our rabbis said, what is this "And the advantage *(yitron)* of the land in all things"? (Kohelet 5:8). Even things you see as superfluous *(meyutarin)* in this world—like flies, fleas, and mosquitoes—they are part of the greater scheme of the creation of the world, as it says, "And God saw all that God had created, and behold it was very good" (Genesis 1:31). And Rabbi Aha b. Rabbi Hanina said, Even things you see as superfluous in this world—like snakes and scorpions—they are part of the greater scheme of the creation of the world.

Here as in so many cases, the Rabbis were ahead of their time. The Rabbinic endeavor, above all, was about creating norms by which the Jewish people should live. Today such norms are needed if humanity is to survive. May we be guided by Rabbinic wisdom as we do our part to repair our beautiful, fragile, interconnected, Divine Earth.

References

All Rabbinic quotes are original translations by Fred Dobb.

Belkin, Samuel. "Man as Temporary Tenant." In *Judaism and Human Rights,* ed. Milton Konvitz. New York: Norton, 1972, pp. 251–58.

Carmell, Aryeh. "Judaism and the Quality of the Environment." In *Challenge: Torah Views on Science and Its Problems,* eds. Aryeh Carmell and Cyril Domb. New York: Feldheim, 1976, pp. 500–25.

Helfand, Jonathan. "The Earth Is the Lord's: Judaism and Environmental Ethics." In *Religion and Environmental Crisis,* ed. Eugene C. Hargrove. Athens: Univ. of Georgia Press, 1986, pp. 38–52. [See also the present anthology.]

Larson, Jeanne, and Madge Micheels-Cyrus, eds. *Seeds of Peace.* Philadelphia: New Society Publishers, 1987.

Leopold, Aldo. *A Sand County Almanac.* New York: Ballantine; 1949/1970.

Merchant, Carolyn. *Radical Ecology: The Search for a Livable World.* New York: Routledge, 1992.

Stein, David E., ed. *A Garden of Choice Fruit.* Wyncote, Pa: Shomrei Adamah, 1991.

Tamari, Meir. *With All Your Possessions: Jewish Ethics and Economic Life.* New York: Free Press, 1987.

NATURE VS. TORAH

Jeremy Benstein

Rabbi Ya'akov omer: hamhaleikh ba-derekh ve-shoneh, u-mafsik mi-mishnato ve-omer: mah na'eh ilan zeh, mah na'eh nir zeh, ma'aleh alav ha-katuv ke-ilu mithayeiv be-nafsho. (*Pirkei Avot* 3:7)

Rabbi Ya'akov says: One, who while walking along the way, reviewing his studies, breaks off from his study and says, "How beautiful is that tree! How beautiful is that plowed field!" Scripture regards him as if he has forfeited his soul. (*Ethics of the Fathers* 3:7)

Jeremy Benstein, a native of Toledo, Ohio, holds a B.A. degree in linguistics from Harvard, an M.A. degree in Talmud and midrash from Jewish Theological Seminary/The Seminary of Judaic Studies in Jerusalem, and is a doctoral candidate in cultural anthropology at the Hebrew University, researching environmentalism and local culture, especially Israeli. He is the co-founder with Eilon Schwartz of the Heschel Center for Environmental Learning and Leadership in Tel Aviv. He made aliyah seventeen years ago and lives with his wife, Elisheva, and twin sons, Noam and Yonah, in Kiryat Tivon, Israel.

If one is a Jew with strong environmental concerns, one is often led to study the Sources with an eye for those particular teachings that are inspirational for—or at least compatible with—one's own predetermined "green" positions, and thus avoid challenging oneself with texts that don't fit current environmental wisdom. All three sides—Judaism, environmentalism, and ourselves—suffer from this sort of superficial understanding of what it means to learn Torah, or to interact with any age-old wisdom tradition. This essay looks at one of those "tough" traditional texts, one that is seemingly antithetical to any sort of sympathetic portrayal of the natural world, along with the ancient and modern commentaries that show how Jews have grappled with it in different generations, in an attempt to understand what it may be saying to us in our generation.

This passage has frequently been understood to teach a rejection of the (natural) World, and any appreciation of it, in the face of the supreme—and ultimately, exclusive—value of Torah study. As such, it serves as a central proof-text for the claim that Judaism, at its core, is spiritually alienated from Nature; that Jewish tradition stands squarely behind Revelation (Torah) as its central religious category of experience, and source of Truth, while Creation (Nature) is seen as a potentially dangerous competitor, as an alternative, and therefore heretical, source of inspiration, or Truth(s), or experience of the Divine, whose seductive charms must be contained, or in this case, vehemently censured.

The text is a saying from that part of the Mishna known as *Pirkei Avot,* literally *Chapters of the Fathers,* often translated as *Ethics of the Fathers. Avot,* as it is also called, is a collection of ethical maxims and moral teachings, of a non–legally binding nature, ascribed to the *tannaim,* the sages of the Mishnaic period, who lived roughly from around the turn of the era, until c. 200 CE.

The teaching, in the original Hebrew, heads this article, but the translation has been deliberately omitted,[1] since like most significant ancient sources it cannot be rendered simply or straightforwardly into modern English. Though the text is not particularly complex or sophisticated in style, any single literal translation will invariably miss allusions and levels of meanings which not only deepen and enrich our understanding of the original, but also occupied the traditional and modern commentators whose interpretations we also wish to study. Therefore, this text, rather than being translated, will be given a close reading and "discussed into English," to use Robert Frost's phrase, in an approach inspired by translations of modern poetry.[2]

This process will both facilitate the introduction of the commentaries (for while it is well known that every translation is, in fact, an interpretation, it is equally true that every interpretation is a translation of sorts) and open up the range of possibilities in the text for our own readings.

THE TEXT

Rabbi Ya'akov omer . . . /*Rabbi Ya'akov [Jacob] says . . .* The first question we encounter is the attribution of the teaching. Some manuscripts relate this saying in the name of R. Ya'akov, some in the name of R. Shim'on[3] This issue is not (just) a pedantic, academic one. It is important to understand this saying—which purportedly denigrates this material World, as compared with the Eternal Torah—in the wider context of the worldview of the sage(s) who allegedly uttered it. Rabbi Ya'akov is Ya'akov ben Korshai, a *tanna* (a sage of the Mishnaic period) of the fourth generation, who lived in the mid-second century, and was a member of the Sanhedrin at Usha. He was a disciple of Rabbi Meir, a contemporary of Rabban Gamliel II, and was chosen to be the tutor of the young Rabbi Yehuda Hanasi, the redactor of the Mishna, and one of the giants of the period.[4] More important is Ya'akov ben Korshai's family background: he was the grandson of the (in)famous apostate Elisha ben Abuya, known as *Acher*, "the Other." The very scenario[5] which was reputed to have caused Elisha ben Abuya to have lost his belief in God and in Divine justice did not shake the faith of his grandson, Rabbi Ya'akov, for it was his firm belief that the poor child who died, though fulfilling two *mitzvot* which should have guaranteed him long life, would receive his length of days and just rewards in the World to Come. This emphasis on the next world seems to be a central axis of his thought, which ties into our mishna as well. Further along in *Pirkei Avot,* he is quoted as saying the following: "This world is like a vestibule to the world to come; prepare yourself in the vestibule that you may enter into the (banqueting) hall" (4:16). And: "Better is one hour of bliss of spirit in the world to come than all the life of this world" (11:17). It makes sense that our mishna came from the same mouth that spoke these anti-this-world teachings.

Were Rabbi Shim'on to have originated this saying, though, that too would be fitting. The Rabbi Shim'on in question is none other than Rabbi Shim'on bar Yochai, a contemporary of Rabbi Ya'akov ben Korshai. He was one of the five remaining students of Rabbi Akiva who survived the failure of the Bar Kochba revolt, and himself had to flee the Romans and eventually hide out in a cave. According to the Talmudic account (*T. B. Shabbat* 33b), he secluded himself, together with his son, for thirteen years, studying Torah day and night. When they finally emerged, they saw people going about their daily affairs, plowing and sowing, and not devoting themselves to Torah. They exclaimed, *"Me-nihin hayyei olam ve-oskim be-hayyei sha'ah?"* meaning, "They forsake eternal life (i.e., Torah study and its rewards) and devote themselves to temporal life?"

When their fiery gazes destroyed all they looked upon, God came to the aid of his Creation, and their passionate devotion to divine Revelation notwithstanding, God rebuked them: "Have you emerged only to destroy My World? Return to your cave!"[6] Elsewhere, in a dispute about the value of labor, Rabbi Shim'on said: "If a person ploughs in the ploughing season, and sows in the sowing season, and reaps in the reaping season, and threshes in the threshing season, and winnows in the season of wind, what is to become of the Torah?"[7]

For Rabbi Shim'on, Torah is an all-consuming and exclusive passion; any diversion, such as taking care of one's physical needs (here, significantly, represented by agriculture, i.e., work in Nature) is a subversion, and must be fought. His anti-this-world stance stems from considerations very different from those of Rabbi Ya'akov's, but our mishna from *Pirkei Avot* dovetails with his value system as well.

These are just the briefest of thumbnail sketches of the sages involved and their beliefs, but hopefully they serve to add some background, or flavor, to the text under discussion. In the end, we relate to a teaching on the basis of its contents, not on the basis of who it was who taught it, but it is important (where possible) to be aware of the larger intellectual context of the "life and times" of the relevant thinker(s), and the interrelationships among their ideas and values. When this is ignored, or deemphasized, as is all too often the case, it is easy to forget that a given statement or teaching is the single voice of a particular sage, one view among many.

A major point of this essay is to argue (by example) for taking voices like the one represented by this mishna seriously because they are *part* of Jewish tradition but not because they *are* (the whole of) Judaism. One need look no further than sections of the book of Psalms, or Job, to discover other voices that speak about Nature in very different terms from these. Part of the richness of Judaism—and the excitement of Jewish learning—is the ongoing dialogue between the frequently very disparate voices of that tradition, a dialogue which we shall soon see continues through to the present day.

Hamhaleikh ba-derekh . . . /*the walker on the road; he who walks by the way . . .* Two things are evident here: the mishna is referring to an individual (not a group), and that person is out-of-doors, and in transit from one place to another. A good example of a Talmudic-style question that some commentators ask is, Is this choice of phrasing *be-davka?* That is to say, is the mishna referring *specifically* to an individual on the road, and therefore excluding a similar occurrence that might happen to someone sitting under a tree or at home? Or is this just meant to be a general example and apply in any situation? Several answers are discussed below.

The other important thing to note is the clear allusion to the Biblical verse (Deut. 6:7): *ve-shinantam le-vanekha ve-dibarta bam . . . u-velekhtekha va-derekh . . .* "and you shall repeat them [these words] to your children, and speak of them . . . when you walk along the way. . . . " If this verse directly underlies our mishna, then the "peripatetic student" is not just engaging in a rather unusual pastime, he is actually fulfilling a *mitzvah.*

Ve-shoneh . . . /*and is studying; while reviewing his studies; repeating [his Torah tradition]* . . . [8] This verb is from the same root, *shanayim, shnei,* "two, second," that is, to do something a second time, to repeat. It is predicated specifically on oral review or verbal rote learning.[9] The use of this single, particular word gives us a very concrete image, perhaps different from what we imagined at first: our traveling learner is not walking around absent-mindedly with his nose in a book, but rather taking advantage of some quiet time alone to go over what he has learnt, what he is trying to memorize—and very possibly fulfilling a *mitzvah* as well.

There is some discussion as to what is permissible subject-matter for the road, even whether it is advisable to study while traveling at all. The conclusion in *T. B. Ta'anit* 10b is that rote repetition *(migras)* is acceptable for wayfarers, but "deep thought," or analysis *(iyunei)*, is potentially dangerous. The danger in excessive engrossment in one's studies is not the failure to be alert to physical risks (of attack or mishap) or simply losing one's way. The "danger" in being diverted *from one's studies* by what one sees along the way— well, that's the subject of our mishna. But this particular word makes it clear that the literal risk is not so much losing one's train of thought as actually forgetting the Torah that one is trying to learn.

U–mafsik mi–mishnato ve–omer . . . /and ceases his repetition; breaks off his study; interrupts his learning and says . . . The strong terminology here seems to imply that this interruption is not a momentary lapse of attention, but a complete shift in the activity and mental state of the subject. The late chief rabbi of England, Rabbi J. H. Hertz, who seems rather ill-at-ease with the mishna as a whole in his commentary (Hertz, p. 53), interprets these words to mean: "What is deprecated here is a willful distraction of the mind from Torah-meditation by the surrounding scenery."

Mah na'eh ilan zeh . . . /How beautiful, or fine, is this tree! . . . The appreciation expressed here seems to be clearly of an aesthetic nature.[10] Many commentators have pointed out that there is a prescribed blessing that is to be recited at the sight of beautiful creatures *(be-riyot tovot)* and beautiful trees *(ilanot tovot)* from *T. B. Berachot* 58b: *Barukh she-kakhah lo be-olamo*, "Blessed is the One whose world is thus."[11] Some claim, therefore, that the person who uttered these words was therefore engaging in an essentially praiseworthy activity, of praising God's creation; while others point out that since the phrase here is not the *matbea berakhah,* the set text of the blessing, as prescribed, the subject here is expressing illegitimate (possibly heretical, at least frivolous) aesthetic expression, that is not divinely-oriented. This will be expanded upon below.

Mah na'eh nir zeh . . . /*How beautiful, or fine, is this furrow; this plowed field!* . . .   While many translations have simply "field," this is inaccurate. As Rashi correctly points out, a *nir* is not a *sadeh,* a field, it is a *sadeh she-nihrash,* a field that has been plowed and made ready for cultivation (see Jeremiah 4:3). This pinpoints the scene described in the mishna once again: the student is not hiking through deep woods, but rather is walking along a country road, through farmland, apparently before the planting. It is reasonable to assume that it is springtime, which would mean the aforementioned tree is probably in bud (making it particularly attractive), whether wild, or part of someone's orchard, as now seems likely.

It is also important to note that a furrow is a distinctly human creation, in contrast to the tree. Some commentators make much of this point—the divine creation together with the human.[12] Others point out, that while there is a blessing for the tree (even if our wayfarer only alluded to it, but didn't actually recite it), there is none prescribed for seeing a plowed field, no matter how attractive.

Ma'aleh alav ha-katuv . . . /*Scripture accounts it to him; regards him; [such a person] is considered by the Torah* . . .   This is another problematic part of our text. Invariably a formulation such as this is accompanied by a proof-text, a verse cited to justify the conclusion: "**Scripture** *regards him.* . . . " But no verse is included here. Rashi claims that that is strong enough evidence to doubt the actual phrasing of the mishna; some versions (see Taylor, p. 48) in fact do omit the word *ha-katuv,* "Scripture," which results in: "this person is regarded as. . . . "

Commentators have taken differing tacks: Herford wrote (p. 73), "it is hard to imagine what text would support such a thesis"; likewise Hertz (p. 53): "No text is, or could well be, quoted in support of this teaching." But earlier than either of them, the authors of the *Machzor Vitry,* a prayer book composed in eleventh- or twelfth-century France by followers of Rashi, commented that there are a number of likely candidates: Proverbs 6:22, "when you walk it will lead you"; Deut. 6:7, "when you walk along the way . . . "; and also Deut. 4:9, "take utmost care, and watch yourselves scrupulously, so that you do not forget the things that you saw with your own eyes. . . . "[13] None of these verses is quite virulent enough, though, to justify the harsh "judgment" that follows.

Ke-ilu mithayeiv be-nafsho. /*It is as if he . . .*   Here we truly run into translation difficulties. A survey of a dozen editions yields more than ten different renderings. The range of possibilities includes "were mortally guilty,"[14] "sinned against his own soul,"[15] "committed a capital offense,"[16] "were guilty against his own soul,"[17] "were guilty against himself,"[18] "has become liable for his life,"[19] "were 'guilty' of death,"[20] "had incurred guilt [expiable] by his life,"[21] "has forfeited his soul (life),"[22] "were guilty of deadly sin,"[23] "(has) hurt his own being."[24] This listing is somewhat random—there are undoubtedly other permutations and nuances that are possible.

There are two main difficulties in this three-word phrase, and they are related. The first is the significance of the modifier *ke-ilu,* "as if." In a previous mishna (3:5) we are told that one who stays awake (or awakens) at night, or travels alone, or turns his heart to idle matters, that person has [actually] *mithayeiv be-nafsho* (choose one of the alternatives above). Why the difference? Why is the "punishment" (or judgment) for this apparent sin only "as if"? Is it less serious?[25] Are there mitigating circumstances?

The other obvious difficulty is trying to figure out exactly what that judgment is. *Le-hithayeiv* is "to become, or to be found, guilty" (connected to *hov, hayeiv*), and by extension, "to sin (with respect to)." *Nefesh,* of course, is "soul," but in pre-modern Hebrew it also refers simply to "self." In the rest of the Mishna (outside of *Pirkei Avot*), the phrase occurs in three other places,[26] all of them in a strictly legal context. All have the force of "receive the death penalty," hence also the rendering here "guilty of a capital offense," i.e., worthy of death. But interpreting the guilt, or the risk (or the damage) involved as *physical* harm seems excessively literal; perhaps this should be understood on a spiritual plane.[27]

The modifying *ke-ilu,* "as if," certainly reinforces this (but in 3:5, without the modifier, the implication seems just as clearly metaphoric—nobody has been sentenced to death for insomnia, or for a penchant for solo travel!).[28] Therefore, in order to express the spiritual nature of the statement, but also retain the legalistic sense of punishment (or loss), the translation "has forfeited his soul" will be used.

This, then, is the reconstructed text:

> *Rabbi Ya'akov says: One, who while walking along the way, reviewing his studies, breaks off from his study and says, "How beautiful is that tree! How beautiful is that plowed field!" Scripture regards him as if he has forfeited his soul.*

THE COMMENTARIES

Commentators over the centuries have related to a wide range of issues connected to our mishna, many of which are beyond the scope of this essay. The focus in the following selections will be the question of the relationship of Nature and its appreciation to Torah study and religious experience. It is important to note, however, that certain commentators did not see this as the central issue at all. For example, Shimon ben Tzemach Duran (Spain, 1361–1444) wrote in his commentary *Magen Avot:*

> And although in our passage the Sages speak specifically of the exclamation, "How handsome is this tree, how handsome this field!"—the same is true of any other chatter. But the Sage is referring to something commonplace, for it is customary for those who walk on the highway to talk of what they see along the way. (Goldin, p. 128)

Most, however, did relate specifically to the issue of Torah and Nature. Regarding the question, we can discern three broad approaches in the classical and contemporary traditional commentaries.[29] All in some way "justify" the mishna: that is to say, interpret the text in such a way so as to extract a message that is acceptable (to them). None reject or negate the passage (as the Zionist Berdichevski did). The differences appear in how they relate to Nature per se. The first is complete subordination—to the point of denigration—of the value of Nature and of appreciation for the works of Creation in the face of the supremacy of Revelation and the study of Torah. Meiri (Menahem ben Solomon HaMeiri, France, 1249–1306) considers such appreciation "vain" and "idle":

> The reason for such strong condemnation is this: by [his] nature man is drawn to vanity *(hevlim)* and idle matters *(shehot batlot).* [If he does not resist his nature] he will be drawn on from such habits to throwing off the yoke of the Torah completely. (Goldin, p. 128)

And Don Isaac Abarbanel, the great fifteenth century Spanish commentator, writes in his commentary *Nachalat Avot* that material concerns such as this are "useless":

> When a person who was walking along the way, and reviewing his studies, stopped his studying in order to pay attention to things that are of no use *(ein ba-hem to'elet)* then he forfeits his soul, because he ceased his study, and made it secondary, peripheral *(tapeil)* and made the other, worldly, material things *(ha-devarim ha-gashmiyim)* central *(ikkar)*.

A second, more moderate—and more prevalent—approach also sees the acts of Creation as subordinate to the words of Revelation but recognizes the act of appreciation of those acts, praising God for the divine handiwork,[30] as correct and valuable in itself, but still not as important as Torah study. Representatives of this approach among traditional commentators are Bertinoro (Obadiah ben Abraham Bertinoro, Italy, 1470–1520):

> And there are those who say that this (particular example) teaches us something significant, that despite the fact that he would be brought to recite a blessing—"Blessed is the One who has such [beauty] in His world"—nevertheless, he is accounted as if he forfeited his life, since he ceased his studying.

and Rabbi Yitzchak Magriso, in *Yalkut Me'am Lo'ez,* an eighteenth century Ladino anthology of commentary and stories:

> The case which he is discussing is not that of a person who puts aside his studies merely to engage in useless chatter, but to praise God for the beautiful tree that he saw. Nonetheless, since this person has stopped studying, it is counted as if he were engaging in useless speech, and it is considered a sin. What one

should do under the circumstances is complete the subject of his study, and then praise God for the beautiful sight. From this one can see how great is the sin of interrupting one's studies, since even praising God is considered a waste of time. How much greater is the sin of abandoning one's studies without good reason, for a real waste of time. (Yerushalmi version, pp. 142–143)

Modern commentators have also adopted this approach, which seems to afford a comfortable "middle road" by allowing affirmation of the World without denying the traditional primacy of Torah study. Reuven Bulka develops this point at length:

If, as has been posited in the previous *mishna,* all is God's, this would include the heavens and the earth, nature, the trees, the fields. One can see in all of this the greatness and majesty of God. Nevertheless, this should not develop into an equation of sameness. There is profound significance in everything, but not everything is the same. There is a scale of values; there are priorities and levels of importance. One who is walking by the way in study and interrupts the study to admire nature by saying *"How beautiful is this tree!"* or another such statement which affirms the majesty of God in the world, has made a priority substitution which is distorted. This distortion in-heres in that such an individual has seen fit to interrupt Torah study to admire nature. Admiring nature is part of appreciating the beauty of the world, but not a priority when juxtaposed with Torah study. Nature is God's work, but the Torah is God's formula for life. Interrupting Torah to admire nature is a value distortion.

The *mishna* ends by saying that the individual who makes the value distortion *is regarded by Scripture as having forfeited one's soul.* It is unclear which verse in Scripture is the proof-text for this. In all probability, it would seem that Scripture in general makes this observation. It is in the very nature of the importance of Scripture. One who denies Scripture's importance by placing primacy on nature, by interrupting Torah meditation to admire nature, Scripture itself sees this as a rejection of the very notion of Scripture's being so vital to life, and being the most crucial of all human pursuits. Placing this pursuit in a subordinate position to admiring nature denies the primary importance of Scripture. It is as if one has forfeited one's soul, because in the process of placing Torah and its values in a secondary position, one has denied its essentiality to life and has thus compromised the value actualization which is so vital for a meaningful life. (pp. 111–112; see also Hirsch).

A third approach, very different from the first two, can be seen in the commentary of Rabbi Yosef Hayyim Caro (1800–1895, Eastern Europe). Though unswervingly Orthodox—he studied under the great halachist, Rabbi Akiva Eiger—Caro had some familiarity with German literature and was also a proponent of Jewish settlement in Palestine. His commentary is strikingly original and will be presented and discussed in detail. He begins by formulating the questions that strike him as most troubling, and to which he plans to respond.

The commentators, he says, have had great difficulty in interpreting this mishna:

> Why should one forfeit his life in saying *"how fine is,"* etc.? If it is because he ceased from his studies, then it should have been phrased simply "he who was studying, and stops his study, it is accounted to him," etc. And also—what is the meaning of the [apparently extraneous] *walking by the way*? Is it permissible, then, to break off one's studies in one's house?

Clearly, the element of being out-of-doors, and the specific re-mark about trees and fields, is not accidental and requires addressing. Caro goes on to explain how he feels that one can know God through natural events:

> It seems to me that Rabbi Jacob's words refer to the follow-ing—There are certain people who know the Blessed Creator through His amazing creations, as in "The heavens declare Your Glory, O God" (Ps. 19). And it is not only in the high heavens that one can discern the actions of the Creator, but also in the seed in the ground, and in the fruit of the tree, that grows in the field, in the lowly mosses that can be seen growing on walls, all the way to the mighty, lofty cedars of Lebanon, be-cause all these express the might of God, and His wonders. . . .

All of Nature—not just the "celestial fireworks"—bears close scrutiny, for it all is indicative of divine action, and instructive re-garding God. Caro's next move is far more radical:

> And were it not for the danger of failure, this way would be the superior one. Not only that, but all the miracles and won-ders through which the Holy Blessed One makes known His might and glory were created solely for the people who have not reached this spiritual level of knowledge of the Creator, and they are the vast majority, but for those few whose eyes are open to see the wonders of nature, these enlightened ones will observe, and reflect, and come to know the wonders of God through the usual order of natural processes. . . . For from these can be seen that everything has been established in wisdom, understanding and knowledge, and they can sense in their souls that this is the work of a wisdom that far surpasses any idea or concept [of ours], and this is our transcendent Creator; but people are fools, for everything that seems to them the usual course of nature, they will pay no attention to—"they have

eyes, but will not see"—unless God creates something totally *new* upon the earth, then they will hop and skip like a ram, on the hind legs of their reason, saying: "Look! Now surely Hashem is God!" Like at the Red Sea, which was a sign for the rebellious among them, that they should believe in God, whereas the insightful sage will say, aren't these great waters which have been flowing for thousands of years a greater testament to the might of their Maker? As King David wrote (Ps. 93:4): "from the crash of great waters, the mighty breakers of the sea, The Lord on high is awesome." What could the miracle of those waters drying up for a few hours at God's command possibly add to that?

Those fancy Biblical miracles—they are for the spiritually short-sighted. The vast majority of people considers those extraordinary events to be proof of God's acting in the world—and needs them, to believe that—while all around them, every day, occur miracles of far greater magnitude, to which they are blind! Those miracles are "invisible" to us because they do not stand out against the background of the natural order—they *are* the natural order. And that order testifies "more faithfully to the power and glory of the Blessed Creator than all that He did against Pharaoh and his armies" (Ibid.). Were it not for a certain (theological) danger, which will be outlined presently, this way, of the study and experience of Nature, would be superior even to Torah study. Caro continues:

> If people's consciousness was fuller, they should know their Creator from the wonder of His creatures, and His acts, but in truth, judging from human nature, this is not the case, for the people's discernment is insufficient to consider and understand the complete significance of those things to which they have become accustomed. . . .
>
> Even though in truth it were better for us to strive to

know God through the wonders of nature, in any event, were the weakness of our understanding not enough, whoever depended solely on this route, is in danger of stumbling, and falling into the trap of denying the belief in a Creation at all, and other true beliefs; therefore, the remarks of the Torah, which tell of the wonders of the Creator in upsetting the natural order, are necessary and fitting, according to our temperament and characteristics, and also safer, and prevent us from [falling into] stumbling and transgression, as we wrote in a previous work for Jewish children: "the words of the Living God are more trustworthy than the testimony of earth and heaven."

Here Caro retreats slightly and begins to lay the groundwork for explaining why our mishna is not in fact mistaken in warning *against* the dependence on Nature for religious inspiration. The idea that God created the World is not something that can be deduced from our experience of it, he claims. It is equally reasonable to assume that the World is eternal, and uncreated—a belief held by the ancient Greeks and considered heinously heretical by the Rabbis. In order for us to understand what we are looking at, we need God's Torah as an interpretive guide. That goes for the sage as well who, unlike the masses of close-minded people, does discern the wondrous nature of all that goes on in the environment—but the natural order, however much appreciated, does not interpret itself.

Caro now turns to the text of the mishna itself, and interprets its particular message:

This, then, is the meaning of the words of R. Jacob in our mishna, *he who walks by the way,* that is to say, that he walks the Way of Goodness, to achieve the object of his desire in knowing God, and establishing in his heart the love and fear of God; and *he was learning, and he breaks off his learning, and says "how fine is this tree,"* etc., i.e., he ceases his Torah study, saying that we have no need for it to achieve this goal, but rather [knowledge and love of God can be achieved] through correct observation of the beauty of the natural order and its creation, he, then, *would forfeit his soul,* for what could be easier than that he should succumb to the disease of heresy, as described above, and he himself would be the guilty party, for he left the Source of Living Waters, our Holy Torah, which comprised his learning according to what human reason is capable of, and to what he is accustomed. . . .

And in saying *"Scripture accounts it to him . . . ,"* the Mishnaic sage was no doubt referring to the verse [Deut. 4:9, quoted in the following mishna]: "Take utmost care and watch yourselves scrupulously, so that you do not forget the things that you saw with your own eyes . . . " in which our Holy Torah warns us to remember the day of the receiving of the Torah, such that we worship God from this perspective, and not from the perspective of the structures of nature. For nature is always visibly present, and it is difficult to imagine forgetting it, but the revelation of the Torah at Sinai, it is only too possible for human beings to forget, and so it is about this that we were warned. Understand this . . .

We were instructed about [the importance of] learning, and the testimony of the Torah, so that we don't rely exclusively on the testimony of nature alone.

So Nature is neither useless nor peripheral; it is clearly on a par with Torah, in the potential it has as a means for reaching God, but it is unfortunately less trustworthy, and needs to be backed up by, or placed within the framework of, divine truth as revealed in the Torah. Torah as Revelation, though, can be forgotten—therefore it requires special attention and care. Nature, on the other hand, is always "out there," Caro claims, and is less in need of human focus to avoid being forgotten. This contradicts in part what he wrote previously, for the inability of masses of people to appreciate the significance of what is always in front of their eyes is certainly a type of forgetting. And the fiery Zionist ideologue Micha Yosef Berdichevski, while admiring many of Caro's sentiments, would certainly disagree with his conclusion.

MODERN AND ZIONIST RESPONSES

Before we turn to Berdichevski and other interpretations inspired by Zionist ideals, it is worthwhile to make mention of two other, very different modern opinions. In his essay, "The Unnatural Jew," the late Prof. Steven Schwarzschild claims not only that, yes, Jews have been alienated from Nature over the centuries, but that this is good. "The main line of Jewish philosophy (in the exilic age) has paradigmatically defined Jewishness as alienation from and confrontation with nature" (p. 349). Any other approach, such as pagan ontologism or Greek-inspired Christian incarnationism "results in human and historical submission to what are acclaimed as 'natural forces'" (p. 347). Anything which smacks of immanentism—from Spinoza and Marx to kabbala and Zionism—is a "specifically Jewish heresy" (pp. 353, 361). Zionism in particular is classed as pagan and non-Jewish, in what he derisively refers to as the "back-to-nature thrust [which] inheres in the Zionist enterprise" (p. 360). It is no surprise, therefore, to find that our mishna is Schwarzschild's "favorite text" (p. 358). For him, Rabbi Ya'akov represents a positive and candid statement of mainstream Jewish dogma.

For Eric Hoffer, on the other hand, Rabbi Ya'akov is only one of a long line of fanatics in the history of the human race, who are characterized by dangerously blind, single-minded devotion to a cause. He cites our mishna, along with the example of the medieval monk and Crusader St. Bernard of Clerveaux, who would pace around beautiful Lake Geneva, lost in thought, never seeing the lake. In *The True Believer,* Hoffer writes:

> The fanatic's disdain for the present blinds him to the complexity and uniqueness of life. . . . In *Refinement of the Arts,* David Hume tells of the monk "who, because the windows of his cell opened upon a noble prospect, made a covenant with his eyes never to turn that way." The blindness of the fanatic is a source of strength . . . but it is the cause of intellectual sterility and emotional monotony. (Sec. 118, p. 141)

For Hoffer, it is partly the fanatically exclusive allegiance to an ideology which he finds repugnant; but it is also specifically that that devotion alienates the "true believer" from the breadth and richness of the world, and it is no coincidence that the examples are drawn from expressions of being cut off from the natural world in particular.

Three other approaches—in the form of interpretations of this mishna—have been expressed in the context of Zionism, the Jewish national return to the Land of Israel. As one might expect, classical Zionist thought, which represented both a secular and a political critique of Diaspora religiosity, seen to be desiccated and overly intellectualized, and an affirmation of the renewed connection with the Land, would have a problem with a teaching such as Rabbi Ya'akov's.

The most extreme reaction is undoubtedly that of Micha Yosef Berdichevski, who later took the name Ben Gurion. Berdichevski was born in Russia in 1865 to a family of distinguished rabbinic lineage. He was soon a recognized scholar in all branches of traditional Jewish learning, including Talmud, Kabbala, and Chasidism. But like many of his generation, the *Haskala* ("enlightenment") and the world of secular learning beckoned him. In 1890 he moved to Western Europe and deepened his exposure to the intellectual currents of the time. He was deeply influenced by Nietzsche and the latter's call for "a transvaluation of all values" in culture.

When it came to the Jewish tradition, Berdichevski had a love-hate relationship, and in his writings "he saw only tension and affirmed only revolt."[31] He certainly expressed that Nietzschean idea in his writings on Judaism (a radical secular Zionist had a lot to "transvalue" in Jewish Europe at the turn of the century), but the love-hate ambiguity is also very present in his style. Even in translation,[32] his luxuriant Biblical language comes across in this paean to nature, which nevertheless does not negate or exclude God:

> The Universe telleth the glory of God, the works of His hand doth Nature relate; for Nature is the father of all life and the source of all life; Nature is the fount of all, the fount and soul of all that live. . . . And then Israel sang the song of the Universe and of Nature, the song of heaven and earth and all their host, the song of the sea and the fullness thereof, the song of the hills and the high places, the song of the trees and the grass, the song of the seas and the streams. Then did the men of Israel sit each under his vine or his fig tree, the fig put forth her buds and the green hills cast their charm from afar. . . . Those days were the days of breadth and beauty. . . . We had thought that God was power, exaltation, the loftiest of the lofty. We had thought that all that walked upon the heights became a vehicle for His presence, but lo! a day came in which we learned otherwise. . . .

That day was the beginning of the other-worldly, Diaspora mentality that prized ethereal spirituality over all else. The value of

political sovereignty, a deep relationship with one's natural surroundings, national pride—all these fell by the wayside.

> Is it any wonder that there arose among us generation after
> generation despising Nature, who thought of all God's marvels
> as superfluous trivialities?
>
> Is it surprising that we became a non-people, a non-
> nation—non-people indeed?
>
> I recall from the teaching of the sages: Whoever walks by
> the way and interrupts his study to remark, How fine is that
> tree, how fine is that field—forfeits his life!
>
> But I assert that then alone will Judah and Israel be saved,
> when another teaching is given unto us, namely: Whoever
> walks by the way and sees a fine tree and a fine field and a fine
> sky and leaves them to think on other thoughts—that man is
> like one who forfeits his life!
>
> Give us back our fine trees and fine fields! Give us back the
> Universe.

Like many Zionists, even in his absolute rejection of them,
Berdichevski remains tied to the texts, and the categories of their
thought, which formed his identity. He is claiming here that Zionism can only be fulfilled when we not only reject the implications
of Rabbi Ya'akov's teaching, but when we adopt the exact opposite
outlook.

If the tradition gives primacy to Torah study over Nature, then
we must reverse the priorities, and make our relationship with the
World in all its manifestations central, and relegate Torah study to the
spiritual back-seat, if we validate it all. If we take his reading at face
value, he seems to be claiming that the Land can replace the Book as
the Jewish people's prime source of sustenance, of identity and existence. According to Hertzberg (p. 292), Berdichevski asserted that

"nature worship and idolatry, not biblical monotheism, had been the real religion of ancient Israel in its days of glory." Other Zionist thinkers and writers, notably the poet Saul Tchernichovski, were sympathetic to this quasi-pagan approach.

Another Zionist understanding of our mishna is provided by Ahad Ha'am and Chayim N. Bialik. They were of the same generation as Berdichevski, but did not call for a radical rejection of all things Jewish.[33] Instead they worked for a secular rejuvenation of Jewish culture, based on the renewed study, and reinterpretation of our age-old Sources. They also believed that a new relationship between Torah and Nature would have to be forged in the rebuilt Jewish society in the Land of Israel. But rather than rejecting or inverting the teaching of our mishna, as Berdichevski had done, they *contextualized* it, making it a teaching that was crucial for our years wandering in the Diaspora, but now was in need of revision. Bialik wrote the following in his seminal essay, "Halacha and Aggada,"[34] attributing the idea to Ahad Ha'am:

> It is not without significance that the people of Israel, or at least the great majority of them, submitted to the iron yoke of Halachah, and not only that, but actually chose to carry with them into exile a heavy load of laws and ordinances. . . . And here is what the Halachist himself says: "If a man studies as he walks, and breaks off his study to say 'How lovely is this tree! How lovely is this field!'—Scripture regards him as guilty of deadly sin." Our aestheticists have spent all their ammunition on this unfortunate mishnah: but even here the sympathetic ear will detect, between the lines, the apprehension, the trembling anxiety for the future, of a wandering people which has nothing to call its own but a Book, and for which any attachment of its soul to one of the lands of sojourn means mortal danger.

So long as the Jews were in lands other than their own Land of Israel, connected not to a real homeland, but to their "portable homeland," as Heine characterized the relationship of the Jews to Torah, then, yes, rejecting that spiritual inheritance for the sake of a tenuous connection with "one of the lands of their sojourn" is potentially spiritual suicide. So, according to Bialik and Ahad Ha'am, this mishna is not talking about all of Nature—only Diaspora Nature.[35] Only that sort of diversion presents a spiritual threat. The implication being that once the Jews return to their land, a new balance can be struck, that can validate both sides of the equation, with neither suffering at the hands of the other. The Land—a metonym of all of Creation, but also the special portion of the Jewish people—would take its place alongside the Book.

CONCLUSION: A NEW VISION?

What is that new balance, and how is it to come about? A complete answer to that question has yet to be worked out—for as the Jerusalem educator Moti Bar-Or has remarked, the Jewish people may have begun to make *aliyah* to the Land of Israel but the Torah has not yet made *aliyah,* has not yet resettled in the Land. In Israel the Abraham Joshua Heschel Center for Nature Studies has been founded to work out the implications of a Jewishly rooted approach to the natural environment, and do educational work in this area. Making our relationship to the World an item on the Jewish educational agenda should be a priority, both in Israel and the Diaspora.[36] Ecological concerns are thankfully becoming more prevalent among many sectors of the population, especially youth. Exploring in a deep and sophisticated way the relevance of Jewish learning to students' deepest personal concerns can only help revitalize Jewish education, and on the other side, give environmentalism significant spiritual roots that can help make it an integral part of our world-view, and not relegate it to the status of a passing fad.

A Jewish environmental ethic should be based on the sense of responsibility that flows from our awe at the wonders of Creation. Regarding responsibility, traditional Jewish teaching has focused on *mitzvot bein adam le-chavero,* the (ethical) commandments concerning our duties to our fellow human beings, and *mitzvot bein adam le-Makom,* the (primarily ritual) commandments which help express our relationship to God.[37] What is needed today is a new, third category: *mitzvot bein adam le-olamo,*[38] the *mitzvot,* and the concomitant sense of commandedness, which can inform and define our piece in the World, and our responsibility towards it.

These commandments bridge, and transcend, the traditional categories of ethics and ritual. The *mitzvah* of *bal tashchit,* the prohibition of inappropriate use and excessive consumption, is not a ritual but neither is it ethically directed at the welfare of other human beings. Similarly, shabbat and kashrut are conventionally considered ritual commandments, yet have significant environmental implications. Once we have a name for something, then we can begin to talk about it on, and in, its own terms.

To this end, Jewish teachers need to learn how to integrate interaction with the natural world, and religious thinking about it, into educational experiences which until now have been classroom-bound, and limited to what can be printed between the covers of a book (or with more creativity and funding, on disk or cassette). We need to reinterpret that other potentially anti-environmental *Pirkei Avot* text, the saying attributed to Ben Bag-Bag (5:24): *Hapokh bah ve-hapokh bah de-khola bah,* "Study it [the Torah], and review it, for *everything* is contained within it." The prevalence of this perspective has made us blind to all those things which are not contained in the books—as wide and deep and rich as our vast sacred bibliography is.

Jewish summer camping has great potential, though too often stunning natural camp settings are treated as no more than static props, or scenery against which the otherwise unaffected drama of camp life takes place. It is not enough just to be "out there," or to take those hikes which have become part and parcel of the Jewish summer camp experience: for true interaction, and integration to take place, the learning that goes on must relate to the apple trees, and not just take place under them. And rabbis, who are accustomed to trying to elicit religious experiences among their congregants in the synagogue sanctuary, and via the *siddur*, the text of the prayer book (apparently they are also used to frequent failure in this department), need to be trained to foster spiritual sensitivity out-of-doors as well, in response to Creation—in the forests, deserts, oceans, and even just the front- and backyards of the World. There may be some surprises in store.

Three Zionist approaches were mentioned above, but only two were presented. The third is a *torah she-be'al peh,* an oral teaching that has defied all efforts to trace it to a written source.[39] This interpretation zeroes in on two words: *mafsik mi-mishnato,* "ceases, breaks off from his study." The force of our mishna hinges on there being a dichotomizing, the breaking off of the Torah study in order to experience Nature. All the commentaries cited above assume this dichotomous reading, whether anti-Nature, like Meiri or Schwarzschild, or moderately or radically affirming of the value of Nature, like Caro or Berdichevski. This assumption results in an either-or, black-and-white worldview; it allows only for a pat acceptance of the *peshat* (in this case, the surface, literal meaning) of the mishna, or a Berdichevskian rejection, leading to the establishment of an opposite, but equally alienating hierarchy of values.

As Jews, whether in the Diaspora or in the Land of Israel, we cannot *mafsik mi-mishnato,* turn our backs on the texts, or cease to define ourselves in terms of them; an *exclusively* nature-based identity is not a Jewish identity. But neither can we afford any longer to accept the dichotomizing of the world and of our own souls. This third interpretation consciously negates that assumption, and proposes a competing version of the *peshat* based on synthesis.

Yes, if in order to relate to the natural environment you have to cease your learning, then your soul is in grave danger. This, then, is the sin that is castigated here: the radical rupture between Torah and Nature, the traditional, Diaspora-Jewish incommensurability of Creation and Revelation. What is called for today is *synthesis,*[40] a supreme effort to mend that gap, to forge a common language for our disparate forms of religious experience.

One who perpetuates this dichotomy, this spiritual feud, is in truth risking great spiritual, and physical harm. But one who walks by the way, engaged in Torah thoughts, and who *mimshikh be-mishnato,* "continues that study," seeing the beautiful tree, and the field, and our relationship to them, as an extension, as an expansion, of that study, that person will have performed a great act of *tikkun* (repair): *tikkun ha'olam,* of the World, and *tikkun hanefesh,* of our (previously endangered) souls.

References

Albeck, H., and H. Yalon. *Shishah Sidre Mishna.* (In Hebrew) 6 vols. Jerusalem: Bialik Institute; Tel Aviv: Dvir, 1952–56.

Berdichevski, Micha Yosef. "In Two Directions." Quoted in *The Zionist Idea,* ed. Arthur Hertzberg. New York: JPS, 1959; Atheneum, 1972, pp. 296–97.

Blackman, Philip, ed. And trans. *Mishnayoth.* New York: Judaica Press, 1977.

Bulka, Reuven. *As a Tree by the Waters: Pirkey Avoth: Psychological and Philosophical Insights. Jerusalem:* Feldheim, 1980.

Bunim, Irving. *Ethics from Sinai.* 3 vols. Jerusalem: Feldheim, 1964.

Caro, Yosef Chayyim ben Yitzchak. *Minchat Shabbat (Solet LeMincha).* (In Hebrew) Commentary to *Pirke Avot.* Krotoshin, 1847.

Cohen, I., and B. Y. Michali, eds. *An Anthology of Hebrew Essays.* Tel Aviv: Massada Publishers, 1966.

Danby, Herbert. "Chapters of the Fathers." In *The Mishna.* Oxford: Clarendon Press, 1933, pp. 446–61.

Goldin, Judah, ed. *The Living Talmud.* New Haven: Yale University Press, 1955.

Herford, R. Travers. *The Ethics of the Talmud: The Sayings of the Fathers.* New York: Schocken, 1945/1962.

Hertz, Joseph. *Sayings of the Fathers.* New York: Behrman, 1945.

Hirsch, Samson Raphael. *Chapters of the Fathers,* trans. Gertrude Hirschler. Jerusalem: Feldheim, 1967.

Hoffer, Eric. *The True Believer.* New York: Harper, 1951.

Israelstam, J., ed. and trans. *Soncino Talmud: Aboth.* London: Soncino, 1935.

Kravitz, Leonard, and Kerry Olitzky, eds. and trans. *Pirke Avot: A Modern Commentary on Jewish Ethics.* New York: UAHC Press, 1993.

Maharil, Aharon Shelomo Katriel., *Pirkei Avot HaOlam HaKadmonim.* (In Hebrew) Jerusalem, 1929.

Me'am Loez. R. Yitzchak Magriso, ed. R. Aryeh Kaplan, trans. David Barocas. New York: Moznaim Publ., 1990.

Neusner, Jacob. *The Mishna: A New Translation.* New Haven: Yale University Press, 1988.

Neusner, Jacob. *Torah From Our Sages: Pirkei Avot.* New York: Rossel Books, 1984.

Schwarzschild, Steven S. "The Unnatural Jew." *Environmental Ethics* 6(1984): 347–362.

Shtal, Avraham. *Pirkei Avot.* (In Hebrew) Tel Aviv: HaKibbutz HaMe'uchad, 1975.

Siddur Sim Shalom, A Prayerbook for Shabbat, Festivals, and Weekdays, ed. Rabbi Jules Harlow. Rabbinical Assembly, 1989. *Pirkei Avot* (pp. 602–665) trans. Rabbi Max J. Routtenberg.

Taylor, Charles. *Sayings of the Jewish Fathers.* New York: KTAV, 1969 (reprint). Originally published in 1897.

Wyschogrod, Michael. "Judaism and the Sanctification of Nature," *The Melton Journal,* no. 24 (Spring 1991): 5, 7.

Ya'avetz (Jabez), Yosef. *Perush LePirkei Avot,* ed. Eliezer Avraham Layzer. (In Hebrew) Machon Ma'oz, 1970.

Yalkut Me'am Lo'ez, R. Yitzchak Magriso, trans. Shemuel Yerushalmi from Ladino into Hebrew. Jerusalem: Wagschel Publ., 1972.

Spiraling into the Future: Sources for Learning and Doing

Imagine that for the next seven generations Jews keep wrestling with God and each other to shape an ever-evolving Torah that can help heal the wounds between *adam* and *adamah*.

As we move into that puzzling future, we will keep learning from historians and biologists, prophetic activists and gentle river guides, farmers and rabbis—from all who have journeyed amongst us these four millennia.

Many of the voices in this book will continue in that conversation, and many others are joining it.

So for me to name those who have helped me birth this book is a statement not about the past, but about the future. I intend to keep consulting these people, working with these organizations, learning these teachings. I urge others to do the same.

This book took its first shape in the process of birthing another anthology—*Trees, Earth, and Torah: A Tu B'Shvat Anthology.* In a way, these two are twins brought forth from a single womb of work—not hostile twins like Jacob and Esau, but friendly like Zerach and Peretz. My co-laborers in that first birthing were Ellen Frankel, Naomi Mara Hyman, and Ari Elon.

But the maturation and birth of the second twin took months more, and a different team of midwives gathered to help birth it—a team brought together by Jewish Lights. First, Stuart Matlins was drawn to the seed of possibility, the glimmer of a new bookshelf in down-to-earth Jewish spirituality as this volume got to stand alongside Ellen Bernstein's *Ecology & the Jewish Spirit*—and possibly, someday, others. Rabbi David Sulomm Stein, as the editor's editor, very much improved these pages with penetrating and persistent questions. Sandra Korinchak took on two tasks: first inviting me to explore new ways of unfolding and connecting these varied essays, and then pulling together all the threads of words, graphics, machines, paper, and people into a book. For me, it was a delight to have her join in the weaving.

Long before I focused on these two anthologies, I was taking part in the swirl of eco-Jewish conversation that began in the early 1970s. I learned with and from all those Jews who committed themselves to healing the relationship between *adam* and *adamah,* the earth and human earthlings. Ellen Bernstein, Barak Gale, Rabbi Everett Gendler, Mark Jacobs, Naomi Steinberg, and Mike Tabor have brought both prescience and perseverance to this work. Among the network of eco-Jewish advocates who have been crucial to me over the years are Rabbi Arthur Green, De Herman, Rabbi Margaret Holub, Rabbi Myriam Klotz, Rabbi Mordechai Liebling, John Ruskay, Rabbi David Saperstein, Rabbi Zalman Schachter-Shalomi, Rabbi David Seidenberg, Rabbi Steve Shaw, Cantor David Shneyer, and Rabbi Dan Swartz.

Since the administrative support of ALEPH: Alliance for Jewish Renewal and The Shalom Center was crucial to the completion of this book, I owe special thanks to Rabbi Daniel Siegel, rabbinic director of ALEPH, Susan Saxe, its chief operating officer, and Annette Epps, its office manager; to those who have been staff for The Shalom Center for some period during the last few years—Miryam Levy, Abby Weinberg, Laurie Schwartz, Rachel Gurevitz, Erika Kotske, and for work on this book especially to Doug Heifetz; and to the Rita Poretsky Foundation, The Shefa Fund, the Nathan Cummings Foundation, the Righteous Persons Foundation, the Alan B. Slifka Foundation, the Dorot Foundation, the Walter and Elise Haas Fund, the Fabrangen Tzedakah Collective, and hundreds of ALEPH and Shalom Center members for their support of The Shalom Center.

In all my work and all my rest, I learn from my beloved co-author, co-davvener, co-storyteller, co-parent, friend, and life-partner: Phyllis Ocean Berman.

ECO-JEWISH
ORGANIZATIONS

In the United States, from year to year, a growing number of organizations and publications provide further information about Judaism and the earth.

Broadest among these is an umbrella organization, the **Coalition on the Environment and Jewish Life (COEJL),** 443 Park Ave. South, New York, NY 10016; (212) 684-6950 x 210, e-mail COEJL@aol.com; or info@coejl.org; website www.coejl.org.

COEJL works under the direction of representatives of the Jewish Theological Seminary, the Religious Action Center of Reform Judaism, and the Jewish Council on Public Affairs. Its sponsors include almost all the national Jewish organizations in the United States.

COEJL works on legislative advocacy, liturgical materials keyed to the Jewish calendar, guides to eco-sensitive living, and conferences of Jewish communal leaders, rabbis, and theologians, and annual training institutes for eco-activists. It has a growing number of local and regional affiliates. Rather than try to list these, we urge people to check with COEJL for such contacts.

COEJL sponsors an e-mail discussion group. People can join by writing listserv@jtsa.edu with the message: <sub kol-chai FirstName LastName>.

It also sponsors an advocacy network and a news distribution list. Sign up to the first by writing the same address as before, but with the message <sub COEJLAction FirstName LastName> and to the second at the same address with the message <sub L-COEJLNews FirstName LastName>.

COEJL is itself part of a broader coalition, the National Religious Partnership on the Environment, website www.nrpe.org. In the larger grouping, other components are the U.S. Catholic Conference, the National Council of Churches, and the Evangelical Environmental Network.

- **The Shalom Center,** 6711 Lincoln Drive, Philadelphia, PA 19119; (215) 844-8494; e-mail shalomctr@aol.com; website www.shalomctr.org. The Shalom Center is especially interested in developing theology and eco-kosher life-practice adequate to the present ecological crisis; in bringing together the next generation of Jews who seek to heal the earth and society; in applying Jewish communal ethics to encourage corporations to act responsibly; and in working with other religious and spiritual communities to end the pressure for overwork that now ravages the earth, shatters regional economies and cultures, disheartens neighborhoods, stresses families, and exhausts individuals.

The Shalom Center sponsors an e-mail discussion group, "Jews Renewing Justice" (JRJ-Net@shamash.org), for those involved in Jewish action for social justice, eco-sanity, corporate responsibility, peace, and community-building. People can join by writing Rabjeff@echonyc.com.

- **Shomrei Adamah,** one of the earliest Jewish earth-oriented groups, is now mainly a support group for **Teva Learning Center,** 50 W. 17th St., 7th Floor, New York, NY 10011; (212) 807-6376; e-mail tevacenter@aol.com. Teva is especially concerned with teaching environmental ethics to young Jews, integrating direct outdoor experience with Torah.
- **Yetziah/Jewish Wilderness Journeys** is housed at Camp Isabella Friedman, 116 Johnson Rd., Falls Village, CT 06031; (860) 824-5991; e-mail yetziah@aol.com. It specializes in river and other wilderness trips that integrate Torah study with nature experience.
- **Center for Tikkun Olam,** 90 West 31st Ave., Eugene, OR 97405; e-mail YHH@aol.com. It is pursuing the creation of an ongoing guide to eco-kosher living.
- **Shalom Nature Center** offers day and residential Jewish environmental education and nature programs to Jewish day schools, households, organizations, and students. 34342 Mulholland Hwy., Malibu, CA 90265; (818) 874-1101; e-mail Shalom_Nature_Center@jcc-gla.org or Josh_Lake@jcc-gla.org; websites www.shalomnaturecenter.org and www.shalominstitute.com.

In the United Kingdom, the **Noah Project,** P.O. Box 1828, London W10 5RT, UK; e-mail environmentally.sound@virgin.net. Promotes environmental awareness and responsibility in the Jewish community through Jewish education, celebration, and action.

In Canada, there is a nascent eco-Jewish group called **Eco-Jews,** c/o Shai

Spetgang, 1057 Steeles Ave. W., Suite 736, Toronto, Ontario M2R 3X1, Canada; (905) 882-7493; e-mail shai@idirect.ca.

In Israel, the most important environmental groups are:

- **Society for the Preservation of Nature in Israel** *(Haganat Hateva)*, 4 Hashfela St., Tel Aviv 66183; for hikes and trails, 03-638-8677; for environmental action, 03-375-063; with an American affiliate at 28 Arrandale Ave., Great Neck, NY 11024; (212) 398-6750; e-mail aspni@aol.com.

- **Israel Union for Environmental Defense** *(Adam Teva v'Din)*, 317 HaYarkon St., Tel Aviv 63504; 03-546-8099. IUED is an active legal support and challenge center for neighborhoods and towns whose ecosystems are being endangered.

- **Jewish National Fund** *(Keren Kayemet l'Yisrael)*, with an American affiliate at 42 E. 69th St., New York, NY; (212) 879-9300. JNF has made tree planting in Israel one of its major programs. It has been criticized by some other Israeli environmentalists for allegedly doing this in a way that contradicts eco-sensitive requirements.

- **Heschel Center for Environmental Learning and Leadership,** Yavneh 1, Tel Aviv, 03-620-1806; e-mail heschel@netvision.net.il. Does eco-theology, applying Torah to issues of the earth.

- **Arava Institute for Environmental Studies,** Kibbutz Ketura, DN. Hevel Eilot, 88840, Israel; 02-735-6666; e-mail arava@netvision.net.il. Regional center for conservation and environmental protection activities; accredited program in environmental studies (taught in English).

- **EcoPeace: Middle East Environmental NGO Forum,** P.O. Box 55302, East Jerusalem, 97400, via Israel; 02-626-0841; e-mail ecopeace@netvision.net.il. Egyptians, Israelis, Jordanians, and Palestinians working together to promote ecologically sound development in the Middle East through research, education, and advocacy.

- **Neot Kedumim,** P.O. Box 1007, Lod, 71100, Israel; 08-233-3840. Nature reserve dedicated to restoring the flora and fauna of biblical Israel; publications.

SUGGESTIONS FOR FURTHER READING

Several books have appeared in recent years to address eco-Jewish concerns:

- Evan Eisenberg, *The Ecology of Eden* (Knopf, 1998). A magisterial examination of the relationship between the actual down-to-earth eco-geography of Israelite life, the evolution of biblical values and teachings about the earth, and the meaning of these for the contemporary ecological crisis.
- Ellen Bernstein, ed., *Ecology & the Jewish Spirit: Where Nature and the Sacred Meet* (Jewish Lights, 1997). Includes essays on how a number of individual Jews have been awakened to and responded to a sense of healing the earth as an aspect of Jewish life and thought.
- Ari Elon, Naomi Mara Hyman, and Arthur Waskow, eds., *Trees, Earth, and Torah: A Tu B'Shvat Anthology* (Jewish Publication Society, 1999). Since Tu B'Shvat, both in ancient days and the last century, has been intimately connected with trees and the earth, almost all the texts and essays in this collection are useful in exploring, past, present, and future.
- Marge Piercy, *He, She and It* (Knopf, 1991). A novel set alternately in the Prague of the famous Golem and in the late twenty-first century (in the newly independent Jewish city-state of Tikva, located on the hills where Boston used to be before global warming), which addresses at political, psychological, and spiritual levels the dangers of out-of control technology and the possibility of a humane technology.
- Richard H. Schwartz, *Judaism and Global Survival* (Atara, 1987).
- Arthur Waskow, *Down-to-Earth Judaism: Food, Money, Sex, and the Rest of Life* (Morrow, 1995). Looks at a number of Jewish life-path issues with special regard to the effects of the earth-human relationship.

- Matt Biers-Ariel, Deborah Newbrun, and Michal Fox Smart, *Spirit in Nature: A Jewish Hikers' Trail Guide* (Behrman House, 2000).
- Arthur Waskow, *Godwrestling—Round 2* (Jewish Lights, 1996). Puts forward a Torah-rooted theology of eco-Judaism.
- Arthur Waskow, *Seasons of Our Joy* (Beacon, 1982; 1990). Views the cycle of Jewish festivals in part as an attunement to the spiritual meaning of the sun-moon-earth cycles.
- Phyllis O. Berman and Arthur Waskow, *Tales of Tikkun: New Jewish Stories to Heal the Wounded World* (Jason Aronson, 1997). Includes "The Rest of Creation," "The Return of Captain Noah," and several other stories with eco-Jewish themes.
- David E. Stein, ed., *A Garden of Choice Fruit: 200 Classic Jewish Quotes on Human Beings and the Environment*. Available from Shomrei Adamah (see "Eco-Jewish Organizations").
- Louis I. Rabinowitz, *Torah and Flora* (Sanhedrin Press, 1979).
- Nogah Hareuveni, *Tree and Shrub in Our Biblical Heritage* (1984). Order from Neot Kedumim (see "Eco-Jewish Organizations").
- Roger Gottlieb, ed., *This Sacred Earth: Religion, Nature, Environment* (Routledge, 1995).
- *Judaism and Ecology,* a study guide produced by Hadassah and Shomrei Adamah. Available from Dept. of Jewish Education, Hadassah, 50 W. 58th St., New York, NY 10019.
- Ellen Bernstein and Dan Swartz, eds., *Let the Earth Teach You Torah.* Available from Shomrei Adamah (see preceding "Eco-Jewish Organizations").
- Martin D. Yaffe, ed., *Judaism and Environmental Ethics* (Lexington Books, 2000).
- In preparation: A series called "Torah Universe" by Noson Slifkin; Targum Press (distributed by Feldheim Publishers).
- *Operation Noah,* two pamphlets on biodiversity and protection of endangered species from a Jewish standpoint—one on contemporary science, action, and program ideas; the other on Jewish texts and sources. Available from COEJL (see "Eco-Jewish Organizations").

There are two excellent handbooks for action in Jewish communities:

- *To Till and to Tend,* published by COEJL (see "Eco-Jewish Organizations").
- *The Green Shalom Guide,* ed. Naomi Friedman and De Fischler.

Available from Washington Area Shomrei Adamah, 706 Erie Ave., Takoma Park, MD 20912; (301) 587-7535.

Special issues of several journals, as well as several videos, have addressed these questions:

- *Melton Journal* of the Melton Center at Jewish Theological Seminary (Spring 1991 and Spring 1992).
- *Conservative Judaism* (Fall 1991).
- *Palestine-Israel Journal* (vol. V, no. 1, 1998), P.O. Box 19839, Jerusalem; 972-2-6282-115; e-mail pij@palnet.com.
- *CCAR Journal* (Winter 2000).
- "Visions of Eden: A Jewish Perspective on the Environment" (1997, VHS, 60 minutes). Documentary on Judaism and ecology produced by the Jewish Theological Seminary, COEJL, and ABC Television. The program follows a group of Jewish leaders, including rabbis and leading environmentalists on an overnight backpacking journey along the Appalachian Trail. JTS Communications Office, (212) 678-8020.
- "The Earth Is the Lord's" (VHS, 60 minutes). Jewish Theological Seminary of America. For all ages. Tells the Creation story and the importance of protecting all of God's creatures.
- "Keeping the Earth" (1996, VHS, 27 minutes). National Religious Partnership for the Environment (NRPE)/Union of Concerned Scientists (UCS). Narrated by James Earl Jones. Middle school–adult. Prominent religious leaders and scientists. Order from UCS, 2 Brattle Sq., Cambridge, MA 02238-9105; (617)547-5552.
- "Green Borders," on several eco-sensitive Israeli kibbutzim and some Palestinian contacts, by Ramona Rubin, 200 Thayer Rd., Santa Cruz, CA 95060; e-mail monamoon26@hotmail.com.

NOTES

PART 1
Biblical Israel

Evan Eisenberg, "The Mountain and the Tower: Wilderness and City in the Symbols of Babylon and Israel"

This paper is adapted from several chapters of my book, *The Ecology of Eden* (New York: Knopf, 1998), in which interested readers will find my argument refined and expanded. I thank Yochanan Muffs, Joel Kaminsky, Daniel Hillel, Ellen Bernstein, and Paul Sanford, as well as my editors Daniel Frank and Jon Beckmann, for reading this material in various forms. The errors that remain are my own.

Unless otherwise noted, translations of biblical passages are from Max L. Margolis, ed., *The Holy Scriptures According to the Masoretic Text,* trans. Marcus Jastrow et al. (rev. ed., Philadelphia: Jewish Publication Society, 1955).

1. On the geography and ecology of the ancient Mediterranean and Near East, see Ellen Churchill Semple, *The Geography of the Mediterranean Region; Its Relation to Ancient History* (New York: Holt, 1931); Yohanan Aharoni, *The Land of the Bible: A Historical Geography,* trans. and ed. A. F. Rainey (2nd ed., Philadelphia: Westminster, 1979); A. Reifenberg, *The Struggle Between the Desert and the Sown: The Rise and Fall of Agriculture in the Levant* (Jerusalem: Jewish Agency, 1955); Daniel Hillel, *Out of the Earth: Civilization and the Life of the Soil* (New York: Free Press, 1991); and the well-illustrated book by David Attenborough, *The First Eden: The Mediterranean World and Man* (Boston: Little, Brown, 1987).

2. Though I have borrowed the concept from Eliade (*Cosmos and History,* trans. Willard R. Trask [New York: Harper and Row, 1959], pp. 12ff.), I have chosen a cruder term than his *axis mundi*. Eliade, by the way, makes no distinction between "cosmic mountains" that are real mountains and "cosmic mountains" that are fakes. "The names of the Babylonian temples and sacred

towers themselves testify to their assimilation to the cosmic mountain," he writes, which is true enough as far as it goes.

For examples of World Mountains and other world-poles, see Eliade; E. A .S. Butterworth, *The Tree at the Navel of the Earth* (Berlin: de Gruyter, 1970); Joseph Campbell, *The Masks of God* (4 vols., New York: The Viking Press, 1959–69), vol. 1; as well as the splendidly illustrated book by Edwin Bernbaum, *Sacred Mountains of the World* (San Francisco: Sierra Club, 1990).

3. To avoid the political freight, as well as the imprecision in an ancient context, of such terms as Israel, Palestine, Syria, and Syro-Palestine, I use the most ancient name for the region that still means something to modern ears. Several thousand years of bad press in Hebrew and Latin sources have helped keep the Canaanites, and their cousins the Phoenicians and Carthaginians, from getting the serious study they deserve. For general treatments, see Donald B. Harden, *The Phoenicians* (rev. ed., Harmondsworth, U.K.: Penguin, 1980); John Gray, *The Canaanites* (London: Thames and Hudson, 1964): Emmanuel Anati, *Palestine Before the Hebrews* (New York: Knopf, 1963). Moscati, *The World of the Phoenicians,* trans. Alastair Hamilton (London: Weidenfeld and Nicolson, 1968). Canaanite texts are translated by H. L. Ginsburg in James B. Pritchard, ed., *Ancient Near Eastern Texts, Relating to the Old Testament* (3rd ed., with supplement, Princeton: Princeton University Press, 1969); short selections are translated, and discussed, by Frank Moore Cross, *Caananite Myth and Hebrew Epic* (Cambridge, Mass.: Harvard University Press, 1973) and Richard J. Clifford, *The Cosmic Mountain in the Old Testament* (Cambridge, Mass.: Harvard University Press, 1972).

4. Clifford, p. 68. Most extant Canaanite poems are found on clay tablets from Ugarit in northern Syria (the modern Ras Shamra) that date from about 1400 BCE. But the myths they relate may be far older. It now seems likely that the Canaanites were autochthonous—that they grew from the soil of Canaan. They were offspring of the first farmers in the region (the first in the world, as far as we know), probably of the first proto-farmers (the Natufians, whose villages were supported by the harvesting of wild grains), and possibly of the first modern humans. The seeds of the myths that bloomed so profusely in late Bronze Age Ugarit may have been planted by farmers of the late Stone Age. While the myths of Mesopotamia are far older in their written forms than those of Canaan, it seems likely that those of Canaan represent an older way of life.

For a more detailed consideration of Canaanite myth, see Eisenberg, chap. 7.

5. Donald O. Henry, *From Foraging to Agriculture: The Levant at the End of the Ice Age* (Philadelphia: University of Pennsylvania Press, 1989); William C. Brice,

ed., *The Environmental History of the Near and Middle East Since the Last Ice Age* (New York: Academic Press, 1978).

6. Ofer Bar-Yosef and Bernard Vandermeersch, "Modern Humans in the Levant," *Scientific American* 268, no. 4 (1993): 94–100. Creatures once dignified (if that is the word) with membership in the human race, and classified as archaic *H. sapiens* and *H. sapiens Neanderthalensis,* are now generally placed in separate species.

7. On the unpromising natural endowments of ancient Mesopotamia, see Hillel, chapter 11; Samuel Noah Kramer, *The Sumerians* (Chicago: University of Chicago Press, 1963). On ancient Mesopotamia generally, see Kramer, *The Sumerians* and *History Begins at Sumer* (New York: Doubleday, 1959); A. Leo Oppenheim, *Ancient Mesopotamia: Portrait of a Dead Civilization* (rev. ed., compl. Erica Reiner, Chicago: University of Chicago Press, 1977); Harriet E. W. Crawford, *Sumer and the Sumerians* (Cambridge: Cambridge University Press, 1991). Sumerian, Akkadian, and Babylonian texts are translated in Pritchard, as well as in the cited books by Kramer; Thorkild Jacobsen, *The Treasures of Darkness* (New Haven: Yale University Press, 1976); Clifford; Helmer Ringgren, *Religions of the Ancient Near East,* trans. John Sturdy (London, S.P.C.K., 1973), and Alexander Heidel, *The Babylonian Genesis* (2nd ed., Chicago: University of Chicago Press, 1951) and *The Gilgamesh Epic and Old Testament Parallels* (2nd ed., Chicago: University of Chicago press, 1949).

8. The best account of ancient Mesopotamian irrigation is in Hillel, *Out of the Earth,* chapter 11. See also Robert McCormick Adams and Hans J. Nissen, *The Uruk Countryside* (Chicago: University of Chicago Press, 1972).

9. "And, by the way, who estimates the value of the crop which Nature yields in the still wilder fields unimproved by man?" To the question posed by Thoreau in *Walden* ("The Bean-Field"), a first effort at an answer was recently made: a systematic attempt to estimate the annual economic value of the earth's (more or less) natural ecosystems. Though the researchers cast their net wide—taking in such varied things as recreation value, pollination services, forest timber, the effect of wetlands on shrimp harvests, and the role of the oceans in regulating atmospheric carbon dioxide—plenty of things slipped through, among them nonrenewable fuels and minerals and the merits of such relatively unstudied ecosystems as deserts, tundra, and urban parks. Despite its conservative assumptions, the study came up with an annual value of $33 trillion. By contrast, the GNPs of all nations on earth total about $18 trillion. In short, the Mountain has challenged the Tower on its home turf, economics, and bested it nearly two to one. See Robert Costanza et al., "The Value of the World's Ecosystem Services and Natural Capital," *Nature* 387 (1997): 253–60, as well as the comments by

Pimm in the same issue, pp. 231–32; see also Gretchen C. Daily, *Nature's Services* (Washington, D.C.: Island Press, 1997).

10. Hillel, p. 83. His account (chapter 11) of salinization in ancient Mesopotamia is both expert and readable.

11. Thorkild Jacobsen and Robert McC. Adams, "Salt and Silt in Ancient Mesopotamian Agriculture," *Science* 128 (1958): 1251–58. First proposed by Jacobsen and Adams in 1958, the theory has intermittently been attacked (for example, by M. A. Powell, "Salt, Seed and Yields in Sumerian Agriculture: A Critique of the Theory of Progressive Salinization," *Zeitschrift der Assyrologie* 75 [1985]: 7–38) and defended (for example, by Michal Artzy and Daniel Hillel, "A Defense of the Theory of Progressive Soil Salinization in Ancient Southern Mesopotamia," *Geoarchaeology* 3, no. 3 [1988]: 235–38) in the years since. What is in question is not the fact that salinization occurred, but whether Mesopotamian farmers had effective methods to arrest, reverse, or soften its effects. Most recently, the trend has been to explain the vicissitudes of farming in various parts of Mesopotamia, and the attendant fates of cities and empires, in terms of climate change: see, for example, H. Weiss et al., "The Genesis and Collapse of Third Millennium North Mesopotamian Civilization," *Science* 261 (1993): 995–1004. While no single factor can explain the whole course of Mesopotamian history, my own (lay) hunch is that salinization played a major role.

12. For a reading of various Mesopotamian myths and epics that brings out their ecological significance—linking, for example, the Sumerian poem "Enki and Ninhursag" to the problem of soil salinization—see Eisenberg, chap. 11. And see chap. 27 of that book to correct the impression I may have given here that I am somehow opposed to cities. To summarize my later conclusions:

> It is easy to chide the Mesopotamians for making the city the world-pole, yet it was a necessary step. They would not have been able to do the remarkable things they did if they had not been able to abstract human culture from nature to some degree. The same can be said of the Western civilization they helped shape. To view human culture as having its own logic, its own map, its own font and its own channels is both useful and true—up to a point. If a child does not assert its independence from its mother, it does not grow up. True independence may be an illusion but it is a useful one.
>
> Despite Arcadian cant, the city is not a place you must escape from if you want to live a fully human life. Cities are natural.

Even their unnaturalness is natural, for it springs from our nature and (if kept within bounds) can meet our quirky needs without doing nature too much harm. And it turns out that the Tower, which figures in this essay as a bastard pretender and enemy of the Mountain, can be its best friend and staunchest defender. Ideally, it concentrates both the warm bodies of humans and their steamy cultural energies in a small, bounded, insulated place, so that wild nature need not take the heat.

13. In the first half of the twentieth century the German school of Alt and Noth predominated: this school denied the historicity of the Bible, and spoke of gradual infiltration of Canaan by seminomadic tribes, which in time formed a loose confederation. About mid-century a counterattack was led by Albright and the more radical Kaufmann, who propped up the patriarchal stories, and those of the conquest of Canaan, with sherds and other evidence newly unearthed. In the last couple of decades the winds have shifted yet again, with Dever, van Seters, Gottwald, and Mendenhall, among others, placing the Israelites more firmly in a Canaanite context. (Mendenhall goes farthest, making the Israelites out to be downtrodden peasants of wholly native origin.) For a clear presentation of this general approach, see Robert B. Coote, *Early Israel: A New Horizon* (Minneapolis: Fortress Press, 1990).

   On the ecology and husbandry of ancient Israel, see Yohanan Aharoni, *The Land of the Bible: A Historical Geography,* trans. and ed. A. F. Rainey (2nd ed., Philadelphia: Westminster, 1979); David C. Hopkins, *The Highlands of Canaan: Agricultural Life in the Early Iron Age* (Sheffield, England: Almond, 1985); Oded Borowski, *Agriculture in Iron Age Israel* (Winona Lake, Ind.: Eisenbrauns, 1987); Reifenberg; Hillel; and the eccentric but interesting works of Nogah Hareuveni, founder of the biblical landscape garden Ne'ot Kedumim.

14. On Eden as the Mountain of God, see Jon Levenson, *Theology of the Program of Restoration of Ezekiel 40–48* (Cambridge, Mass.: Scholars Press, 1976) and *Sinai and Zion* (San Francisco: Harper and Row, 1985).

15. This was the received opinion in Philo's day, though Philo himself was unconvinced. "Questions and Answers on Genesis," cited by Frank E. Manuel, Fritzie P. Manuel, *Utopian Thought in the Western World* (Cambridge, Mass.: Harvard University Press, 1979), p. 43. Those modern scholars, such as Speiser and Zarins, who take the four rivers to be tributaries, and situate the Garden at the point where their joined waters debouch—that is, at the head of the Persian Gulf—have the weight of ancient tradition against them.

16. See Daniel Hillel, *Rivers of Eden: The Struggle for Water and the Quest for Peace in the Middle East* (New York: Oxford University Press, 1994).

17. Louis Ginzberg, *The Legends of the Jews,* trans. Henrietta Szold and Paul Radin (7 vols., Philadelphia: Jewish Publication Society, 1909–38), vol. I., p. 70; Josephus Antiquitates Judaicae 1.39; Rashi ad loc.

18. True, the word *midbar,* when used to mean "desert"—an arid or desolated place—is sometimes set in opposition to Eden; but to conclude from this (as, for example, Roderick Nash does in *Wilderness and the American Mind* [3rd ed., New Haven: Yale University Press, 1982]) that Eden and wilderness in the more general sense are opposites in Hebrew thought is a misunderstanding.

19. W.H.I. Bleek and L. C. Lloyd, *Specimens of Bushman Folklore* (London: George Allen, 1911), pp. 54ff.

20. By "the Fall of Man" I mean the expulsion from Eden; there is no reference to the concept of original sin.

21. Gesenius, the great nineteenth-century Hebraist, notes that *avur* can also mean "produce" or "yield" (cf. Joshua 5:11f). Thus the phrase might be read, "Cursed is the ground in (i.e., with respect to) thy produce"; or, more intriguing for our purposes, "Cursed is the ground by thy produce."

22. My translation. There are, of course, many other licit interpretations of the two Hebrew words. Among the more interesting is Cassuto's: he makes *l'ovdah* refer to "divine service" (following *Bereshith Rabbah* 16:5: "These denote sacrifices"). And he makes *l'shomrah* refer to the task of guarding, which was formerly (in Babylonian tradition and the lost epic tradition to which Ezekiel alludes) that of the cherubim—to whom it reverts when Adam is expelled.

23. On the tangled web of writ and legend that connects Sinai, Zion, and Eden, see Raphael Patai, *Man and Temple in Ancient Jewish Myth and Ritual* (2nd ed., enl., New York: Ktav, 1967); Levenson; Clifford.

24. Source criticism of the Pentateuch teases its rough weave into five strands: J, the Yahwist; E, the Elohist; P, the Priestly source; D, the Deuteronomist; and R, the Redactor, who also did the weaving. For a fine summary of recent thinking about who these authors were, when they wrote, and why they wrote what they wrote, see Richard Elliot Friedman, *Who Wrote the Bible?* (New York: Summit Books, 1987).

25. *Midrash Hashem Bekokhma Yasad Arets,* Jellinek 5:63; *Yoma* 54b; *Tanhuma: Kedoshim* 10. See Levenson, *Sinai and Zion,* p. 118.

26. It should be noted that Mt. Horeb plays the role in the E and D sections of the Bible that Sinai plays in J and P.

27. The word for wilderness, *midbar,* has been related to the root *dbr,* "to speak."

The Midrash comments, "Whoever does not make himself like a wilderness, open to everything, will not be able to acquire wisdom and Torah" (*Bemidbar Rabbah* 1:7).

28. How exactly this might have jibed with the biennial fallow common in the ancient Near East is something of a puzzle: see Hopkins.

29. By far the least famous of these figures, Marshall is by no means the least noteworthy. A New York Jew—son of the jurist and Jewish leader Louis Marshall—he became a botanist, a devout backpacker, founder of the Wilderness Society, forestry official under Franklin Roosevelt, and architect of wilderness protection in America. A great wilderness in Alaska bears his name.

30. Alexander von Humboldt, *Cosmos,* trans. E. C. Otte (2 vols., London: George Bell, 1886), vol. 2, pp. 411–13.

31. *Iliad* 1.5.

32. See, for instance, *Abot de Rabbi Nathan* (Schechter) 46a; *Midrash Tehillim* 19: 2; and even the dyed-in-the-wool rationalist Maimonides (*The Guide of the Perplexed,* pt. I, chap. 72). See also Patai, *Man and Temple* and *The Hebrew Goddess* (3rd ed., enl., Detroit: Wayne State University Press, 1990).

Tikva Frymer-Kensky,
"Ecology in a Biblical Perspective"

1. Lynn White, Jr., "The Historical Roots of Our Ecologic Crisis," *Science* 155 (1967).

2. See, e.g., Jeanne Kay, "Concepts of Nature in the Hebrew Bible," *Environmental Ethics* 10:4 (1988): 309–27, and recently J. Baird Callicott, "Genesis Revisited: Murian Musings on Lynn White, Jr. Debate," *Environmental History Review* 14:1–2 (1990): 65–90.

3. This copy of the *Atrahasis Epic* was published by Lambert and Millard, Cuneiform *Texts from Babylonian Tablets in the British Museum,* XLVII, 2965. Lambert and Millard published the edition and English translation in *Atrahasis: the Babylonian Story of the Flood* (Oxford, 1969).

4. Moran constructed the text differently, understanding the "one god" in the tablet who instigates the rebellion not as "a god," but as a specific god, whose name may have been in a break, and who is identical to the god We-ilum, who was killed in the creation of humankind. See William Moran "The Creation of Man in Atrahasis I, 192–248" BASOR 200 (1970): 48–56.

5. For Moran, it is not "a god" but "the god"; instead of "one who has sense" he translates "the one who had the plan."

6. For a study of these wordplays, see Steven Geller, "Some Sound and Word

Plays in the First Tablet of the Old Babylonian *Atrahasis Epic*," in *The Frank Talmage Memorial Volume I,* ed. Barry Wahlfish (Haifa University Press, 1993), pp. 137–44.

7. In the Sumerian King List (ed. Thorkild Jacobsen, *Assyriological Studies* II), the kings before the flood had reigns into the thousands of years; after the flood, their reigns were more normal.

8. Jacob Klein, "The 'Bane' of Humanity: A Lifespan of One Hundred Twenty Years," *Acta Sumerologica* 12 (1990): 57–70.

9. This is not the view of Genesis 2, where the earth is barren until humanity is created. Genesis 2 is a farmers' myth, Genesis 1 is not.

10. Or "this one will give us rest," reading the Hebrew word as *yenihemenu,* which would conform to the Greek, as the standard *yenahamenu,* "will comfort us," also matches the Greek, for the technical use of the word *nhm* means to have release from work-bondage. However, since Noah's name is not Nahum, "give us rest" fits his name better.

11. See Tikva Frymer-Kensky, "The Atrahasis Epic and its Significance for Our Understanding Genesis 1–9," *Biblical Archaeologist* 40 (1977): 147–55.

12. For a further discussion of the nature of human responsibility, see Tikva Frymer-Kensky, *In the Wake of the Goddesses* (Macmillan, 1992), pp. 83–107 and 243–49.

13. The closest rite is the ritual of the decapitated heifer, performed when a corpse is discovered and the murderer cannot be found. This ritual seeks to prevent the pollution from settling in; once it does, nothing can remove it and it builds up until it reaches a critical mass. For further understanding of this concept of pollution, see Tikva Frymer-Kensky, "Pollution, Purification and Purgation in Biblical Israel," in *The Word of the Lord Shall Go Forth: Essays in Honor of David Noel Freedman,* ed. Carol Meyers and Michael O'Connor, (Winona Lake, Ind.: Eisenbrauns, 1983), pp. 399–414.

PART 2:
Rabbinic Judaism

Norman Lamm, "Ecology in Jewish Law and Theology"

1. *The New York Times,* May 1, 1970.
2. Gen. 1:29: "And God said: 'Behold, I have given you every herb yielding

seed which is upon the earth, and every tree in which is the fruit of a tree yielding seed—to you shall it be *for food.*'"

3. Ibid., 9:2–6.

4. Ibid., 3: 15–19.

5. Ibid., 4:12.

6. Ibid., 6:11–12. Alternatively, the last phrase may be translated "I will destroy them *from* the earth" (see Rashi), both implying the reciprocity between man and nature.

7. Isa. 11:6–9.

8. Exod. 23:29–30, and see Deut. 7:22 and II Kings 17:25.

9. See Deut. 23:13–15. This has been brought to my attention in a paper by Eric Freudenstein, since published in *Judaism,* Fall 1970, who also points to air pollution legislation in the early talmudic period. The Mishnah (*B.B.* 2:8, 9) prohibits establishment of a permanent threshing floor within fifty cubits of the city limits, because the chaff borne by the wind may jeopardize the health of the city dwellers. Similarly, animal carcasses may not be deposited and tanneries and cemeteries not set up, within the same distance of the city.

10. For illustrations of the Halakhah's insights into the nature of Sabbath rest, see Lamm, *Faith & Doubt* (Hoboken, N.J.: KTAV, 1971), ch. 7; on the Kabbalistic conception of the Sabbath, see Lamm, *Faith & Doubt,* ch. 2.

11. *Tamid,* end.

12. Lev. 19:19. The verse begins with the admonition, "Ye shall keep *hukotai,* My laws," upon which the Talmud (*Kid.* 39a) comments: "Laws which I have legislated in My world," implying that these laws protect the integrity of the world. See Ramban and Seforno and commentaries of Chief Rabbi Hertz and R. Samson Raphael Hirsch. Of the various forms of forbidden intermingling of species, only two are specifically prohibited to Noahides as well as Israelites—grafting branches of diverse species, and interbreeding livestock. The *kilayim* of garments, seeds, and vineyard are forbidden only to Israelites. *Sanh.* 56b; Maimonides, *Hil. Melakhim* 10:6.

13. Lev. 19:18.

14. *Shabbat* 53b.

15. Deut. 20:19, 20.

16. *Sefer Ha-hinnukh,* No. 529.

17. R. Yaakov Zvi Meklenburg, *Ha-Ketav Ve'ha-Kabbalah* to Deut. 20:19. He interprets the phrase *ki ha-adam etz ha-sadeh,* etc., not as above ("For is the tree of the field man that it should be besieged of thee?"), but as: "For as man, so is the tree of the field when it is besieged of thee," i.e., just as the enemy

who has surrendered and is willing to pay tribute must not be destroyed, so the fruit tree that gives you tribute (fruit) must not be cut down.

18. II Chron. 32:2–4,30.

19. *Pes.* 56a. See Rashi.

20. II Kings 3:17–20.

21. Commentary to the Mishnah, Introd. to *Seder Zera'im.*

22. *Shabbat* 77b.

23. *B.B.* 26a; *B.K.* 96b; *Mak.* 22a; Maimonides, *Hil. Melakhim* 6:8.

24. *Hil. Melakhim* 6:9.

25. Commentary to *B.K.* 91b.

26. Commentary on the Torah, to Deut. 20:20; supplement to Commentary on Maimonides' *Sefer Ha-mitzvot,* Pos. Com. # 6.

27. Indeed, Nahmanides *(ibid.)* appears to permit this too, considering it necessary destruction and hence justifiable; the prohibition is limited to unnecessary and pointless devastation.

28. Sifre to Deut. 20:19. Maimonides, *Hil. Melakhim* 6:8–9.

29. Maimonides, *Hil. Melakhim* 6:10. Apparently this passage implies that destruction of material other than fruit trees entails a Rabbinic violation, and so did most commentators read Maimonides. Earlier, however, in his *Sefer ha-Mitzvot,* Maimonides held that other objects were equally included in the biblical proscription. Others, too, hold that all objects are included in the biblical commandment, so *SeMaG, Sefer Yere'im,* and apparently *Sefer Ha-hinnukh. Minhat Hinnukh,* however, reads this passage in Maimonides to mean that *all* objects are covered by the biblical prohibition, but whereas the destruction of fruit trees takes flogging as a biblically prescribed penalty, because it is explicit, the ruining of other objects is forbidden by biblical law, but no punishment declared for it. Such punishment (flogging) is, however, ordained by Rabbinic decree.

30. See *Hullin* 7b; Tos *B.K.* 115b, s.v. *ve'lo yashkeh; Sh. A. Harav, Hil. Shemirat Guf Va'nefesh* 14.

31. *B.K.* 91b; Maimonides, *Hil. Melakhim* 6.

32. *B.K.* 92a; *Tzemach Tzeddek,* cited in *Pahad Yitzhak* on *Bal Tashchit.*

33. *Turei Zahav to SH.A.Y.D.* 116:6.

34. Responsa *Havot Yair,* no. 195.

35. *Shabbat* 140b. The reason given is not the usual one, namely, that danger to life cancels out most other obligations. Such a rationale would limit the dispensation to severe illness entailing danger to life. Rather, the Talmud reasons that *bal tashchit* applies to one's body as well as to one's possessions, indeed more so, and, therefore, it is preferable to harm a tree than one's health. This reasoning is not limited to critical illness.

36. *Yevamot* 44a.

37. Ibid. Cf. SeMaG, Neg. Com. 229.

38. Supra, n. 16.

39. Ibid. The source for this is B.B. 25b. Cf. Maimonides, Hil. Melakhim 6:9.

40. Supra, n. 28.

41. *Hazon Ish* to Maimonides, *Hil. Melakhim* 6:8.

42. *Sh. A. Harav, supra,* n. 30. However, a problem is posed by the commentary of R. Asher to *Middot* 1:2 (and *Tamid,* chap. I, end), who says that destruction of property countenanced by the law for disciplinary purposes is not in violation of *bal tashchit* because of the principle that the courts declare such property ownerless *(hefker bet din hefker).* This implies the reverse of the ruling of *Sh. A. Harav.* But see Responsa *Noda Bi'Yehudah,* II, *Y.D.* 10; and appendix to Responsa *Devar Avraham,* Part I.

43. *B.K.* 92b.

44. *B.K.* 89a.

45. Exod. 25.

46. *Exod. R.,* 35.

47. Supra, n. 33.

48. *Sefer Hasidim, Tzavaot R. Yehudah Ne-hasid,* 45, and gloss of R. Reuven Margoliot.

49. Cited in *The New York Times* report, *supra,* n. 1.

50. Isa. 6:3.

51. Cited in R. Shneur Zalman's *Shaar ha-Yihud ve'ha-Emunah,* chap. I. Cf. R. Shneur Zalman's teaching of divine immanence by equating the numerical value of the divine Name *Elohim* to *ha-teva,* nature.

52. Mishnah *Kelim* I:6.

53. See my article on the *Metzaref Avodah* in the Professor Joshua Finkel Festschrift (Yeshiva University, New York).

54. Gen. R. 68:10.

55. For further discussion on the question of monism–pluralism and the Halakhah, see Lamm, *Faith & Doubt,* ch. 2.

56. See, for instance, R. Elimelekh of Lizensk's *Noam Elimelekh, Hanhagot Ha-adam,* no. 20; and cf. chapter 2 of my book on the study of *Torah Lishmah* in the works of R. Hayyim of Volozhin, in English (Feldheim, New York), and in Hebrew (Mosad Harav Kook, Jerusalem).

57. R. Nahman of Bratzlav, *Likkutei MoHaRaN,* II, 12.

58. In *Tzavaat Ha-RiVaSH.*

59. *M. Tanhuma, Tazria.*

60. *Ber.* 35a.

61. *Sanh.* 38a.

62. See Nahmanides to Gen. 1:1.

63. *B.K.* 98b.

64. See Maimonides, *Hil. Mekbirah* 10:4.

65. *Tosefta, B.K.,* Chap. II.

66. On man's responsibility for his intellectual achievements, expressed as a law forbidding the scholar to destroy the records of his academic contributions, see R. Naftali Zevi Yehudah Berlin, Responsa *Meshiv Davar,* 1:24.

67. Gen. 2:15.

68. See the commentary of Benno Jacob, *Genesis,* to this verse. I am indebted to the paper of Mr. Eric Freudenstein for this reference.

Jonathan Helfand, "The Earth Is the Lord's: Judaism and Environmental Ethics"

1. Arnold Toynbee, "The Genesis of Pollution," *New York Times,* 16 September 1973, sec. 4. This essay was based on an article that appeared in *Horizon Magazine* at that time.

2. For an excellent sketch of the literature of the *halakhah,* see David M. Feldman, *Marital Relations, Birth Control, and Abortion in Jewish Law* (New York: Schocken Books, 1974), pp. 3–18.

3. George Foote Moore, *Judaism in the First Centuries of the Christian Era* (New York: Schocken Books, 1971), vol 1., pp. 161–63.

4. Ibid., vol. 2, p. 212.

5. Rabbi Samson Raphael Hirsch in his commentary to Psalms 5:3 and 31:6 emphasizes that the process of prayer entails self-cognition on the part of the worshipper.

6. *Tosefta, Berakhot,* 4:1.

7. Philip Birnbaum, ed., *Daily Prayer Book* (New York: Hebrew Publishers, 1977), pp. 773–75.

8. *Tanhuma, Berakha,* sec. 7. This theme is particularly stressed in the liturgy for New Year's Day, which, according to tradition, is not only the Day of Judgment, but also the anniversary of creation.

9. *Shabbat,* 77b.

10. *Kilayim,* 1:7. Cf. the tana'itic midrash to Leviticus, *Sifre.*

11. *Sefer Ha-hinukh,* no. 244. Maimonides, recognizing the source of this law in the "natural order," rules that this prohibition applies to gentiles as well in the cases of grafting and interbreeding. "Laws of Kings," *Mishneh Torah,* 10:6.

12. *Sefer Ha-hinukh,* no. 62.

13. *Shabbat,* 53b.

14. For a detailed discussion of these laws, see *"Bal tashchit,"* Encyclopedia Talmudit

(Jerusalem, 1963), 3: 335–37. Also see Jonathan I. Helfand, "Ecology and the Jewish Tradition," *Judaism* 20 (1971): 331–33.

15. See, for example, the commentary *Da'at Zekenim mi-ba'alei Ha-tosefot* to Deuteronomy 20:19.

16. "Laws of Kings," *Mishneh Torah* 6:8. See also the *Kesef Mishneh* (commentary to Maimonides, code): *Sefer Mitzvot Gadol* [= *SeMaG*], negative commandment no. 229; and Rabbi David Kimhi's commentary to 2 Kings 3:19.

17. *Bava Kama*, 91b. Some commentaries, however, interpret it as meaning "all trees."

18. *Shabbat*, 140b; *Kiddushin*, 32a; *Shabbat*, 129a; *Yevamot*, 11b. In the latter case the text reads: "A man should not pour the water out of his cistern while others may require it." The *SeMaG* interprets this as being based on the law of *bal tashchit*. On the question of the pollution of water resources, see Nahum Rackover, "Protection of the Environment in Hebrew Sources" [in Hebrew], *Dine Yisrael* 4 (1973): 18–19.

19. "*Hilkhot shmirat ha-guf ve-nefesh.*" *Shulhan Arukh Ha-rav*, par. 14.

20. The *Sifre* (a tana'itic midrash) to Deut. 10:19 includes the cutting off of water supplies to trees as a violation of the rule. See also Maimonides, "Laws of Kings," *Mishneh Torah* 6:8. Incomplete destruction is cited by the Talmud in *Kiddushin*, 32a (see Rashi) and *Bava Kama*, 91b.

21. *Sanhedrin* 108b.

22. Nahmanides, commentary to Deuteronomy 22:6. See also his comments in Leviticus 19:19 on the laws of *kilayim:* "He who mixes kinds denies and confounds the act of creation." These comments contrast with and undoubtedly modify his strong statements in Genesis 1:26, 28 regarding man's mastery over creation.

23. *Sefer Ha-hinukh*, nos. 194, 545.

24. *Shulhan Arukh, Orah Hayyim*, 233:6. On the Jewish attitude toward hunting and killing for sport, see Sidney B. Hoenig, "The Sport of Hunting: A Humane Game?" *Tradition* II, no. 3 (1970): 13–21.

25. *Bava Kama*, 79b and Rashi.

26. *Mishnah Tamid*, 2:3.

27. *Tamid*, 29b; Maimonides, "Laws of Things Banned from the Altar," *Mishneh Torah*, 7:3.

28. This principle is also invoked in numerous other instances. For a review of this literature, see the *Encyclopedia Talmudit* (Jerusalem, 1956) 2: 225–26.

29. Numbers 35:2–5.

30. "Laws of Sabbatical and Jubilee Years," *Mishneh Torah*, 13:5.

31. See the commentary of Rashi to Numbers 35:2 and to *Arakhin*, 33b.

32. *Encyclopedia Talmudit,* 2:226.

33. *Tur Hoshen Mishpat,* par. 175 (based on *Bava Metzi'ah,* folio 108b).

34. Ibid. See Bet Yosef (commentary of Rabbi Joseph Karo), no. 43, and the comments of *Prishah* to this paragraph in the *Tur.*

35. *She'ilat Ya'avetz,* pt. I, responsum 76.

36. Birnbaum, *Daily Prayer Book,* pp. 15, 51ff.

37. *Berakhot,* 43a.

38. *Tosefta, Bava Kama,* 10:2. Cf. *Bava Kama,* 50b.

39. *Pirkei Avot,* 4:21.

David Ehrenfeld and Philip J. Bentley, "Judaism and the Practice of Stewardship"

1. Even the ownership of family pets—dogs and cats—was, until recently, uncommon among both Ashkenazic and Sephardic households.

2. Norman A. Stillman, *The Jews of Arab Lands: A History and Source Book* (Philadelphia: Jewish Publication Society, 1979).

3. Satish Kumar, *No Destination* (Wales: The Black Pig Press, 1977).

4. David Ehrenfeld, *The Arrogance of Humanism* (New York: Oxford University Press, 1981).

5. Nahum Glatzer, ed., *A Jewish Reader* (New York: Schocken Books, 1961).

6. Trude Weiss-Rosmarin, *Judaism and Christianity: The Differences* (New York: Jonathan David, 1943).

7. Aldo Leopold, *A Sand County Almanac* (New York: Oxford University Press, 1966). See, especially, the essay on "A Land Ethic."

8. Compare this with E. F. Schumacher's similar statements about the necessity and divinity of work, in his essay on "Buddhist Economics" in *Small Is Beautiful* (New York: Harper & Row, 1973).

9. Richard Hirsch, "There Shall Be No Poor," in *Judaism and Human Rights,* ed. M. Konvitz, (New York: Norton, 1972).

10. Wendell Berry, in his brilliant essay, "The Gift of Good Land" (*Sierra Club Bulletin,* Nov.-Dec., 1979), actually defends both Jewish and Christian traditions against the charge of anti-environmentalism. One of the first and most comprehensive defenses of the Jewish position was by Robert Gordis, in an essay entitled "Judaism and the Spoliation of Nature" (*Congress Bi-weekly,* April 2, 1971, pp. 9–12). A more recent evaluation of the charge of anti-environmentalism has been given by Nigel Pollard, "The Israelites and Their Environment," *The Ecologist* 14, no. 3 (1984), 125–33, who has assembled many sources and, unlike Berry and Gordis, views the subject from an

entirely secular perspective—at least as far as Judaism is concerned. (See also the essay by Lamm, referenced in note 21.)

11. A. Cohen, ed., *The Soncino Chumash: The Five Books of Moses with Haphtoroth* (London: Soncino Press, 1947), p. 6.

12. Some commonly cited examples are Deuteronomy 10:14, Psalms 24:1–2, Job 19:26–27 and 40:15, 19 as well as Isaiah 47:10.

13. J. Goldin, ed. and trans., *The Living Talmud* (New York: Mentor, 1957).

14. The antiquity of this theme is demonstrated by its appearance in *Avot* 3:16 (attributed to Rabbi Akiva) a thousand years before Janah's time. That an association between the idea of stewardship and that of accountability to God is not unreasonable, is borne out, for example, by the talmudic midrash that Moses and David were not fit to be leaders of Israel until they, themselves, had been shepherds (*Talmud Yerushalmi, Kilayim* 9:3, 32a; *Bava Metzia* 85a).

15. H. Freedman, and M. Simon, eds. and trans., *Midrash Rabbah,* Vol. 8: *Ruth, Ecclesiastes* (London: Soncino Press, 1939).

16. Eric Freudenstein, "Ecology and the Jewish Tradition," in *Judaism and Human Rights,* pp. 265–74; Jonathan Helfand, "Ecology and the Jewish Tradition: a Postscript," *Judaism* 20 (1971): 330–35.

17. Samson Raphael Hirsch, *Horeb: A Philosophy of Jewish Laws and Observances,* trans. I. Grunfeld (New York: Soncino Press, 1981), pp. 279–80.

18. For example, see the discussion of bird diversity at a farmed oasis and at a nearby protected oasis in the Sonoran Desert, in Gary Nabhan's book, *The Desert Smells Like Rain* (San Francisco: North Point Press, 1982), pp. 87–97.

19. *Jewish Vegetarian,* quarterly publication of the Jewish Vegetarian Society, London. See also, R. Schwartz, *Judaism and Vegetarianism* (Smithtown, NY: Exposition Press, 1982).

20. Garrett Hardin, "The Tragedy of the Commons," *Science* 162 (1968): 1234–38.

21. For the ecological significance of the difference between human and divine creativity, see N. Lamm, "Ecology in Jewish Law and Theology," published in *Faith and Doubt* (New York: KTAV, 1971) [and reprinted in this anthology]. Lamm also discusses the issue of Genesis 1:28 and the subject of Hasidic immanentism.

22. Gerald J. Blidstein, "Man and Nature in the Sabbatical Year," *Tradition* 9, no. 4 (1966): 48–55.

23. Joseph H. Hertz, ed., *The Pentateuch and Haftorahs,* 2nd ed. (London: Soncino Press, 1978), p. 531.

24. Abraham Joshua Heschel, *The Sabbath: Its Meaning for Modern Man* (New York: Farrar, Straus and Giroux, 1951).

Jeremy Benstein, "Nature vs. Torah"

I would like to thank Noah Efron and Noam Zion for their helpful critiques of the form and content of this essay; and the participants of the Beit Midrash Elul workshop on "Nature and the Human Spirit: Jewish Perspectives on the Environment," co-led by myself and Eilon Schwartz during 1993–1994 in Jerusalem.

All translations of passages from the Babylonian Talmud are taken from the Soncino translation, ed. Rabbi Dr. I. Epstein (London: Soncino Press).

1. For those interested in getting the overall sense of this short passage before we begin to dissect it into its component parts, the conclusion of this translation process is given on p. XXX (((MS PG 89, PART 2))).

2. *The Poem Itself: 45 Modern Poets in a New Presentation* (New Yorki: Holt, Rinehart and Winston, 1960) and *The Modern Hebrew Poem Itself*, ed. Stanley Burnshaw, T. Carmi, and Ezra Spicehandler (New York: Schocken books, 1965). The pithiness of Mishnaic texts like *Avot* lend them a poetic compactness that invites this sort of treatment.

3. There are even editions with the name of Rabbi Akiva, but this seems particularly implausible. The weight of scholarly opinion seems to support R. Ya'akov. See, in the References, Herford and Albeck, who has R. Shim'on in the body of the text but writes in his notes: "A different version, which is correct, has: Rabbi Ya'akov."

4. See *T. J. Shab.* 10:5, 12c,d; *Pes.* 10:1, 37b.

5. Recounted in *T. B. Kiddushin* 39b, and again at the conclusion of *Hullin* (p. 142a). The mishna (*M. Kid.* 1:10) which that particular gemara is relating to seems to be claiming that there is direct and immediate reward in this world for the performance of mitzvot. Rabbi Ya'akov disagrees, saying: "There is no reward for precepts in this world . . . there is not a single precept in the Torah whose reward is [stated] at its side which is not dependent on the resurrection of the dead" (i.e., the next world). A Rabbi Joseph is quoted as saying there that if *Acher* had interpreted as did his daughter's son, Rabbi Ya'akov, he would not have come to sin.

6. It is interesting to note that the conclusion of this tale is that Rabbi Shim'on bar Yochai (or RaShBi) is eventually reconciled with the Jewish people and the world when, as Shabbat eve is approaching, he sees an old man running with two myrtle branches in his hand. He asks the old man what they are for, and he tells him that they are in honor of the Shabbat, one symbolizing *zachor* (remember)—the aspect of the Shabbat emphasized in the Ten Commandments in the book of Exodus—and the other representing *shamor* (observe)—the aspect of the Shabbat emphasized in the Ten Commandments in Deuteronomy. In other words, the (apparently original,

unprecedented) ritual use of the branches of a tree in the context of Shabbat has put his mind at ease about the fate of the world.

7. *T. B. Berachot* 35b. In part because of his mystical, fiery character, and also the mysterious isolation in the cave, Rabbi Shim'on bar Yochai is traditionally considered to be the author of the great mystical masterwork, the *Zohar.*

8. This last is Neusner's rendition, in his *The Mishna: A New Translation,* p. 679.

9. The Mishna (from the same root) was the first great codification of the Oral Law, and though we are familiar with it in book form, it was originally oral, meaning that people learned it by heart (hence the need for constant repetition) and taught it solely verbally. Those people were the *tannaim,* which is also from the same root, with an Aramaic transposition of *t* for *sh.*

10. But there are other uses of this interesting word *na'eh.* For instance, in a well-known passage from *Midrash Tanhuma* (*Tazria,* sec. 5, and *Tanhuma,* Buber ea., sec. 7) the Roman curate Turnus Rufus asks Rabbi Akiva: Whose works are more *"na'im"* those of God or those of human beings? From the rest of the story, and the examples bandied back and forth between them, it seems unlikely that they are talking in purely aesthetic categories; specifically, Rabbi Akiva's *coup de grâce*—the superiority of cakes and cloth to raw wheat and flax—seems to imply functional value as well. In-depth study of this *aggada* can reveal a great deal about rabbinic attitudes towards Nature, culture, and the human role in Creation.

11. This is the Talmudic phrasing. As codified in the *Shulchan Aruch* (O.H. 225:10), the full standard blessing ("Blessed are You, Lord our God, Sovereign of the Universe . . . ") is required. It is explained there that the blessing is to be recited upon seeing beautiful creatures of all sorts: this includes people (non-Jews, even idolators, as well as Jews) and all sorts of beasts. In *T. J. Berachot* 13b,c, it is related of Rabban Gamliel that he recited this blessing upon seeing a beautiful Roman woman, no less one of God's handiworks.

This is one of the *birkot hanahanin,* the blessings of "enjoyment." As opposed to other forms of benedictions, which are to be recited at prescribed times, either during a prayer service, or before the performance of a *mitzvah,* these *berachot* are essentially a set form for spontaneous reactions of wonder and thanksgiving for experiences of various aspects of Nature. These blessings potentially have the power to cultivate a deeper appreciation of elements of the world around us, but sadly, they are rather underemphasized in contemporary Jewish spiritual education. This particular blessing, in fact, is apparently no longer said at all by Ashkenazic Jews, according to the *Mishna Berura,* the authoritative Eastern European law code published less than a hundred years ago (though it still appears in most prayer books that include a section on "blessings for various occasions"). In any event, writes [the author of *Mishna Berura*], if said at all it is best recited in an abbreviated form, without mentioning the Name of God or God's sovereignty *(b'li shem u'malkhut)*. See *Mishna Berura,* vol. 2, 225:10, note 32; and *Chayei Adam* (Avraham Danziger, 18th c. Lithuania) 63:1. The latter gives the astonishing reason that, since we are only required to make blessings of this sort upon the very first contact with the creature or object in question—"when the enjoyment is still intense, and the difference [from one's usual routine] is great"—it is no longer appropriate to do so, since: "We are always accustomed to this, and we don't experience any striking contrast." Even if Vilna of 1790 were exceptionally beautiful (all year round) it is hard to fathom this rationale. This sort of blessing is designed precisely to foster a sense of wonder at things we might otherwise take for granted. If Danziger had read Caro's commentary (see the following section, "The Commentaries"), he certainly didn't take it to heart!

12. Neusner (*Torah From Our Sages,* p. 105) presents a particularly interesting midrash on the interaction of human and divine here: "This is a stern message. It emphasizes that the beauty of the tree, the beauty of a field one has worked to plow—the creation of God, the creation of humanity—must not take our minds away from the labor of Torah, which belongs both to God and humanity. God created the tree, humanity plowed the field; we as earnest students of Torah take God's creation and make it humanity's."

13. Used here is the New JPS translation of this verse. This is considered particularly likely by many commentators, since it is explicitly quoted directly in the following mishna.

   Rabbi Yosef Ya'avetz (or Jabez, Spain-Italy, 15th c.) presents a fascinating alternative understanding of what it might mean for "Scripture" to accuse (p. 77). To the modern ear, however, it sounds slightly whimsical:

   > The Torah gets angry with him: for this reason it does not say simply "forfeits his life" as it does above (3:5), but rather *Scripture accounts it to him*—because it is the Torah itself that is angry at him [for abandoning it].

14. Goldin, p. 127.

15. Ibid., in translation of Aknin's commentary, p. 128. Also Hirsch, p. 47.

16. *Siddur Sim Shalom,* trans. Routtenberg, p. 623. He adds, in note 15 (p. 664): "Literally, 'guilty against his own soul.'" However, in a previous mishna (3:5), where the identical phrase occurs, he translates: "endangers his life."

17. Danby, p. 451. Also Blackman, vol. 4, p. 523. The latter however renders the

other occurrence (according to his numbering, 3:4) "such a one is guilty against himself."

18. Herford, p. 73. Also Hertz, p. 53. He, too, renders this phrase otherwise in 3:5, "such a one sins against himself" (p. 51).

19. Neusner, *The Mishna*, p. 679.

20. Taylor, p. 48 (inner quotation marks in the original).

21. Israelstam, *Soncino Talmud*, p. 31. An alternative is added there in a note: "or incurs guilty responsibility for his life."

22. Bulka, p. 111. Cf. also Hirsch, who adds in his comments (p. 47): "is as if he had sinned against his own soul, or rather, as if he had forfeited his soul." See also Berdichevski, translated by Hertzberg.

23. This appears in Sir Leon Simon's translation of Bialik's essay "Halacha and Aggada", in Cohen and Michali, eds., *An Anthology of Hebrew Essays*, p. 378.

24. From the epigraph to Cynthia Ozick's short story "The Pagan Rabbi" in the collection of the same name (New York: Knopf, 1971), p. 1. That story is a fascinating literary treatment of some of the themes suggested by this mishna. The "pagan rabbi" of the story's title goes much further than abstract appreciation of the beauty of inanimate nature.

25. Avraham Shtal (p. 148) claims that there is a crucial difference: "There he was engaged in acts that are completely unacceptable, whereas here, he praises God by glorifying the Creation. Even so, this too is forbidden, because Torah study is more important." See the following section, "The Commentaries," which presents other commentaries on this issue.

26. *M. Ketubot* 3:2; *M. Bava Kama* 3:10; *M. Hullin* 1:1. In addition, the phrase occurs in the Babylonian Talmud approximately another dozen times, also with the same sense.

27. There are, of course, commentators who do read this in a physical sense. Rashi comments: "Risks his life, for Satan is not able to harm one who is occupied with Torah." Duran makes a similar comment (*Magen Avot*, in Goldin). And Rabbi Yitzchak Magriso, a compiler of the eighteenth century Ladino *Yalkut Me'am Lo'ez*, says that the danger involved is that the traveler is liable to be hurt by wild animals, "for wild animals can have no power over a human being unless he becomes like an animal; and a person who does not engage in Torah study is likened unto an animal . . . " (Yerushalmi version, p. 125).

28. In the *Encyclopedia Judaica* entry on "Law and Morality" (vol. 10, p. 1484), Saul Berman writes of the 'didactic' use of the death penalty threat:

> While the Bible lays down the penalty of death at the hands of the court for a variety of crimes, the *tannaim* had already begun

using the ascription of the death penalty to crimes for which clearly no court would prescribe such punishment. This exaggerated penalty was an effective way of communicating rabbinic feelings about the enormity of misbehavior. The *amoraim* made extensive use of this device to indicate their indignation at immoral behavior. Thus, in a passage which makes manifestly clear that it is aimed at emphasis rather than true legal liability, the Talmud says, "A mourner who does not let his hair grow long and does not rend his clothes is liable to death" (*T. B. Mo'ed Katan* 24a). Similarly the rabbis asserted that "Any scholar upon whose garment a [grease] stain is found is liable to death" (*T. B. Shabbat* 114a).

29. I am indebted to my friend and colleague Eilon Schwartz for the suggestion of this analysis of the commentaries, as well as many other insights that contributed to the development of the ideas in this essay.

30. Of course, even this minimal acceptance of the value of the appreciation of Nature is on the condition that it is not for its own sake, but as a means to praising God and acknowledging the greatness of the Creator. Two twentieth-century Orthodox commentators address this point. Aharon Shelomo Katriel Maharil is particularly clear about this, in his *Avot Ha'olam Hakadmonim:*

> . . . since he said "how fine is this tree, how fine is this field" and did not include God's name (i.e., did not say an actual blessing), this then is idle talk, and constitutes a break from his studies, and he forfeits his life, as it says in the *Zohar* (*Lech Lecha,* 92): one who leaves the Torah, even for a single hour, is like one who leaves the life of the world.
>
> Another aspect: there is actually no problem in saying "how fine is this tree," for one can claim that his intention was for the sake of the blessing. But as for "how fine is this field"—there is no blessing, and so that (illegitimately) diverted his mind from Torah, and for that he forfeits his life.

And Irving Bunim, in *Ethics from Sinai,* says:

> The exclamation of rapture, "How beautiful is this tree," etc., comes forth not as part of religious expression but as an interruption of Torah study, in contrast and opposition to it. Basically,

> Judaism wants us to enjoy life in this world and experience the pleasures which stem from a contemplation of the beauties of nature. But too many of us appreciate nature merely as nature, as something separate and apart, out of any larger context. We fail to see in nature's great beauty, in its wonder and mystery, the hand of a Creator, the Master of the universe. (Vol. 1, p. 267)

31. This characterization is from Hertzberg, p. 291. He places his selections from Berdichevski in a section entitled "Rebels at their most defiant."

32. This translation is from Hertzberg, pp. 296–97. The original essay, called *Du Partzufim* ("Two-Faces," or "In Two Directions" according to Hertzberg), written c. 1900–03, can be found in Berdichevski's collected works (Tel Aviv: Dvir, 1960), the *Essays* volume, p. 45.

33. Actually, neither did Berdichevski. He spent the last years of his life working on a massive collection of Jewish *aggada* and folklore *(Mimekor Yisrael),* not unlike Bialik's *Sefer Aggada.*

34. Translated by Sir Leon Simon, in Cohenand Michali, eds., *An Anthology of Hebrew Essays,* pp. 368–388. This passage appears on p. 378. The Hebrew original, written in the early years of this century, can be found in the collected writings of Ch. N. Bialik (Tel Aviv: Dvir, 1938, reprinted 1971), p. 219.

35. This need not sound too strange to the contemporary ear. One of the hottest topics in environmental thought today is bio-regionalism and "a sense of place"—the importance of one's connection to one's immediate area and its environment. As Jews, can we seriously speak of establishing a deep sense of place, of totally integrating with our environment—making it a part of ourselves, and ourselves a part of it—in New England, or the American Southwest, or the pampas of South America—without always having in the back of our mind that something is not quite right? that we Jews once had a *monumental* "sense of place," and it has been renewed, for some, with the re-establishment of the State of Israel in the Land of Israel? This is the (unabashedly Zionist) question for the reader to ponder: can we speak of "Jewish bio-regionalism" anywhere else but there, in what is known in our tradition as *ha-aretz, the* Land?

36. Important pioneering work in this field is being done by the American group Shomrei Adama. Clearly, Jews need to be approached educationally where they are (physically, and otherwise), and ethically speaking, a universal vision is essential—but see the reservations expressed in the previous note.

37. The literal translation of this epithet for God—*makom*—is "Place." A full exploration of the history and implications of this fascinating term are beyond

the scope of this essay, but the potential for "green midrash" is clear. It might even be claimed that the best Hebrew translation for the ecological term discussed in note 35, "a sense of place," is precisely this: *bein adam le-Makom,* the relationship between humans and the(ir) Place—theological ramifications intended. It should be noted, though, that a classic midrash (*Gen. Rabbah* 68:9) explicates this phrase as a negation of pantheism: "God is the place of the World, but the World is not the Place of God," i.e., all of creation, the entire universe, does not—*cannot*—contain Divinity.

38. Literally, "the commandments between man and his world." Of course, the possessive pronoun, expressed in the Hebrew suffix "-o" should be interpreted as indicating *relationship,* not *possession,* as in the phrase "between people and their fellows." For the midrashically minded, the theologically suggestive possibility exists of interpreting that little suffix as referring (possessively) to "'His' world," i.e., God's world—*kemo she-katav,* as it is written, *"L'H ha'aretz üëm'loah,"* "the Earth is the Lord's" (Ps. 24:1).

39. Many people attribute the following teaching to Rav Kook, the great thinker and spiritual teacher of the early part of this century, and first Chief Rabbi of Israel. Though this is very much in the spirit of his thought, the only place he relates expressly to our mishna, he says something very similar to Reuven Bulka. In his *Orot Ha'Torah* (9:7, p. 45) Kook writes:

> The Light of Life shines forth from all parts of the world, but the Torah's effluence is the Light of the Life of Life. Torah is the forceful and original holiness, while Nature in comparison is only a "lighter" and secondary source of holiness.

Though I have found no written reference, the interpretation may have been an oral teaching of his son, Rabbi Tzvi Yehuda Kook.

40. Does this call for synthesis risk pagan eclecticism? On the whole issue of the possibility of the sanctification of nature within Judaism, I find inspiration in the closing paragraph of Orthodox scholar and theologian Michael Wyschogrod's seminal essay on that topic (p. 7):

> It is difficult to return to the religion of nature. It is difficult and dangerous, particularly for Jews, to worship nature again. At the same time the destruction of nature, which seems to follow to some extent from the desacralization of nature, has reached a stage that cannot continue. So we must try to combine these two themes. To be perfectly honest, I have long felt that the religion against which the prophets expounded so eloquently in the

Hebrew Bible did not get a full hearing from them. I wonder whether the prophets gave a really fair representation of the point of view and theology of the worshipers of Baal and Ashteret . . . Perhaps it would have been better if the prophets had occasionally sat down with them and said, "Tell us how you see the world." Could there be some insights in what they taught which we need to learn? I am convinced there were; and even if we don't agree with much of what they believed, I think we would profit by better understanding their point of view.

ABOUT THE
CONTRIBUTORS

Jeremy Benstein, a native of Toledo, Ohio, holds a B.A. degree in linguistics from Harvard, an M.A. degree in Talmud and midrash from Jewish Theological Seminary/The Seminary of Judaic Studies in Jerusalem, and is a doctoral candidate in cultural anthropology at the Hebrew University, researching environmentalism and local culture, especially Israeli. He is the co-founder with Eilon Schwartz of the Heschel Center for Environmental Learning and Leadership in Tel Aviv. He made aliyah seventeen years ago and lives with his wife, Elisheva, and twin sons, Noam and Yonah, in Kiryat Tivon, Israel.

Rabbi Philip J. Bentley is Rabbi of Temple Sholom in Floral Park (Queens) New York. The author of many articles on justice, peace, the environment and other issues in the Jewish tradition, Rabbi Bentley is honorary president of the Jewish Peace Fellowship.

Rabbi Fred Dobb was ordained in 1997 from Philadelphia's Reconstructionist Rabbinical College. Ever since an environmental education walk across the United States ten years ago, he has been writing, teaching, and organizing around ecology and Judaism. He serves on the board of trustees of COEJL and the Teva Learning Center and as Rabbi of Adat Shalom Reconstructionist Congregation in Bethesda, Maryland.

Dr. David Ehrenfeld is a professor at Cook College, Rutgers University, where he teaches courses in ecology at the undergraduate and graduate levels. His books include *The Arrogance of Humanism* and *Beginning Again: People and Nature in the New Millennium.* He was a scientific organizer of the first World Conference on Sea Turtle Conservation.

Evan Eisenberg is the author of *The Ecology of Eden* and *The Recording Angel.* His writing on nature and culture has appeared in *The Atlantic, The New Republic, The Nation, Natural History,* and other publications. A sometime cantor and former gardener for the New York City parks department, he lives in Manhattan with his wife, an urban planner, and their daughter.

Tikva Frymer-Kensky is professor of Hebrew Bible at the University of

Chicago Divinity School. She has been the director of biblical studies at the Reconstructionist Rabbinical College and visiting professor at both the Jewish Theological Seminary and Hebrew Union College. She is the author of *In the Wake of the Goddesses* (Free Press) and *Motherprayer* (Riverhead) and the English translator of *From Jerusalem to the Edge of Heaven* by Ari Elon (from the Hebrew Alma Dee). She is completing a book on women in the Bible and writing a commentary on the Book of Ruth.

Dr. Jonathan Helfand is professor of modern Jewish history at Brooklyn College of the City University of New York and also has rabbinic ordination from the Isaac Elchanan Theological Seminary. Professor Helfand has authored numerous works on the social and religious history of French Jewry, his field of specialization. He was one of the first Jewish scholars to write extensively and lecture on ecology and the Jewish tradition.

Rabbi Norman Lamm is president of Yeshiva University and the author of *Faith and Doubt*. He was the founding editor of *Tradition: A Journal of Orthodox Jewish Thought*.

Rabbi David E. Sulomm Stein is a Reconstructionist rabbi who edited *A Garden of Choice Fruit: 200 Classic Jewish Quotes on Human Beings and the Environment* (Shomrei Adamah). Now a project editor for the Jewish Publication Society, he lives in Redondo Beach, California.

Rabbi Arthur Waskow, editor of *Torah of the Earth,* founded and is director of The Shalom Center and is a Pathfinder of ALEPH: Alliance for Jewish Renewal. He is co-editor of *Trees, Earth, and Torah: A Tu B'Shvat Anthology* (Jewish Publication Society). His other books include *The Freedom Seder; Godwrestling; Seasons of Our Joy; Down-to-Earth Judaism: Food, Money, Sex, and the Rest of Life; Tales of Tikkun: New Jewish Stories to Heal the Wounded World* (with Phyllis Ocean Berman), and *Godwrestling—Round Two: Ancient Wisdom, Future Paths* (Jewish Lights), winner of the Benjamin Franklin Award. He and his wife, Phyllis Ocean Berman, teach, lead Jewish renewal davvening, lecture, and do storytelling in many synagogues, campuses, retreat centers, and interreligious conferences. Waskow lives in Philadelphia.

www.ingramcontent.com/pod-product-compliance
Lightning Source LLC
Chambersburg PA
CBHW060332100426
42812CB00003B/963